Data
Collection

SAGE has been part of the global academic community since 1965, supporting high quality research and learning that transforms society and our understanding of individuals, groups, and cultures. SAGE is the independent, innovative, natural home for authors, editors and societies who share our commitment and passion for the social sciences.

Find out more at: **www.sagepublications.com**

Data Collection

Key Debates and Methods in Social Research

Wendy Olsen

Los Angeles | London | New Delhi
Singapore | Washington DC

First published 2012

Apart from any fair dealing for the purposes of research or private study, or criticism or review, as permitted under the Copyright, Designs and Patents Act, 1988, this publication may be reproduced, stored or transmitted in any form, or by any means, only with the prior permission in writing of the publishers, or in the case of reprographic reproduction, in accordance with the terms of licences issued by the Copyright Licensing Agency. Enquiries concerning reproduction outside those terms should be sent to the publishers.

SAGE Publications Ltd
1 Oliver's Yard
55 City Road
London EC1Y 1SP

SAGE Publications Inc.
2455 Teller Road
Thousand Oaks, California 91320

SAGE Publications India Pvt Ltd
B 1/I 1 Mohan Cooperative Industrial Area
Mathura Road, Post Bag 7
New Delhi 110 044

SAGE Publications Asia-Pacific Pte Ltd
33 Pekin Street #02-01
Far East Square
Singapore 048763

Library of Congress Control Number: 2011921429

British Library Cataloguing in Publication data

A catalogue record for this book is available from the British Library

ISBN 978-1-84787-255-5
ISBN 978-1-84787-256-2 (pbk)

Typeset by C&M Digitals (P) Ltd, Chennai, India
Printed in India by the Replika Press Pvt. Ltd
Printed on paper from sustainable resources

Contents

About the Author

Wendy Olsen works at the University of Manchester. She has taught in the areas of development studies, sociology, development economics, applied statistics, and research skills. Her research interests include gender and British labour markets; economic and social aspects of labour markets in India and in South Asia generally; moral economy of child labour; gender pay gaps; and research methods. Her specialist areas include the regulation of labour markets; feminist analyses of labour relations; labour supply; and mixed methods cutting across the qualitative–quantitative 'divide'. Her publications include *Rural Indian Social Relations* (Oxford, 1996); *The Politics of Money*, with F. Hutchinson and M. Mellor (Pluto, 2002); and *Realist Methodology* (ed., 4 volumes, Sage, 2010). She is currently working on fuzzy set causal analysis, causes of gender pay gaps, institutional change and people's habitus, and moral reasoning strategies.

Preface

In this book, data-collection methods are highlighted across a wide range of examples. I explain a variety of exemplars and then use them to examine the main concepts related to data collection. The empirical examples come from the USA, South Africa, UK, India, and other countries. The key concepts covered support data collection for all kinds of qualitative research, surveys, question-naires, in-depth quantitative research, integrated mixed-methods research, inter-pretation, and case-study research.

This book is distinguished from others in avoiding a rigid split between dif-ferent schools of thought within methodology. I question the usefulness of the quantitative–qualitative divide in particular. The chapters are organised to be useful to those who want to bridge this supposed divide.

I am grateful to several anonymous reviewers of the manuscript who helped me to refine the ideas. Thanks also go to the editors and copyeditors, especially Vince Hunt. I also thank the University of Manchester for providing a sabbatical semester, the University of Göteborg, and the Arnold Bergsträsser Institute for Cultural Studies at the Albert Ludwig University of Freiburg which provided a great atmosphere for writing.

Wendy Olsen
Manchester 2011

Introduction

As a reader of a book like this, you may want to know about cheap and easy data collection, sophisticated data collection, interviews or ethnographic data collection or mixed-methods forms of data collection. All these forms are mutually consistent and can be readily made feasible in practice. The best time to read this book is at the beginning of a research project, but even in the later stages it is worth using it as a handbook to review your progress and to hone in more closely on that main, clearly-seen, well-focused research question!

Part 1 describes what good research is all about: how to validate findings and explore important topics. Key concepts covered include **research and data collection** (1.1), **data** (1.3) and **findings** (1.2). These concepts underpin a strategic approach to data collection.

Part 2 explores qualitative data-collection methods. It includes internet data collection and text-based document gathering. Part 3 covers observation and involved methods of data collection. In these parts, which cover **interviews** (2.1), **representations** (2.7), **participation** (3.1) and **online data collection** (3.5), I explain that the 'stages' of research do not follow a rigid order. Instead, even during the analysis stage you can return to data collection to get more data. It is useful to consider **coding** (2.3) of data because the intentions about coding affect how the data collection should be organised. Use good project management to make sure that when considering a return to the field you do not miss important project deadlines. This book helps focus your mind on the kinds of data that will give you useful representations, helpful insights, and in-depth transcripts of just the right kind.

Part 4 covers experimental data and randomised controlled trials. Part 5 is about surveys and secondary data. Data collection here includes developing a questionnaire, doing **data cleaning** (5.4), or organising some survey data from a larger public data resource (**data extraction**, 5.5). I have covered key concepts such as **operationalisation** (5.1) and **measurement** (5.2) in order to help you develop a questionnaire or make survey data. Special topics such as **data extraction** (5.5), **subsetting** (5.7) and **survey weights** (5.8) help with the secondary use of large-scale datasets. Since many of these datasets are free, the researcher just needs quick and easy access methods such as NESSTAR to get wonderful small datasets. From these one can make accurate charts and tables. In this sense data 'collection' is taken to include the reuse of secondary survey data.

Case-study research (6.1) and **comparative research** (6.2) methods are described in Part 6. This exciting part examines a variety of mixed-methods research design strategies in so far as they require data collection. However, the whole book can help a mixed-methods researcher to choose and refine their methods, so there is no single chapter about mixing methods together.

The book concludes in Part 7 with some suggestions about some practical aspects of a research project, such as using field notebooks in research. The deep issues of **facts** (7.1) and science are taken up in a practical way here. Aspects of ethics are noted throughout the book, with a special chapter on research ethics (2.11 **ethical clearance** in Part 2).

This book offers important help to many kinds of researchers. Evaluation experts, market researchers, students doing research projects, doctoral researchers, management researchers, and people working in education settings who want to research an educational site or find patterns in sets of exam results will discover plenty of depth in it for them.

Health and psychology researchers will find it of special relevance because its methodological basis in realism is consistent with both natural science and social science methods. These details are explained in Part 1, and it is reassuring to think that the social model of health and the biological model of illness can be made to work in tandem in a research project.

According to my approach there is no schism between the natural sciences as fact-finding and the social sciences as exploring representations. Both offer representations which can be contested, but both rest on a foundation through their grounding in human and natural reality. Different standpoints that (really) exist can be reconciled and tolerated, with a growing awareness of when people are actually promoting falsehoods or using ethically undesirable frames of reference. Standpoints and representations are strong themes in Part 2. Having taken this stance, like many other realists, I support a strong ethical approach to choosing the purposes and methods of research.

Best wishes for your research adventure!

Wendy Olsen
Manchester 2011

Part 1

Data Collection: An Introduction to Research Practices

1.1 Research and Data Collection

Doing research is much more than just gathering information or writing a description as a journalist would. Research consists in more intensive study, usually involving getting information that would surprise some audiences, and analysing the information carefully before writing up the results. The best research uses data in an original way or offers some new and exciting interpretation of existing data. Excellent research has to use evidence very carefully. Sophisticated data collection offers ways to plan and execute the best kinds of research. Many research outputs take a written form, but excellent research also results in soundbites that can be offered to practical audiences or in the media. These soundbites (punchy sentences) are only useful if the reader or listener can trace back to the original detailed research outputs, and perhaps even scan and scrutinise the data and data analysis themselves. The best researchers develop a strong reputation for systematic, logical and well-grounded research methods.

Some people argue that scientific research includes all the kinds of research that use data in sophisticated ways. But data are neither necessary nor sufficient for research to be scientific. Data are not sufficient because one also needs a carefully developed scientific argument. In this book, ways of developing good arguments are suggested and these rely in part on planning the whole research process before one starts to collect data. In some areas of research the phases of data collection and data generation are hard to distinguish because the data may already exist in newspapers or government publications, but one needs to be selective and propose that we use some of these resources. We then say that we are generating a dataset as a subset of the existing information. A good scientific researcher is likely to be able to generate or create datasets that are useful for scientific arguments. Data are also not necessary for all scientific arguments, because some arguments take the form of a normative or theoretical statement. Deductive arguments in particular may not require data at any stage. This book focuses more on other forms of scientific inference than deduction.

Research typically begins with the identification of a problem. After some general reading, one sets up a narrow research question which can easily be addressed during a constrained period of research. A literature review must be conducted and this review may include the close study of existing data and data analyses. The researcher then proceeds to gather fresh data or reanalyse and transform existing data. For most projects, a few weeks or months of doing more analysis usually follows. This book focuses more on the data-generation stages and less on the analysis stage, but the two are a little hard to separate because of the planning involved.

Systematisation is common in research. To systematically gather data might mean to run a parallel series of interviews on two sites, or to run several focus groups on the same theme. The choice of the research theme and the narrow research question is crucial. A few researchers in areas of sociology or philosophy may succeed merely by thinking about the issues and the works of previous thinkers. Even here, however, the works of earlier writers appear as a kind of data for the analyst. The vast majority of other researchers across the social and management sciences, medicine and health research, psychology and other topics have to collect and manage data as a crucial part of their research effort. Doing research may require the production of a project proposal to underpin a successful funding bid. Data collection may arise within the project proposal or may occur across a wider set of activities which we might call a programme. For example, one laboratory or institute may focus on how to utilise a longitudinal dataset or a set of cases arising from clinical meetings with patients. The research programme will then typically involve a series of smaller projects. Doctoral research often fits within wider research programmes. The degree of Ph.D. is awarded for scholarly research contributing new knowledge in a particular subject area. This degree requires between three and seven years of study. Other research projects take just weeks or months of work.

These brief notes on research do not do justice to the huge debate about what counts as scientific research. I have aimed here to introduce the various roles that data collection can play within the whole research process.

1.2 Findings

When a research project is written up and nearing completion there is often a moment of angst and concern about the main findings. Some of the stumbling blocks at this stage of a project can be over what to say, what nuances to place on different findings, who takes responsibility for these findings and how to integrate teamwork into an agreed document or presentation. The final stage needs to be foreseen during the data-collection stage so that when there are doubts, there is some recourse to the data or the data-analysis artefacts. Perhaps the data are a bit like the map that helps steering a course in a boat. The captain and crew decide where they want to go, then use the map to ensure they choose a reasonable and sensible way to reach the safety of harbour and complete their journey. Avoiding falsehoods, overcoming difficulties of comprehension, and translating between different dialects or lay idioms are all important ways that 'data' can help the researcher or research team avoid ending up like the *Titanic* – that is, at the bottom of the ocean.

The findings from a good study can usually be represented concisely on a single page in a diagram or other summary statement (as advised by Miles and Huberman, 1994). This advice given by Miles and Huberman was meant for qualitative researchers only, but it is good guidance for all kinds of social researchers. It helps to think of this aim as requiring conciseness, focus and a certain narrowness of the main topic of the research. Most researchers base their 'findings' closely on their research question (see Wisker, 2008: ch. 5). Some, however, revise the research question as they go along. These people tend to get into difficulty when writing up because it may become unclear what exactly they are focused on. Therefore, in writing up your findings a good guidance is first to answer the original research question and then make additional comments about exploratory aspects of the findings and new proposals for future research.

It is often easier for a lone writer to achieve a good write-up or presentation because they do not have to be monitored or influenced by others. On the other hand, the lone author runs a risk of making arguments that others will find ridiculous or unsubstantiated. It is always a good idea when developing a draft to ask at least three people to read it early on. For those working in teams, individuals can write drafts and sections and pass them around. Guidelines for co-authoring can set out the roles team members may play (British Sociological Association (BSA), 2002). For example, one person might be a ghost writer and not want attribution, while another who collects data may want to be a named co-author. In general, the BSA tends to discourage ghost writing and suggests instead that the lead author may have a number of named co-authors, including the paid writer, who then get to claim joint authorship and take a fuller role in finalising the report. The BSA also encourages data enumerators and interviewers to become named authors. The guidelines argue that to be a named co-author of findings, each person needs to be aware of the whole paper's arguments and to have gone over the whole text in detail at a late stage to make comments, insertions and corrections. As long as this has happened, some co-authors can have a relatively minor role in writing up but may have had important roles during data collection.

Some findings will probably 'emerge' from a study without being expected or predicted in advance. The 'expected' findings might follow the usual pattern of normal science. 'Normal science' is a special phrase referring to the use of standard, pre-planned methods on a routine study topic to get results that to some extent (in broad outline) could have been predicted from the start. Kuhn (1970) saw normal science as rather conventional and pointed out that the very best science goes beyond normal science. Anomalies and situations that are new, unique or difficult to explain cause scientists to seek new, creative, innovative explanations or interpretations. Now the same dataset could be the basis of a new set of findings! This exciting vista, set out by Kuhn as paradigm change but also studied by many other authors since Kuhn's time (Fuller, 2003), offers researchers a wide range of ways to deviate from normal science.

Although there are connections (and rootedness) between the data collected and the findings, there is not a single mapping from one to the other. If we stay with our sailing analogy, there are many ways to reach the other side of the ocean. Social science archives (where data are held for future users) offer opportunities for reanalysing older data, comparing it with new data and perhaps applying new interpretive strategies. Thus there is not a single set of findings from one study. Tolerance, pluralism and even-handedness are needed when we realise that different researchers might develop different findings from the same dataset.

According to Kuhn (1970), the hypothesis-testing tradition led to a great pretence of attempts at falsification when in fact the underlying basic theoretical premises were never questioned. As a result, some scientists now avoid the hypothesis-testing methodology. I offer several approaches to this issue in this book. For example, you could be a qualitative researcher developing new hypotheses. You would, of course, test them at the same time and offer sensible claims. But no quantitative research would be involved. If you were a quantitative survey researcher you might test a wide range of hypotheses and tell the reader what you have found out. A mixed-methods researcher has to weave a pathway delicately around these options. Some researchers now do a little of both. In rough terms we might call the first 'exploratory' findings and the second 'tested' findings or simply 'hypothesis-testing'. In order for it to make sense to do both, one needs to leave the tradition described by Popper in which falsification played a central role. One should take responsibility for choosing theories and decide on which set of basic assumptions to work with. Kuhn argued correctly that falsification was not value–neutral in general (Fuller, 2003, 2005). Researchers today, such as the textbook authors on research design, see mixed methods as highly feasible and desirable (De Vaus, 2001; Teddlie and Tashakkori, 2009; Creswell and Plano Clark, 2007; Creswell, 2003, 2009). Advice has tended to move away from the traditional separation between a value-neutral survey method and a value-saturated qualitative method.

I wonder whether the word 'findings' tends to suggest a consensual set of conclusions and so denies the possibility of contesting the results? In recent years it has become clear that many of the basic words and phrases used in social science are essentially contestable. Examples such as human rights, civil society, rational choice and market optimum are obviously controversial for those who do (or do not) adhere to the underlying values that they imply. Social science is not generally considered to be value-neutral any more. Specific concrete sentences may be factual but an overall argument usually has values (whether explicit and/or implicit), a purpose, underlying assumptions and a persuasive undertone (Olsen, 2009).

The most exciting writing certainly has a purpose. This chapter on findings is meant to excite you about the prospect of doing research, even knowing in advance (with trepidation) that the findings are going to be contestable! Having this clear purpose, I can write in a well-informed, focused and informative way: that is what good research is like too. Researchers use evidence as part of their arguments but in a way that other writing does not. So there are necessary connections between the data-collection plan and the goal or horizon of the kinds of findings that are expected from your study.

To summarise: research findings may be controversial but need to fit into an argument that is clearly stated, well grounded with evidence and suitable for further discussion and development by others. Research data can be put into a data archive to enable early findings to be reassessed later. Using tolerance, researcher teams can develop agreed findings even when they are not wholly unanimous about some aspects of policy or values. Using pluralism (which will be discussed in more detail later on), researchers can explore the usefulness and validity of competing theories in an environment that accepts that more than one theory may have a 'purchase' on events or a telling insight to offer. Hypothesis testing and falsification are not the bread and butter of social science even if they are, at times, very important.

1.3 Data

Data are disembodied information. Data are not the same as knowledge. My favourite type of data is interview transcripts. These are rough and raw – often embarrassingly so – but they reveal a lot about a scene to the close reader. The data type I use most often is survey data. Examples of these two data types, shown in Table 1 and Box 1, illustrate how top-quality researchers in the UK frame these two types of data.

Table 1   BHPS data on ID, age, sex, marital status, and flexitime – six-row sample

pid	age	female	married	flextl
167020423	25	yes	yes	0
958518444	51	yes	yes	0
168083472	45	yes	yes	0
520740483	44	yes	yes	1
971938955	45	yes	yes	0
115014131	49	yes	no	0

Note: The data are anonymised here.

Box 1   Extract from a Transcript of a Three-way Interview

Topic: Television industry contractual terms

Length: 18 pages single spaced

Interview ITV Company 15 March 2000

Interviewees:

Person 1:   Researcher in the TV industry, female aged 22. Single. Recently graduated from Cambridge with good degree in politics. Short term contract.

Person 2:   Post-production/video tape library, male aged 43. Married with one child. Permanent staff in the TV industry.

'Me' is the interviewer Valerie Antcliff.

Me: The first thing I'd like to ask you is how secure you feel in your current position?

Person 1:   Not very at all! I graduated last year so this is my first sort of proper job and to begin with I was clearly – oh well this is what happens, you're on three month contract, I mean I've just been told that my contract ends at the end of April and my next contract sort of goes up until the end of June and that's it, so essentially from June I'll be unemployed. Now that's because the series I work on will finish in June, but other things will come up that I can possibly go on to that will last over the summer, but there isn't that guarantee and actually it is rather an odd feeling, yes technically I could be unemployed in June. The way I've sort of looked at it is, well I do actually enjoy the job I do but if something else comes up I'm not tied to it because I've not signed a year-long contract like a lot of my friends who got jobs when they graduated have. They sign these great big, long contracts to sort of be there for ever and ever and me, I'm kind of in the reverse of that. But it is slightly unnerving because there is that sense that you think well if they think I'm totally terrible, well they will just get rid of me overnight.

Me: So do you think it could work to your advantage? If a better job comes up....

Person 1:   It works to my advantage because I come into the job knowing I'm not going to be there for very long...

These two examples are chosen to illustrate the two extremes of 'hard' and 'soft' data. People usually mean by hard data the highly structured questionnaire data types. The hardness comes from answers being placed rigorously into categories, as seen in Table 1. These categories are set up to have the same meaning across the whole sample. In the case of the British Household Panel Survey (BHPS) this would be across the whole United Kingdom (Taylor, 2001). Little adaptation is possible within the table, called a 'matrix of data', to allow for possible variations in Wales or Scotland compared with England or Northern Ireland. Thus a kind of universalism of meaning within the population is assumed in so-called 'hard data'.

The 'soft data' of the interview is framed sequentially by a delicate balancing act of the three actors – the female interviewer Valerie Antcliff, the female respondent and the male respondent. All interviews vary in their content, and words are not assumed to have any specific (stipulated) meaning. Even a semi-structured interview like this one has a softness to it in the mapping between words and meanings. Instead of universalism, there are assumptions like concrete local specificity, subjective variations of meaning and exploration of tacit meanings in the construction of the interview. Interviews have flexible sequence so that any idea or claim can be explored. In this example we see that the idea of job security is being explored by the respondents.

An interview is a mutual construction. By contrast, the content of a highly structured questionnaire – and its flow – are dominated by the people who constructed it.

In the interview, any attempt to change the subject, dominate the flow of topics or push further into a given subject is evidently going to be 'led' by somebody. It is a very personal, messy, interactive business. In a survey the 'leading' is done institutionally at the questionnaire preparation stage. This 'leading' is usually managed through careful piloting (i.e. interviews) around blocks of draft questions. Once the questionnaire is printed up, the questions and the flow leading away from certain topics are fixed for all respondents. To a respondent, the leading is invisible. It has hardened into printed instructions, which may seem rather authoritarian. For the questionnaire 'enumerator' or face-to-face interviewer there is very limited room for manoeuvre.

The survey method is also not 'soft' in the way it is delivered. Surveys are often delivered by hand and then collected by post, or even conducted on the internet. But the best survey data, like the BHPS, are collected by hand during a face-to-face interview. This interview is so institutionalised that some of it is now captured immediately on a laptop computer. The face-to-face method enables the questioner to help the respondent navigate the flow of the survey. The questioner can also clarify any ambiguities that may arise. The basic idea of a survey, though, is that the viewpoint of the questioner (enumerator) cannot colour the way the questions are phrased. This supposed absence of the enumerator's subjectivity helps ensure national or even international homogeneity of the data that are recorded. The homogeneity of meaning is only valid, of course, if it is both feasible and realistic to use a single question to tap into an area of experience right across the whole space being sampled. The survey method depends heavily on this homogeneity assumption. By contrast, interview methods are robust to local variations in meaning. Interviews can also handle the situation where people hold contradictory views at a single moment. In a survey, by contrast, as everyone knows, the respondent is supposed to put up a consistent self-image. The data simply records that image.

These two data types – surveys and interview transcripts – are sometimes confused because we often use an interview to fill out a questionnaire. The usual way to distinguish them is to say that structured interviews are used with questionnaire surveys, but semi-structured and unstructured interviews are used to generate interview transcripts. For an unstructured interview you might not even produce a transcript, preferring instead to follow a topic through a series of visits to one or more respondents.

There are many different data file types that correspond to the different forms of data. Here are some of them:

- documents, with file extensions .doc, .rtf or .txt, for interview transcripts;

- images, with .jpg, .tif or .wmf, for photos;

- spreadsheet data, with .sav, .dat or .xls, for survey data;

- sound and video, with .mp3 or .mpg, for interview sound files.

I will take a moment to briefly describe each of these types of data. Note, however, that there are many other types which are not computerised! Examples include handwritten maps, focus-group tape recordings, art drawn by children, interim action research memoranda, and field notebooks. As this book progresses, most of these data types will be discussed.

The .rtf format is a substitute for a Microsoft Word document. RTF stands for 'rich text format'. This format is transferable between computer packages, and can retain some computer graphic images, such as logos, even when moving away from the original software. There are some formats the .rtf file cannot be moved into, such as Adobe Acrobat .pdf format, without buying the proprietary software that corresponds to that format. Adobe Acrobat .pdf format files are nicely encap-sulated to present the graphics, page margins, font and footnotes consistently, no matter what computer the file is opened on. The .pdf file is highly portable because the user does not need to have Microsoft Word software. Indeed, the user typi-cally cannot edit the .pdf file, and is a passive reader rather than being a co-writer on the document. As a result, the .pdf format is very common but is not usually a desirable 'data' format and does not appear in my list. Instead, the older and more basic standard '.txt' format appears. The .txt file is simply a text file and cannot hold graphic images or logos. Microsoft Word can create a text file but it will drop complex layouts such as page numbers or footnotes. From a .pdf source file, using cut and paste, one can create a .txt file that contains usable data. The 'usable' data are easily edited, moved, translated, annotated, and so on: it is a writeable as well as readable file. The .doc format is usually fine for such text files. For open source software users, a variety of other file types can be used too.

The images taken by digital cameras are mixed in with logos and other com-puterised pictures and graphics in the filetype .jpg. Many other file types exist for holding images, including bitmaps (.bmp) and tagged image format files (.tif).

Social scientists often learn to use a spreadsheet during their basic training. The spreadsheet is a table with numbered columns labelled A to Z and AA, AB, AC, and so on. Potentially, several hundred columns and many rows can be filled with detailed data. The data can be words or numbers. These spreadsheets take a special format in social science, where the numeric data can be mapped into a coding scheme to give each value a word or phrase as its value label. For example, 'yes' would be 1 and 'no' would be 0. In the example in Table 1, the variable flext1 ('flexitime work arrangement in paid job') is coded thus. The coding scheme for gender (female = 1 and male = 0) and the coding scheme for marriage have been entered into the computer, giving words in the table but with numbers stored in the computer spreadsheet. In this case I used STATA software (see Hamilton, 2004; STATA, 2003). Because the coding scheme for FLEXT1 is not yet entered into the machine, the numeric values show up in the table. I can declare the value labels, and the table will then appear as shown in Table 2.

Table 2   BHPS data after further coding

pid	age	female	married	flextl
167020423	25	yes	yes	no
958518444	51	yes	yes	no
168083472	45	yes	yes	no
520740483	44	yes	yes	yes
971938955	45	yes	yes	no
115014131	49	yes	no	no

Note: The last column now shows the value labels rather than the raw code values.

A dictionary summarising the coding can be produced from the special software such as SPSS (Field, 2009). One of the simple tasks this package does is to produce a list of variable names – which are not the same as value labels – as shown in Table 3.

Table 3   A data dictionary segment

Variable Name	Variable Label
pid	Person identifier
age	Age at Date of Interview
female	Female
married	Married/Living as Couple/Partnership
flext1	Work Arrangement: Flexitime

Sound and video files can be held temporarily on a minidisc player or MP3 player. Dictation machines can be used to record sound. The .mp3 or other sound files can be uploaded to a computer afterwards. Another alternative is to put a microphone into the input socket of a computer and make a recording directly onto the personal computer. This will generally appear as an .mp3 format file. Video files take many formats and researchers using a digital camera may decide to make short shots of video using .mpg format to capture a glimpse of respondents – with their prior per-mission, of course. Observation studies can use the .mp3, .mp4 or .mpg format to keep a detailed video record, including sound, of various activities, again with prior permission. Compact discs (CDs) generally use a different file format such as the .cda format. The material on CDs can be 'ripped', i.e. uploaded with a new format, to make an .mp3 file. If the source data are speeches recorded on CD, then a simple computer operation can rapidly create .mp3 files from the original files. Similarly, sound on phonograph records or cassette tapes can be converted.

During a research project computer data files are generally complemented by handwritten 'field notebooks' that are gradually filled by each researcher during a project. Field notebooks pile up over the years and form a crucial backup copy of raw data, contact addresses and the researcher's initial thoughts. I usually start off a field notebook with my name and address on the front so that if it gets lost, it – and the crucial research notes, phone numbers and ideas I've jotted down as I go – can be returned to me. Then I put the 'research question' – the one that identifies what is really special and unique about this study. Next, I start making lists of contacts and what they do and where, when and how to reach them. When I visit an 'informant', I open the book and say that this is where my notes go. If they want to remain anonymous I use a pseudonym for the notes pages. I keep a list that matches pseudonyms with real names in a separate, secret place. The field notebook gradually fills up with notes and reflections. The interview plan is taped into the notebook, interviews that are taped do not go into the notebook, but I will make a note of the cassette number or MP3 file name and who I have spoken to, when and so on. The notebook can then be used as the question source and it is no longer necessary to take notes once the data are recorded as sound.

A sample of an interview plan is shown in Figure 1. This plan is very concise and would be put into the notebook and handed out to respondents. Data from

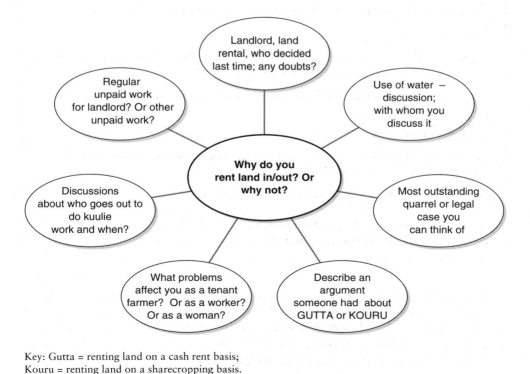

Key: Gutta = renting land on a cash rent basis;
Kouru = renting land on a sharecropping basis.

Figure 1 Plan of a semi-structured interview

this particular plan were used for writing several short articles. There were four interviewers: three native Telugu speakers and me. We did not try to make all the interviews the same, but we tried to cover all the topics shown in Figure 1 and Box 2 in each interview. I will discuss this exemplar more later.

Box 2   Interview Plan Used in Rural India

INTERVIEW PLAN EXTRACTS

Would you agree that we tape your interview so that Wendy can improve her knowledge of Telugu and also write about the situation in the villages? _____Thank you.

Were there any doubts about decisions that were made last year about the renting of land?

How and when was the crop choice made last time, for putting crops on the tenanted land? This can refer either to last year *kharif* or to the current *rabi* season.

Basically why do you rent land?

(or why do you not want to, if you have doubts about renting it?)

[8 questions omitted]

Think of a situation when someone wanted to do kuulie [casual paid] work, and there was a disagreement about it. Tell me about that.

Think of a situation where it is routine to do kuulie work. Tell us who decides about that.

[7 questions omitted]

Etc. prompting till some disagreements are described, and some household-level agreements are described.

[3 possible supplementary questions omitted] End.

Note: The interview plan is shortened for the sake of brevity. *Kharif* and *rabi* refer to the winter and spring planting seasons, respectively.

In discussing 'data' at a more abstract level I will now consider impartiality and validity. Impartiality is important because most people think that hard data create an impartial and unbiased source of information. This is not generally true. Being disembodied records, the 'data' do have three qualities that make them less personal than the usual face-to-face interview:

1. Reliability. No matter which enumerator did the questioning the answers are still harmonised around the same core meanings.

2. Validity. During piloting there were careful checks that the meanings are consistent or homogeneous among different subgroups of the population, e.g. young and old, north and south, and different language groups.

3. Authenticity. There are checkable, disembodied historical artefacts recording what 'was actually said':

   (a) The advantage of the survey method is that we know exactly what has been recorded. *X* per cent of respondents said *This* in response to *That* prompt. $100 - X$ per cent did not say *This*.

   (b) The disadvantage of the method is that we cannot be sure what they meant to convey by giving or choosing that response. Close-ended multi-answer questions are the worst culprits here.

Data as historical artefacts have great advantages for the study of change over time. But in a revisit study or 'longitudinal study' the questions would have to be framed the same way the second time around for the comparison of answers over time to be valid. Validity and verification are important areas for survey research.

Reliability has a specific meaning in the context of social research. It means that a study's findings would be the same even if it had been conducted by a different person. There are two levels of reliability: the reliability of data and the reliability of the findings of the survey.

When considering the reliability of data, the survey method helps to ensure harmonisation and homogeneity. The delivery methods also help. Having literate respondents complete their own questionnaire is a useful method, termed 'self-completion'. If interviewers are used, they should be non-interventionist and should not vary the wording of questions. They should not introduce their own opinions between questions or at stages of the questionnaire. If they do, this will reduce data reliability. The data obtained from each delivery of the questionnaire should not vary from one enumerator to another.

The issue of the reliability of the findings of the survey, on the other hand, is much more problematic. Given a single survey data table, each separate author might write divergent themes and findings from that table. Their differences might arise from theoretical differences, cultural assumptions or selective use of different parts of the data. Beginners often think that findings or results should be reliable. I would advise that this position reflects a misunderstanding of social science. The results might be reliable between different interpreters, but this is not necessarily a good thing. When a new interpretation arises, it can be invigorating, democratic, interesting, innovative, helpful and creative! So I do not idealise 'reliability of findings' in the same way that most survey researchers aim for 'reliability of data'.

Validation should not be confused with reliability. Two forms of validity are often referred to in survey research. Firstly, internal validity occurs where measures conform to the stipulated meanings that the researchers intend to associate with the words used. Internal validity can be developed through a convincing argument about how the questions used relate to the research question and the topic of research in general. Internal validity also requires consistency among a research team's writings. The meaning of key terms must not be changed in mid-stream.

Internal validity is contrasted with external validity. Here the data are supposed to be constructed in such a way as to have consistent meanings both for the researchers and for the respondents. It is also important that the intended audience of the research understands the central concepts in consistent ways. External validity is hard to achieve in a world of contested concepts such as 'social capital' and 'cultural values'. Some social science disciplines like psychology and management put higher value on external validity than other disciplines do. Sociology and politics are particularly willing to allow for multiple interpretations of the same data. If multiple interpretations are possible, and different standpoints of interpretation have their own way of constructing their internal validity, then the phrase 'external validity' will not make much sense. In these disciplines, and for qualitative researchers more generally, there is sometimes impatience with the sweeping generalisations made by survey researchers. Nevertheless even the qualitative researchers have concepts of validity. These are described elsewhere in this book.

Having looked briefly at reliability and validity, we come back to the basic core concept of 'data' in social research. Data are artefacts. Datasets are like mini-museums. Carefully constructed, managed and displayed, data can be a rich resource both for knowledge and imagination.

Data archiving helps retain these data artefacts for future generations and for use by outsiders. Many countries run a national data archive. In the UK the institutions include the Economic and Social Data Service (www.esds.ac.uk) and the UK Data Archive (www.data-archive.ac.uk). The US Census is held on a data archive (www.archives.gov). International organisations such as the International Labour Office and other parts of the United Nations manage data release as a regular part of their operations. The ILO's data can be found online at www.ilo.org. These archives are carefully managed to retain verifiable links between the survey documentation, the validation or piloting activities and the sampling methods used and the datasets themselves. Data archives for survey data help to ensure that we can retain the anonymity of respondents even in the face of concerted attempts to link up datasets to discover people's addresses or identities.

On the qualitative side, too, new data archives have been created to enable the retention and reuse of interview data and other qualitative data types. Both qualitative and quantitative data archives offer some resources free to academic users. Commercial users and those wanting data on hard media and other services are typically charged fees at around the cost of production. These days costs can be minimised by having data transferred through the internet. A common method, known as file transfer protocol (FTP), allows the archive to release the file to the user for a limited period, for example one week, using a password sent to the user via email. The user simply downloads the file from the Internet. The user is restricted in their freedom to copy or pass on the data to others. A signature is usually required to ensure they agree to all the restrictions on their use of the data. Using FTP means the transfer of the data can be extremely quick but might be preceded by a period of a week or so during which emails and signed documents are passed around between user and provider.

So far I have discussed the management and validity of some data types. There are no hard-and-fast rules about the validity of data, so 'beauty is in the eyes of the beholder'. Each researcher will have to develop their own viewpoint about validity and the knowledge that can be gained from research using data. Within a team, there may even be disagreements about knowledge. Ideally each researcher will have well-developed views about it.

1.4 Causes

For some researchers, planning a data-gathering project revolves mainly around notions about how to explain certain outcomes. An explanation involves cause and effect relations. Both survey data and interview data can help us learn about causes and their effects. In both quantitative and qualitative social research there are also times when we do not want to study things causally: we may want to just explore a phenomenon or look at all aspects of it. But when we do want to look at the causes of things, it gets very complicated very quickly.

In this chapter I will define a cause and give some examples of causes and causal factors. Then I will illustrate the data that we collect about such situations and raise some implications of the 'epistemic fallacy' so that you will not get caught out resting an argument too heavily upon a spurious correlation.

A way to define causes is to recognise that social life is changing over time, and that all new events have their origins in the past. We call something causal if it is one of the factors that contributed in the past or present to an event in the present. Causal conditions include structural factors such as the social class you were born into, and, perhaps, are still in; government policy and institutions; and the kind of city you live in. Furthermore, in any chain of events there are direct and indirect causal factors.

There are growth spurts, and the food for growth is causal. There are newly emerging institutions, and the institutional history is part of the causality of the new ones. There are unique and new events, and the creativity of the inventor may be causal there. There are obstacles to certain outcomes and whatever removes the obstacle is a cause of the outcome. Finally, there are enabling factors. These are causes but often only work in the presence of other factors. So you can see there are many types of causes. Some people like to think of deep causes, indirect causes, direct and proximate causes. Of these, the proximate cause is the one nearest to the outcome in time or space. But actually it is hard to distinguish these types of causes because some causes are simply background factors which coexist with – and thus pre-date and post-date – specific causal events. It may be hard to say which is most important. Discerning causes has a subjective element to it.

For me, a cause is mainly interesting if it is not both necessary and sufficient for the outcome. For some empiricists, the opposite is true: for them a cause is only interesting if it is proven to be a cause by being both necessary and sufficient for the outcome. I look at this issue separately and in more depth in the chapter on **causal mechanisms** (6.5) in Part 6. If something is always necessary and sufficient for an outcome, then it is just part of that outcome's pattern: 'letting the lions into the ring' is causal for 'having a lion show in the circus'. It does not really explain why one circus has a lion show and another does not. Taking divorce as an example, marriage is a necessary condition for divorce but is not really an enabling factor since marriage simply lies in the background of all marriages, whether they ended in divorce or not. The type of marriage, date of marriage, mode of marriage, and so on are much more interesting factors in explaining divorces. Divorce papers are not a very interesting cause of divorce either. These are the papers that one partner receives, usually by post, to inform them of the divorce proceedings occurring. They are of course a cause, and both necessary and sufficient to 'cause' divorce, yet the divorce papers are inherently part of divorce. They are not a contingent factor at all. I should point out that this divorce example is based on Western Judeo-Christian systems where divorce goes through a court, not on Islamic systems where the paperwork is not as important.

In summary, the most interesting causes are contingent causes, not inherent background factors. Because causes are contingent and outcomes may occur either accidentally, unpredictably or only in certain patterns or mixtures of causes, discerning causes from empirical data is quite tricky. Even when causes A, B and C are real, they do not work in tandem all the time to cause outcome Y. Therefore evidence about the co-incidence of A and Y may be misleading about whether A causes Y. Even if A really causes Y, it may not co-occur with Y in all situations. If there is a partial association of A and Y, does that mean we refute that A can cause Y? I do not think so. But on the other hand, data about the association of A and Y do not 'prove' that A causes Y either. Proofs of causality are hard to develop.

To be really definite about this, let us look at three examples of causality. Firstly, breast cancer does not always cause death. But it can cause death. So I say: 'Cancer tends to cause death.' This places the causality as a *tendency* of the cancer, not as a deterministic statement or as a fact about all cancers. Intervening factors such as discovery, treatment, food intakes, prior health, and co-occurrence of another cancer are all relevant causal factors. These make data collection a complex task for studies about death from breast cancer. Studies of epidemiology – the causality of illness – stress that if we are to successfully and thoroughly study the causality we need to have survivors of breast cancer in our study as well as those who died (Kreiger, 1994). Studying the causality of death from breast cancer can lead to a strong focus on healthy lifestyles, because survivors may tend to share one common trait, such as healthy lifestyles or a healthy attitude to their body. As examples of this, women with healthy lifestyles survive chemotherapy better than those with prior health problems. Those women who check their breasts frequently are more likely to detect a small cancer before it becomes life-threatening.

Secondly, in social work, it is often observed that poor school outcomes are associated with broken families and economic deprivation. But what is causal in those children's backgrounds? The 'nexus' of their conditioning is complex and has developed over many years. Their interaction with teachers is affected by the teachers' experience of local schools. Maybe the teachers are the cause of poor school outcomes for such children. Maybe teachers cause some outcomes, and children cause some outcomes, but the poor performance outcomes are the same ones. It becomes hard to isolate and measure any single outcome.

Some research papers argue that divorce is bad for children's schooling, while others say that marriage is positively good for schooling. It is important to see that these are different arguments, not merely symmetrical opposites. On the other hand, there is also evidence that children with richer or service sector parents do well even if there is only one parent. (One detailed illustration is provided by Fuller et al., 2002.) The social worker wants to know whether interventions in a child's life can improve school outcomes. But the interventions are themselves unique, personal, interpersonal, hard to record (in detail), and often unrecorded. Scientific survey research may not capture the real effects of transformative meetings of children with social workers and may falsely draw attention to spurious causes, such as the parents getting a good job, which actually arise (also) as outcomes of the social workers' interventions. Thus there is complexity.

Speculation about all these causes is actually a very good way to plan and proceed with widening the data-collection process. That way, no important factor will be left out. Qualitative researchers tend to argue that following single cases over time is an excellent way to understand what factors are transformative. For them, the causality that matters is what transforms a child 'inside', and what makes a household begin to work more functionally (i.e. be less dysfunctional). These things are unique. They also want to understand the dynamics of classrooms and do not think this can be simplified down to 'class size' or the 'curriculum and testing regime'.

Thirdly, in economics we get notions of causality at other levels; that is, beyond the individual. Here you may find that the bankruptcy of a single bank causes a wave of fears of recession and that these fears then cause a strong recession, and then that recession causes unemployment and lower incomes. The causality cannot work the other way, says the economist. But the argument about causality of recession is still contested. The same recession could be attributed to any number of factors: monetary policy, industrial policy, global competition or a protective trade policy on imports and exports. In economics, as in other areas of life, there are so many potential causes that explanatory arguments are highly contested. The role of markets, the emergence of new characteristics in markets and, in general, large-scale 'aggregate' or social properties of markets are offered as alternatives to individualistic explanation (Lawson, 1997). Some economists ultimately commit themselves to reducing everything to individual action by tracing large-scale phenomena backwards until some individual action is found. For example, a poor lending decision by a banker might have indirectly caused the bank to go bankrupt, or a poor risk-management policy by a bank policy-maker might have contributed to the wave of fear, and so on. Again, complexity rears its head, because we have so many different actors on different levels. In economics, as in health and social work, there are multiple stages rather than just a single drama with a few actors.

These three examples show that many causes contribute to outcomes, and that focusing on an outcome and its causes leads us toward studying the history of the present day. We also see that factors exist at many levels which all contribute towards the configurations – or situations – that we are trying to explain (Lawson, 1989).

Ultimately a 'cause' is best thought of as a mechanism which has the capacity to generate some outcome. This capacity is a tendency, but is not always activated. Other causal mechanisms, such as social structures and institutional factors, also intervene. Therefore, the context is part of how a causal mechanism actually generates a particular outcome. For further reading about causality and its measurement I recommend Pawson and Tilley (1997) and Pawson (1998). The latter is quite critical of survey measurement. Summary arguments can be found in Byrne (2002). Nevertheless the consensus is that causality exists.

In the British Household Panel Survey, numerous incidents in a person's life are recorded year after year through a series of annual house visits. The first visit includes a short life history of the person's employment experience, the second visit consolidates this history, and then annual visits create a panel dataset in the standard survey-data format. The BHPS is unusual in having different segments – some done as face-to-face interviews, some using computer-aided interviewing and some using self-completion questionnaires in the home. The rows of data – one row per case – are computerised and made anonymous. We can then trace through the sequences of events from 1991 to 2007 in the lives of any of thousands of respondents. If you are at school or university, a teacher or researcher, see www.esds.ac.uk for free access. Commercial users have to pay a fee.

This is how we can organise the BHPS data assuming variables can act as traces of real causes. The BHPS columns are the variables, and I can list several types of causal variable from BHPS (Table 4). The causality of an outcome such as divorce or poor school performance might be constructed by looking at all the other explanatory factors shown. The outcome might be caused not just by personal but also institutional and social factors as listed.

Table 4   Variable types drawn from the BHPS

Structural factors	Institutional factors	Personal factors
• social class of father • social class of respondent • service class job • household income • age group • marital status • ethnic group • region • rural/urban • home owner or tenant	• whether employer has a union • hours worked per week • whether the hours are flexitime or not • whether job has a pension • whether attends church • whether a member of a voluntary organisation • whether self-employed	• whether respondent is a member of a union • whether person wants to work more hours per week than they currently work • gender • response to an attitude question about managing early-years child care • division of domestic work

So if we put to an interviewee the question 'How strongly do you agree with the statement that a young child suffers if its mother goes out to work?' we need to prepare for a much wider analysis. We cannot just pick any causes we like out of a hat. We need to gather data on structural, institutional (e.g. membership) and event-based causes of different attitudes in answering this question (see Crompton et al., 2005; Crompton and Harris, 1998).

The epistemic fallacy is the tendency to confuse the data with the reality. This fallacy often starts by a statistical method which focuses on given data and does not collect primary data. Being restricted in the variables available, the researcher tends to look only to these to get answers to an explanatory question. The fallacy arises when cause is attributed to what is present (e.g. ethnicity), rather than to the deeper unrecorded factors (e.g. discrimination). In the 'child suffering if mother goes out to work' question, the recorded cause of a strong belief that children suffer might be found in the variable 'age', when the real cause is much deeper, i.e. beliefs about housewifery that were taught to the older generation when they were young. Those who have new training or ideas will tend to disagree with the statement, and those who retain their beliefs over a long period may tend to agree with the statement. To attribute cause merely to 'age' is to misspecify the cause. Bhaskar (1989) is attributed with calling this the epistemic fallacy. His contribution was to show that retroduction can offset the dangers of the fallacy of using only pre-given data. Following loosely Bhaskar's line of thinking, we can advise that retroduction plays a part in scientific research using a typical research design or protocol (shown in Box 3).

Box 3   A Protocol for Hypothesis Testing within a Petroductive Methodology

- State the theory or theories.

- List the hypothesis or hypotheses.

- Collect and analyse the data.

- Test the hypotheses.

- Do more data collection to explore the situation.

- Reflect for a moment.

- Frame new hypotheses.

- Revisit existing theories and draw conclusions.

- Start the next project.

This protocol for hypothesis testing within a retroductive methodology accurately describes what many researchers do, whether using survey data or not. It encourages all researchers to acknowledge their search for a broad expertise and for qualitative and theoretical knowledge. Getting more knowledge (during the middle of a project) is obviously desirable as the learning process proceeds. Even without individualised survey data, we can study history and documents to understand the real causes behind a pattern. Unpicking the epistemic fallacy was a major contribution to the improvement of research designs that try to explain social outcomes. More detail about 'getting the data' is given in other chapters of this book.[1] See also 6.1 **case-study research** and 7.3 **retroduction**.

Note

1. Some readers may wonder whether hypotheses are necessary for a research project. They are not. All projects need to have an initial research question, but this can be modified and is open to change. But having hypotheses or testing hypotheses is not well suited to all projects. The protocol in Box 3 is offered mainly to help those who wish to study through the use of hypotheses, so that they can do it well. 'Doing it well' may involve asking hard questions about where data are coming from, what causal processes or structures could have caused the data to appear as they do, whether the hypothesis is refuted, and so on. Data collection does not exhaust the research process, and in itself the data cannot guarantee good research.

1.5 Sampling

Sampling is a cost-saving way to create sets of cases. For instance, you might sample households randomly in a city, then select individuals non-randomly from those households. If you were doing a study of young people you might choose only those between the ages of 16 and 30, for example. The two main methods of sampling, non-random and random, can be merged only at the cost that the result is usually considered to be non-random. However, non-random sampling plays an important role in so much social research that I propose to discuss it first. Then when describing random sampling the possibility of multi-stage sampling makes a lot of sense. The chapter concludes by suggesting ways of using weights if the sampling scheme does not suit the population of cases that you wish the data to represent.

Non-random selection of cases cannot be called sampling at all. Instead we use the word 'selection' and a number of strategic decisions are normally made. For instance, one may decide *a priori* how many cases are desired, what the geographic area is, what unit is to be considered a case, and whether cases are to be seen in their nested location within larger units.

The first method of non-random case selection is snowball sampling. Snowball sampling refers to extending the network of known cases outward using contacts offered by those within the existing sample. Snowball sampling for small studies may stay within a tight geographic area. Suppose you were studying skiing accidents. You might pick up some cases from an indoor skiing facility, then ask them to name some other skiers. Using the phone or email, you would try to contact these skiers and ask them, among other things, for more contacts. During this process you would normally make a list containing basic details about each case (person, skier). If you decided to use the 'accident' as the case instead of the 'person', then you would amend the notes to suit the characteristics of the new case unit. Accidents are usually nested within skiers. In a few cases a skier may give you contact details of another skier involved in the same accident. By creating an N-to-N relationship, with N representing any number above 1, this makes a non-nested relation between skiers and accidents. Your task in qualitative research is usually to focus on one or the other of these. For survey research it might be easier to insist on a 1-to-N relationship, hence a nested relationship, in which each skier can have multiple accidents but each accident is associated with just one of the skier cases. Snowball sampling does not give a random representation of the population. Indeed, the whole population's characteristics (and location) need not even be known.

An example of snowball sampling (Eldar-Avidan et al., 2009) shows that in selecting 22 respondents it is possible to claim to have touched upon a wide variety of groups in society. The small-scale study by Eldar-Avidan et al., was focused on adults whose parents had been divorced while they were young. On the design of the sample they write:

> Twenty-two Israeli young adults participated in this study, aged 20–25 years (average: 23), whose parents divorced before they were 18. … Participants were chosen to ensure variability and sampling was terminated when saturation was reached …. Heterogeneity was achieved in regard to age (within the predefined age group), age at the time of divorce, time since the divorce, education, occupation, parents' current marital status, number of siblings, and place of residence. Thus some came from big cities, while others were from smaller towns, villages, or the kibbutz (communal settlements); some were still doing their mandatory military service, while others were working, studying, or both. Some participants were referred ('snowball') by colleagues or other young people. (Eldar-Avidan et al., 2009: 2)

The claim being made here is not that the sample is representative. For just $N = 22$ there can only be one or two from several of the groups that are named. It would be hard to justify claiming that this is a representative sample in the usual statistical sense of enabling inferences from sample to population. Instead, however, behind this sampling strategy is a mild assumption that most young people in Israel of the age group 20–25 whose parents were divorced would exhibit some homogeneity on some of the relevant characteristics. However, the authors are open to diversity; in the findings, there is more than a hint that tapping into a subgroup, such as rural Israeli residents, with just a handful of cases will give interesting and perhaps even representative information about them. The paper rightly avoids making generalisations across broad swathes of Israeli people. Instead most of the general statements in the paper are simply about the 22 young people interviewed. Like most grounded theory, the paper is highly concrete and the findings are specific to the selected cases chosen.

In the conclusions of the study, to some extent a distinction is made among three types of young people: those left more vulnerable after divorce, those more resilient after divorce, and those who are survivors of divorce. The results of this study are carefully couched in grounded theory as a method of data gathering and analysis. In grounded theory, purposive stepwise sampling goes hand-in-hand with developing a theory about outcomes. In this instance the stepwise sampling included some snowballing and some purposeful deviation into contrasting groups. The word 'saturated' is used in grounded theory when the sample selection is considered to be complete and the theory development has firmly started, but data are still being collected and analysed.

Snowball sampling can also be done via the internet. Internet groups and online sites such as dating sites offer additional opportunities for qualitative sample selection. Another form of qualitative non-random sample selection, quota sampling, depends upon making some decisions about the types of respondents that are wanted, making a grid of basic characteristics and distributing the desired sample size among them, and then going out to a specific area (or the internet) and finding people or other cases of the desired types. Quota sampling is often confused with random sampling by the less initiated. It is critical to realise that when filling a quota – from the street, from among students in a classroom, from among visitors to discussion groups or wherever – there is a strong tendency for a bias in sample selection to arise from among the cases available. This bias will differ for different researchers; to give two examples, young women might avoid tall older men in one scenario, while researchers of one linguistic group such as French might avoid speakers of another language group in some other scenario. The quota table might specify what sex and age group to choose, and what occupational category to accept into each quota. If it specifies the areas that are at risk of bias, then the tendency to bias can be compensated for. If it does not, then this bias risk remains.

Random sampling, on the other hand, attempts to avoid bias by asking the enumerators or researchers to select specific cases from a given list of available cases. An obvious example is to use the electoral register (which contains adults who are registered to vote in a specific geographic area, and their addresses), selecting a certain random sample of pages and then a random sample from each page. One can generate random numbers in Microsoft Excel with =RAND(). For instance, using Excel, one can generate 60 random numbers from 1 to 12 using the formula =INT(RAND()*12+1. (The function starts at 0 by default so needs 1 to be added to get positive integers.) If the register has 96 names per page, one may choose names by counting downward using the first random number to a name, then to the next, e.g. down 6 lines and then down 4 lines. For each page, on average, 8 names will be chosen. If 7 pages had been random selected to begin with, then $7 \times 8 = 56$ would be the achieved sample size (nearly 60). By adjusting the formula, a sample of any target size can be achieved. From the 56 individuals, only a very small handful will be living together in the same household. This sampling frame is thus said to be a list of individuals, not a list of households. If the list is randomly ordered, then a simpler method called systematic sampling can produce a random sample. Take every nth name, e.g. every 12th name, on each selected page.

After generating the sample frame, one calculates the sampling fraction as n/N, where n is the number in the whole sample and N is the number in the list which is being taken as the population. The sampling fraction is irrelevant to the degree of statistical significance you will have in calculating statistics from the study. What really matters is sampling non-response (where cases are not available, or individuals refuse to answer) and the absolute size of the final sample. The non-response rate is the number of refusals divided by the total n in the desired sample. We need to denote the actual sample size by n', indicating that n' is less than n by the number of refusals, and the effective sampling fraction is n'/N rather than n/N. In social science a sampling fraction such as 85% is considered good, and 95% excellent, while in market research and business studies some lower sampling fractions are considered acceptable. Postal surveys and those projects where respondents are considered to come from a homogeneous population are areas where a lower sampling fraction is considered more acceptable. If bias is suspected in the non-response rate, the rate should be high. If bias is not considered a problem, perhaps because of homogeneity, then the non-response rate can be allowed to be low. Homogeneity of the cases might exist, for example, if all taste-buds worked the same general way and consumers were being tested for how sweet they thought particular foods were. The homogeneity that matters is only on all the characteristics that matter for a given study. If, instead, one is looking at consumer preferences for high- and low-alcohol drinks, and the level of alcohol is not easily perceived but instead is being guessed at using labelling clues and past experience, then we would have to assume a heterogeneous population and try to get a sample with a high response rate and no researcher selection biases.

Cluster sampling refers to choosing cases from particular places or groups which are named and listed prior to setting up the next stage of sampling. If there were 30 bowling clubs in a region, and the cases desired were Saturday night bowlers, then one could choose five bowling clubs randomly and move to a second-stage sampling strategy on Saturday nights of taking all the bowlers on three lanes at random in each club once per hour from 7 to 11 p.m. In the cluster sampling strategy, the next stage can instead cover the entire population within each cluster, e.g. all bowlers present on Saturday night over a three-week period. Cluster sampling runs the risk of missing heterogeneity in the clusters not chosen. It also depends upon some prior information such as a list of bowling clubs. Cluster sampling is usually considered to cause wider confidence intervals when sophisticated statistical software is allowed to integrate the information about clustering with the rest of the detailed survey data. However, for some studies cluster sampling is a highly efficient way to target the visits of researchers to specific areas, and for this cost-saving reason it is desirable even if it leads to a risk of poor representation of a geographic region overall.

Stratified sampling is more complicated. To stratify a sample, one decides first on the overall sample size, then breaks this n down into subgroups. Prior information about the prevalence of certain characteristics, relevant to the study, in each subgroup is used to decide on the percentage of cases which are to come from each stratum. The strata can be of different sizes, and a simple mode of stratified sampling is to use the inverse of the proportion in the group to set the proportion of *n* that will be in that stratum. Small strata thus get better representation, and large strata worse representation, than in simple random sampling. It can be proved that if the strata are set up well to encourage large strata only where there is case-wise homogeneity on relevant characteristics, then stratified sampling will tend to give a better representation than simple random sampling over the chosen population. However, there are often difficulties getting the relevant information. Once the strata are set up, it is also possible to manipulate the sample sizes and make a post-sampling weighting adjustment (see 5.8 **survey weights**) to give unbiased averages and other statistical results for the whole *n* overall. The use of post-stratification survey weights can also be a way to adjust for non-response and leads to design-based statistical inference. Cluster sampling can be used in conjunction with stratified sampling. Just when cluster sampling has reduced the overall accuracy of a survey sample, stratification within each cluster can attempt to increase it and thus improve accuracy again. The mixing of cluster sampling with stratified sampling is usually called multi-stage sampling.

If multi-stage sampling includes a non-random stage, such as snowballing, then the sampling method overall is not considered random. If it is not random, then generalisations based on the sample *n* should not be considered to apply to the wider population from which the sample was drawn. Care needs to be taken not to confuse these basic rules if random sampling is considered desirable. In general, random sampling is more expensive than non-random case selection. However, the overall ambitiousness of a study – its geographic and social extent – is an easy factor to vary if cost savings are needed. In the case of Israel, for example, one could have had an urban-only study with a higher number of cases for the same cost.

If non-random sampling is used, including carefully manipulated sampling strategies such as cluster sampling and stratified sampling, then a weighted average of the data in the rows can be used to generate an estimate of the average overall among a sample as a representation of the average in the population. The error in this estimate will tend to be increased where cluster sampling is used, but on the other hand error is decreased where stratified sampling is used. The researcher who has either cluster or stratified sampling may choose to use post-stratification weights. These weights imply design-based inference. Furthermore, those who have any noticeable non-response rate may create and apply post-sampling weights by comparing the actual sample with a gold-standard data source, such as a census or a full hospital register. Post-sampling weights are usually called post-stratification weighting, but there are three sub-kinds of these weights. One is an identifier for each cluster; the second is an identifier for each stratum and furthermore a weight attached to the stratum that compensates for higher or lower sampling in that one relative to overall; and thirdly the non-response weighting adjustments. All the weights average out to 1 and they can be multiplied by each other. The result is the overall weight given to each case for design-based inference. For example, this would produce the mean of age for the sample with a 95% confidence interval.

Model-based inference is slightly different from design-based inference. A researcher who has access to enough variables that relate either directly or indirectly to the main axes of sampling bias, and who wants to use regression or another multivariate modelling technique, can avoid using post-stratification weights. For example, the data could have a large bulk of students, and then a variable 'student' is put into the model and variation according to this is thus controlled for. The remaining variation in an outcome is examined for how it varies with some other variable – perhaps body size, or previous training. Cleaning out underlying sources of variation in a model-based framework is most frequently done in econometric and panel-data contexts (Greene, 2003; Wooldridge, 2002). It may be comforting to know that it is possible to examine experimental data or other survey data without random sampling. In general, it is best to do so only after making explicit several assumptions about the nature and diversity of the cases and the population. There must also be sufficient cases in the sample n. Another approach would be to make statements that are purely descriptive of the actual sample, but this interpretive stance would not involve inference. Inference is defined as making a valid statement about a population based on a random sample from that population.

Further Reading for Part 1

Data gathering and data analysis are difficult to disentangle. The works I would suggest for further reading also link up these tasks, so that the researcher cannot just automate a data-collection process or follow a rigid rule-book. Instead, people tend to think about how they might attack a problem, develop a research question around that, plan the data collection and data analysis, embark on data collection – perhaps with a pilot study – and then revisit the earlier stages before completing the whole data-collection stage.

Blaikie (2000) and Danermark et al. (2002) strongly support this overall approach which integrates data collection with a holistic well-managed research project. Blaikie (2000) walks you through all the stages of research design. Danermark et al., (2002) have provided a protocol for research which gives an overarching map of the contours of progress through a project. A useful book of comparable scope, with more technical detail and less on the methodology side, is DeVaus (2001). Layder (1993) takes up the issues in a very straightforward language, suitable for undergraduates and the newest entrants to the research scene. This lucid book helps the reader choose methods suited to their particular kinds of research topics.

For those working in Third World or comparative contexts, Laws (2003) provides a book on data collection and methods. In this general area there are two full-length sources of more concrete guidance, both very lucid and helpful. One is written entirely by one author (Mikkelsen, 1995, 2005). She takes into account the difficulty of separating development research from development practice. Although she covers quantitative and qualitative primary data collection practice in some detail, she also has a wonderful section on participatory data collection and encouragement to mix methods. An edited volume on development research as a form of practice is Thomas et al. (1998).

Participation in research is explained in technical detail by Mikkelsen (1995). I recommend the edited volume by Carroll et al. (2004) for anyone wanting to do engaged research, or participatory or action research in any social context. The overview by Flyvbjerg (2001) says much less about practical methods, but it does help by making sense of the whole scene, with researchers being purposive people participating in a social and political landscape.

See also Barnett (2002) on sampling.

Part 2

Collecting Qualitative Data

2.1 Interviews

Interviewing involves an interaction of at least two people. The semi-structured interview schedule is centred around the concept of a prompt. In this chapter I will discuss prompts and a few other details about semi-structured interviews. Then I will turn to the other two major sources of interview data – unstructured interviews and structured interviews. Questions about the practice of constructing and typing the transcripts are dealt with separately under that heading (see 2.2 **transcripts** and 2.10 **accuracy**).

I have already given one example of a three-way semi-structured interview (see 1.3 **data**). That interview was planned ahead of time in conjunction with the rest of Antcliff's doctoral research (see also Antcliff, Saundry and Stuart, 2007). A short extract from the interview, provided below, helps to illustrate how a semi-structured interview moves forward from one topic to the next. The two types of statement uttered by the interviewer are questions and prompts. The questions are planned in advance (see also 1.3 **data** and 2.5 **interpretation**), and they tend to be open-ended questions such as why, what, who, where, or even less structured questions. Examples might include statements such as 'Tell me about how you came to think of taking a step toward divorce' or 'Why did you begin to think of changing jobs at that point?'. The prompts are even less well defined; a list of prompts is invaluable when planning and preparing for doing an interview:

'Why was that?'

'Tell me more.'

'Can you remember more about that?'

'And then?'

'So?'

'and who else, and why?'

It is useful even to simply encourage the speaker (and then go silent), as in:

'I see …'

'Really …'

'It seems to feel that way to you …'

'at the time you looked at it that way …'

These prompts reassure the speaker that you are listening, but they do not turn the conversation aside. The use of questions is reserved for the start of the interview and the moments when, in view of the time and the plan of the interview, the interviewer thinks it is important to move on.

Such an interview is called 'semi-structured' because the basic scaffolding that fills out the allotted time is set up in advance. Unstructured interviews just have a topic. Unstructured interviews usually have no time limit because a revisit is possible and indeed likely. No recording is made. Notes are written down just afterwards from memory. If an unstructured interview is recorded it will be difficult to locate the important segments and distinguish them from the unimportant segments. In general, the semi-structured interview is a more systematic and slightly more pre-planned method than the unstructured interview.

The slave narratives that I discuss in the chapter on **transcripts** (2.2) are unstructured interviews.

On the other hand, a structured interview is usually a face-to-face encounter supported by a questionnaire. This questionnaire is carefully planned. In typical survey methods, the questionnaire would have a lot of closed questions and perhaps some 'showcards' or pre-coded response options (see also the chapters on 2.10 **accuracy** and 5.1 **operationalisation**). The interviewing methods for surveys require a lot of practice, careful time-keeping, explicit guidance to the respondent, and following the guidelines to interviewers carefully. The interviewer is likely to be called an enumerator because they are meant to be capturing mainly quantifiable (easily recorded) answers. (To enumerate means literally to count.) The use of enumerators in the context of harmonised surveys enables a variety of survey employees in different places to conduct a similar survey in comparable ways, and thus generate harmonised data (see 1.3 **data**, 5.1 **operationalisation** and 5.2 **measurement**).

In general, in the context of survey research, an enumerator tries to be non-influential, and they cannot use prompts because they are not capturing answers to open-ended questions. The enumerator has to follow the standardised pathway through the questionnaire and try to treat each respondent the same. That way, answers will correspond to the same questions. This is the very essence of 'structured interviewing'. Nevertheless they can be called an 'interviewer' and it can be confusing that both structured and semi-structured interviews are sometimes conducted by the same staff. If a semi-structured interview is what you intend to do, then do not create a questionnaire for that interview. Do not pre-plan it to such an extent that there is no freedom in the response pattern (see the chapters on 1.3 **data** and 2.2 **transcripts,** where interview plans are described).

In recent years some adventurous mixed-methods researchers have merged aspects of unstructured, semi-structured and structured interviewing. One way is to have open-ended questions (and a recording device) in the middle or near the end of a closed-question survey. The person administering the survey is no longer merely an enumerator, but is interviewing the respondent with a view to both filling in the survey and getting some textual data. It may be wise to have a series of open-ended questions in a group, and to keep the closed questions in a coherent group too. The interview needs careful time-keeping and planning to ensure that it does not take too long.

The semi-structured interview leads to a transcript which may vary from 6 to 40 pages in length. Typing the transcript is a large job whose difficulty varies according to the languages, slang and dialects used as well as the quality of the recording. Without making a tape recording, the analysis of semi-structured interviews is strongly limited. The original first-person narrative is corrupted when it is converted into a third-person narrative of brief notes. It is common for the metaphors, idioms, abbreviations and elisions of language to be changed when the interviewer writes them down afterwards. If they can be remembered verbatim, then note-taking is a good substitute for recording. If the interview is too long to remember, then note-taking is a poor substitute for a transcript.

The interview transcript allows insight into mechanisms, processes, reasons for actions, and social structures as well as many other phenomena.

The introduction to the interview conducted by Antcliff (2000; see also Antcliff and Saundry, 2005) went something like this:

Me: The first thing I'd like to ask you is how secure you feel in your current position.

Here the transcript leaves out the earlier introductions prior to the start of recording. This question clearly indicates an attempt to elicit commentaries about job security and the length of the current contract. Recall that the first interviewee (called Person 1) is a female, temporary casual staff member, and the second (Person 2) is a mature male staff member on a permanent contract who is much older. The interview continues:

Me: So you think the only reason that you got the staff job was because of the skills that you'd learnt elsewhere?

Person 2:   Oh yeah. I refused initially and then they made me an offer I couldn't refuse, they pay me decent money and put me [down as] staff and [gave me] the access to the company pension scheme ...

Person 1:   It's the opposite way round for me. From what I was told, a thousand people applied for the job, that gives them tremendous leeway, they offered me a ridiculously low amount of money compared to other people ... You sign a contract that says I will work all the hours there are in the day for no perks, you sign away the European Time Directive ...

Me: So you actually sign away that right?

Person 1:   Yeah, you sign away that, ...

Me: So you're in completely opposite positions then. [*referring to both interviewees*]

Person 1:   I had more rights when I was temping. ...

Person 2:   ... Bizarre

Person 1:   And as I say for me it just makes me feel like well, I can just go off and do other things because I'm not beholden to them because they're not making an investment in me, they're not saying what we're going to do is train you up in all these things in TV ...

Person 2:   [*laughs*] Yeah, it's a problem, and the problem is that there's quite a big skills gap and that's getting worse and worse. If you look at the people who're actually called in to do the big shows, ... they're all freelance, they're not staff people anymore ... [*gives an anecdote*] The jobs are still going to these [freelance] people and people aren't being trained into it, there's such a skills gap ...

Person 1:   ... My boss tells me I'm good at my job, but there's no reason for me to stay ... I think every one wants to be somewhere where they think, you know, there's an investment in them, and that they're valued. You're not really valued, and you're paid a pittance ... you're coming in at six in the morning and you're thinking – remind me again why I'm doing this job.

Me: So have you received any training at all?

In this extract, the interviewer, designated 'Me' in the transcript, has revealed two interests – first in skills brought to the job, and secondly in training on the job. The interviewer uses a 'prompt' to show an interest in the contrast between the first and second interviewees. The interviewer is careful not to say too much. Nevertheless their prompts move the interview along.

The use of a semi-structured interview approach in this particular case allowed the research to have a joint focus on the organisation and the career of each employee. A joint interview is an interesting twist on the usual face-to-face interviewing method. No doubt using a three-way interview has costs and benefits in terms of how openly people talk, what they choose to talk about, and how sensitive issues are dealt with.

In the particular case of the transcript sample about working on fixed-term or permanent contracts in the television industry, much of the interview material is about social relations within large organisations, including the subcontractors' role. In addition, the career of the junior employee (who is a subcontractor and works on a series of fixed-term contracts) becomes part of the core subject of the research. The female employee's subjectivity becomes very important.

If the TV career interview were being coded according to themes, as in content analysis, then the codes might include money, skills, screening for jobs, power, casual contracts, permanent contracts, flexibility of worker, flexibility of employer, gender, terms of contract. If it were being analysed using discourse analysis then some of these topics would be subsumed under broader headings, such as power assumptions, hierarchical relationships, social networking, agents handling the work contract, assumptions about work contracts, and so on. In the discourse analysis method, one might have more detailed codes for specific metaphors. Using a longer extract, I noted a few of the details that would need to be coded:

- verbs – imposing conditions, asking for help, suggesting training, enticing freelancers;

- archetypical nouns – freelancers, staff people;

- idioms – you're paid a pittance, working all hours, proper staff;

- sarcasm – well that's really nice you know, remind me again why I'm doing this job;

- metaphors – core and peripheral workers, God given gift, those who are looked after by the company;

- exaggeration – they're there for no money all day all night [referring to cheap young interns].

If more interviews were studied, a wider range of these small elements would be coded, and patterns would be discernable. Eventually the main discourses would become evident to the analyst. One might find a 'flexible working discourse' and a 'permanent staff corporate atmosphere' discourse, perhaps. There might also be a 'flexible working freelance resistance' discourse.

When planning to do interviews, all these different sorts of analysis issues should be considered carefully. A pilot interview can be a useful basis for running through all the research procedures (i.e. first transcription, then coding and analysis) that are planned. It is not good to do interviews without knowing what kind(s) of analysis methods will be used. On the other hand, there is no need to limit oneself to a single analysis method. For interviews there are at least seven methods available:

- phenomenology (the study of how a set of events happens, and how it feels or works from inside);
- interpretation;
- thematic content analysis;
- discourse analysis;
- critical discourse analysis;
- narrative analysis;
- conversation analysis.

Merely describing the events that the respondent talked about is not a 'method'. A 'method' is a technique for bringing fresh knowledge out of the interview material. A methodology is a much broader set of assertions, such as constructivist or realist assertions. Thus in this chapter, by giving an example and some instances of 'coding', I have illustrated the 'method' of analysing interviews without specifying which of several methods one might use.

2.2 Transcripts

The creation of a transcript involves writing down or typing out the text of an interview or other sound file. Focus-group transcripts, market research discussion-group transcripts and semi-structured interview transcripts are just three of many possible kinds. Transcripts may be typed out in the original language or translated. I will deal with the basic creation of a transcript first, then take up some issues of translation in order to highlight the crucial role that metaphors and idioms play in the way people talk about the world. The chapter will be helpful for international research, as well as for local research, since idioms of local or dialect origin are prevalent in most lay language situations.

In the transcript it may be important to use abbreviations or pseudonyms. This has to be thought through from the viewpoint of the relevant country's data-protection legislation and the ethical informed consent that you have developed with the respondents. An abbreviated name may be comprehensible to involved persons, and thus not adequately protect the confidentiality of respondents. Therefore, decide at the start whether or not pseudonyms are to be used. If you use pseudonyms, then do not use any abbreviations. Insert the pseudonym at the start of each segment of that person's interview. Furthermore, watch out for them naming other people in their area or organisation. Develop a 'wider pseudonym' list which covers these people in case they are named multiple times. Your 'core pseudonym' list may also have case numbers, interview numbers, cassette identifiers and a list of MP3 sound file names. The pseudonym list needs to be handled carefully as a confidential artefact. Set up password-protected files on your computer and store this information here.

Do not use pseudonyms if you do not need to. They are hard to remember and create a challenge of style and creativity in order to avoid reusing existing names. Thus if someone is called Patrick then you cannot sensibly use 'Patrick' as one of the pseudonyms, at the risk of causing someone to think this is the real Patrick's segment of interview. If you do use pseudonyms, get local advice to ensure they have reasonable nuances. Many names have religious or regional connotations. Try to choose more innocuous ones. Thus 'David' or 'Patrick' may be suitable pseudonyms in Ireland, but 'Skip', 'Felix', or 'Trig' might have the wrong connotations. (Skip sounds like a dog's name to some people; Felix is the name of a cartoon cat character; and Trig is the name of a child of the American politician Sarah Palin.)

If pseudonyms are not being used, then abbreviations may be useful. My own experience is that using 'Q': and 'A': (question and answer) throughout an interview is confusing. It is better to abbreviate each speaker's name and repeat this consistently through an interview text. These abbreviations can be used later if you need to search text documents for relevant passages. You may also decide to be sure that each abbreviation is unique in the survey. Thus 'Th' for Theodore, and 'Tr' for Tracy. This enables future computer searches to locate each speaker successfully.

Silverman (2000, 2001) has given much detailed advice for transcript creation. The book by Bauer and Gaskell (2000) is another useful source for the handling of the data, and that by Lewins and Silver (2007) helps with taking the transcript into a computer software package. Transcripts are normally created with detailed punctuations to show verbatim. For example, use … (3) for a pause indicating the length of the pause. However, this should not be confused with the omission of a segment, where we also put an ellipsis (…) to indicate the omission of contiguous material.

Looking at either of two interesting sets of transcripts (of very different kinds) can give you an idea of the length of a transcript and its potential complexity. The first set of transcripts gives lecture materials in a transcripted format without any question-and-answer format. The BASE (British Academic Spoken English) and BASE Plus Collections project website (see http://www2.warwick.ac.uk/fac/soc/al/research/collect/base/) presents the transcripts using the pause notation [1.2] for a 1.2 second pause, and very little formatting other than that. The raw .txt files such as one from a development economics lecture, illustrated below, have not been punctuated into grammatical English because the aim of the project is to analyse the spoken language's structure without forcing it into standardised formats.

same things are happening in Ghana in the early nineteen-eighties

[0.7] so [0.7] the operation of your large [0.2] parastatal [0.5] is snookering

the whole economy [0.9] there's a whole series of vicious effects here [0.5]

which push you into a bigger and bigger mess [0.7] not surprisingly [0.6] the I-M-F and the World Bank looked at this kind of thing and said [0.3] for heaven's sake privatize these state enterprises [0.6] er [0.2] they're doing you no good at all [0.7] er [0.2] they're probably inefficient [0.5] er [0.3] well it's not obvious that they were all inefficient but the general feeling was that government was inefficient [0.4] and they're messing up your economy in all kinds of ways [0.9] they also wanted key economic institutions reforming [0.6] and those included the tax system

In this example we see that the run-on sentences are used to stress certain phrases and to let the listener think about certain points the speaker is making.

A one-hour lecture on this kind of material could result in a transcript of about 35 or 40 pages using double line spacing and a 12-point font, because the speaker moves quickly from point to point and speaks volubly. For interviews with reluctant speakers, or where some translation is taking place or there are pauses, a minimum per hour of sound is 20 double-spaced pages. From these length estimates, it is possible to work out the cost of transcribing each interview. For example, if each interview is 45 minutes and the speakers are voluble (fluent), and if the typist can audio-type smoothly at 8 pages per hour (double-spaced, 250 words per page), then the time for transcribing each interview is about (30 pages per interview /8 pages per hour) = 3.7 hours. An estimate of less than two transcripts per day would be reasonable for such a typist once the final editing, use of pseudonyms, and insertion of substitute names for identifiable places is included. If you have 40 such interviews you will need at least 20 days of audio-typing time. A non-expert typist will take much longer.

A second example is from the Slave Narratives website (http://xroads.vir ginia.edu/~hyper/wpa). The oral histories of more than 2,000 people who were slaves in the USA during the 1850s and 1860s were transcribed and put into an online resource area without using pseudonyms. The Slave Narratives website gives access to these materials. An oral history is a data-collection method that involves relatively unstructured interviews and the researcher typically meets the respondents several times and does a wide range of background research both before and after the interviews. The slave interview material shows a strong dialect that arises both from the time and the place of the interviews. I put three of the interviews into the NVivo computer software and started to code moments when the former slaves talked about their masters of the time. They refer mainly to the master's behaviour just before and during the Civil War. In the next few paragraphs I present an extract from a coding query in NVivo. A coding query is a way to recover extracts of text which have been coded previously by the researcher. The coding 'node' was Talk About Masters. Three interviews were studied in detail. The extract of the results shown in Box 4 contains one extract from one interview. The usefulness of NVivo is that the various transcripts can be studied by comparing what each slave, such as Walter Calloway, said about the masters – and for the way the transcripts were prepared. None of the interviewers' statements appear here since they were limited to innocuous prompts.

Box 4   Ex-Slaves Talk about Masters

<Internals\3.Narrative Fountain HughesRaw> – § 4 references coded [12% Coverage]
Reference 4 – 2% coverage
  Now, if, uh, if my master wanted sen' me, he never say, You couldn' get a horse an' ride. You walk, you know, you walk. An' you be barefooted an' col'. That didn' make no difference. You wasn' no more than a dog to some of them in them days. You wasn' treated as good as they treat dogs now. But still I didn' like to talk about it. Because it makes, makes people feel bad you know. I could say a whole lot I don' like to say. An' I won't say a whole lot more.

<Internals\3.Narrative TempeH DurhamRaw> – § 6 references coded [41% Coverage]
Reference 6 – 8% coverage
  Freedom is all right, but de niggers was better off befo' surrender, kaze den dey was looked after an' dey didn' get in no trouble fightin' an' killin' like dey do dese days. If a nigger cut up an' got sassy in slavery times, his Ole Marse give him a good whippin' an' he went way back an' set down an' 'haved hese'f. If he was sick, Marse an' Mistis looked after him … Maybe everybody's Marse and Mistis wuzn' good as Marse George and Mis' Betsy, but dey was de same as a mammy an' pappy to us niggers.

<Internals\3.Narrative Walter CallowayRaw> – § 2 references coded [30% Coverage]
Reference 1 – 20% coverage
  Marse John hab a big plantation an' lots of slaves. Dey treated us purty good, but we hab to wuk hard. Time I was ten years ole I was makin' a reg'lar han' 'hin de plow. Oh, yassuh, Marse John good 'nough to us an' we get plenty to eat, but he had a oberseer name Green Bush what sho' whup us iffen we don't do to suit him. Yassuh, he mighty rough wid us be he didn't do de whippin' hisse'f. He had a big black boy name Mose, mean as de debil an' strong as a ox, and de oberseer let him do all de whuppin'. An', man, he could sho' lay on dat rawhide lash. He whupped a nigger gal 'bout thirteen years old so hard she nearly die, an' allus atterwa'ds she hab spells of fits or somp'n. Dat make Marse John pow'ful mad, so he run dat oberseer off de place an' Mose didn' do no mo' whuppin'.

Source: NVivo project created by Wendy Olsen from Slave Narratives website text, http:// xroads.virginia.edu/~hvper/wpa. The extracts have been shortened. Key: 'Reference' means a coded quotation. 'Coverage' is a ratio of the text in the reference to the text in a wider group of sources (either one interview or all the sources for a case). 'Internals' refers to sources that are held within NVivo's project. 'Marse' means master.

In the extract, we see that a lot of words are pronounced in particular non-standard ways, as illustrated by apostrophes and 'misspellings'. The extract illustrates the importance of verbatim transcription. If the words had been converted to standard English of the 1990s, they would look very different and they would have less authenticity. The information content is increased by the idioms and expressions that are reported. For example, Fountain Hughes used the word 'lawdy', which is a shortened form of 'Lord!' or 'Good Lord!' as one might express it now. Fountain Hughes used a strongly southern form of this expression. Merely by its pronunciation, we know that this is a quote from the deep south of the USA. Experts can also discuss the way different social class and ethnic origins will influence the pronunciation. Another example of exact transcription is 'Ole Marse' (spoken by Tempe Durham). This phrase could be rewritten as 'Old Master'. It does not mean 'Mister' but is an abbreviation of the slave term for their 'Master', though these two words are closely related. The history of the title 'Mr.' could be followed up by a researcher wanting to examine the hermeneutics or meanings of the master–slave relationship from the slave's standpoint.

The extracts above show how NVivo can be used to organise a direct comparison of segments of narrative across huge long transcripts. The direct comparison I have created about the slaves talking about the masters makes it much easier to think about similarities and contrasts. NVivo helps in giving a measure of how much of each interview transcript is taken up by each quotation. These percentage measures were correct when the query was run, but become inaccurate when I shorten the quotation using ellipses (…). In any case, in qualitative research, percentages are just rough and ready indications of the prevalence of a coded node's appearance because the transcript lengths are affected by many factors such as interruptions, irrelevant side-talk and how the interview topics vary from one respondent to another.

The availability of oral history material like the slave narratives is increasing. Materials from long ago are now widely available via the internet without filling in any permission forms. The reason for this is that the respondents are unlikely to be injured by the modern-day use of data gathered years ago. Materials from the present data which are kept in 'data archives' are much more carefully guarded, either by a system of pseudonyms or by a gateway of permission forms which clarify the terms which the user has to adhere to in using the data.

If you feel curious to exercise your skills with transcripts, go through the extracts in Box 4 again and see if you can locate the idioms and metaphors used by the three speakers. Here is my list of tropes (i.e. plays on words) they used:

- comparing slaves to animals, common in the days of slavery in USA (see the references to dogs and cattle in these extracts);
- slaves imitating the ceremonies and rituals of their masters, valuing what the masters routinely have (ring and white dress and gloves) – the phrase 'a pretty ring' here means much more than just that it is physically attractive.

Metaphors are a sub-type of tropes, and you can pick out specific metaphors by examining the text closely. Idioms are figures of speech that are embedded in usual language and which are used routinely across a wide range and not just created 'on the fly' by a speaker. Among the idioms used here are 'worth a heap'. Although a heap is in one sense a pile, this may also be a reference to heaps of agricultural produce which were being produced on the farms. Looking closely at the transcript with these analytical headings in mind is a good exercise which forces us to study the narrative closely. One also wants to examine the succession of topics in each text. The study of narratives includes both the content and the processual features of how a text is structured.

With a set of texts like the ones in Box 4 we can also take advantage of the length and free-flowing nature of the talk to examine the overall themes put forward by different respondents. A theme that one might write about is whether the slaves trusted the masters. Trust can be broken down into a series of sub-areas. Could masters be trusted to punish slaves in a fair and consistent way? Was it perceived as fair by the respondent? Were feasts provided whenever slaves wanted them? Was there trust that if a slave behaved well they would be rewarded?

A rich analysis of the text would not limit itself to the narrative structure or the small-scale linguistic features. It would also become a social commentary on how the masters were perceived from the standpoint of the slaves. Moving into the ambitious sphere of the meaning of each text, however, is helped if we spend time looking at the tiny units of text, such as idioms, before moving to the bigger picture. There is no guarantee that a generalisation, such as 'slaves in the USA in 1860–5 thought masters were trustworthy' would emerge. It is more likely that a rich set of contrasting general statements about different subgroups *within the interviewed group* would be valid. These empirically grounded claims could later be woven into a theory of the master–slave relationship of the time.

An example illustrating the creation of unique abbreviations can be found on the BASE website in its interview section (http://www2.warwick.ac.uk/fac/soc/al/research/collect/base/interviews/ireland.doc). Here is a segment of a verbatim transcript of a taped interview with Dr Stanley Ireland:

Key: TK   Tim KELLY

        HN   Hilary NESI

        SI   Dr Stanley Ireland

HN   I'd like to begin by asking you: 'What do you think a seminar is for?'

SI   Well, in many ways a seminar doesn't have a single purpose. I think that's one of the first things you've got to realise. Rather like lectures don't have a single purpose.

In this extract you can see that a question arising from the interview plan is presented in quotation marks. The rest of the talk is recorded verbatim. Even if a sentence is grammatically incomplete, it is still recorded word for word just as it was spoken. This is only possible with recorded sound. Using repeated play-back, you can create an accurate verbatim transcript. Third person summaries such as 'SI said that seminars don't have a single purpose' are not suitable for further research. Verbatim transcripts are exactly that: word for word, even if the speaker goes off the subject for a while. The interviewer's job in a semi-structured interview is to bring them back onto the main topic or draw their attention to the next interview question. Prompts can be used to remind them of the main or current topic.

The transcriber or interviewer may want to add comments into the transcript. Suggested marks for comments include [ ], { } or / /. In Microsoft Word, comments can be inserted but they can be difficult to remove later and will tend to crowd the text on the page by creating a very wide right-hand margin. Annotations are another specialised Word mechanism for putting notes onto a text which may appear (or not) when the text is printed out, depending on the printing settings. If a project is begun using Word Comments or Word Annotations, it will be very difficult to convert these back into .txt or basic text-file components such as / / notes later on. That is why the basic characters which appear on the computer keyboard may be preferable to software-specific annotations. Characters that are useful for transcript notes include * * (for interjections from unknown outsiders), " " for words from a foreign language (inverted commas being preferable to italics since the italics may get lost in moving from one file format to another), ! and ? to indicate the stress presented by the speaker, and finally the keys #~+&@ if swear words are being represented but are not wanted in detail. I suggest you avoid ( ) because parentheses will not be easy to understand. It may appear ambiguous whether the parentheses refer to a parenthetical comment made by the speaker or are insertions by the transcriber later on. The only exception is (sic) which is a standard insertion meaning 'just as is'. My view is that [sic] is a better way to highlight the 'just as is' annotation. That way it is clear that no one actually said 'sic'. [sic] would be used if the speaker made a mistake which one wants to keep and take notice of. In a discussion of the nuclear industry, someone might say 'I think nucular power is useful'. Your transcript would read:

I think nucular [sic] power is useful.

Their mispronunciation is now available for further analysis. Again, italics are optional since the standard square brackets are sufficient to indicate that this is an insertion.

2.3 Coding

Coding refers to making a database of connections between various terms and data items selected from among the whole basket of evidence. Before coding, you might have developed a hand-written booklet of field notes, a survey, an interview plan, some note cards about the relevant literature, and other types of evidence. You might also have a small or large survey (perhaps in the form of a pile of questionnaires, all with their unique identification numbers written on them; or in a matrix form based upon existing case data), or interview files in MP3 format. To do 'coding' means to take the computer-based version of some data and apply codes to it.

A code is a summary term which helps you to recover or retrieve some of the data in a highly purposeful way. There are many kinds of code. I have already explained how one might code the slave narratives data (see 2.2 **transcripts**). Very basic and very advanced systems of coding can be used. In most projects, the coding scheme is original. As a result, whole books exist to guide you in planning your coding (Lewins and Silver, 2007; Gibbs, 2002; Richards and Morse, 2007). The purpose of the present chapter is to show how your coding plans affect the data-collection stage. There are particular points related to qualitative, case-study and survey data in particular. There is no substitute for advance planning.

First of all, if you wish to create a detailed list of all the words that are used in your computerised dataset, you can parse the text material. In the NVivo software (see www.qsrinternational.com), for example, parsing gives a count of each word. The words in the dataset could be used as codes, which will then be called nodes in NVivo, but it would not be efficient to have equal numbers of codes and words. Instead one might choose the most frequently used words as the main codes. If you are performing content analysis you would add to this list any themes which are not explicitly named in the text but which are clearly present in phrases or in the meaning of the text. When using computerised methods, you can automate the coding of the dataset by searching for explicit and literal phrases in the data. Several software packages can serve this purpose, including MaxQDA, ATLAS.ti, NVivo and Ethnograph. These packages differ slightly in their more advanced functions. The book by Lewins and Silver (2007) helps you choose which software to use.

The coding of qualitative data must be done carefully so that it does not become an exhausting activity. It is useful to plan three kinds of coding and to focus particularly on the second kind as the moment of creativity in studying the data. The first kind is retrieval coding, as described earlier. The codes are mainly used in order to be able to move directly to sets of texts which are extracted precisely because they match the code word. Browsing a code by clicking on it will bring you to a concise document which brings together these segments or quotations. Retrieval codes are useful when searching for quotations which one recalls and wants to use in a written piece. Upon retrieval, the text segment will include its document source details.

The second kind of coding is more interpretive. Here we are setting up the code to summarise the meaning of a sentence or phrase. The analysis of meanings has been approached broadly in three ways: ethnographically, through grounded theory, and through discourse analysis (there are many variants on each of these methods). In my experience, it was crucial to choose just one analysis method in order to conduct the method very well. For ethnography, one should be immersed in the scene which one is observing, and the field notes may be coded because they are very important. For grounded theory, one tries to have a two-stage coding method: firstly, coding the basic themes found; and secondly, using axial coding which brings together, in either an explanatory or process-related structure, a theory that relates to the data. A grounded theorist might interpret the process of moving towards divorce, for example. This is not just an explanation of divorce but an interpretation of how the phrases used relate to the outcome and to how the outcome is reached. A grounded theorist might use legal documents along with interviews or other sources (see also the helpful book on document analysis by Scott, 1990). The coding for grounded theory might consist of two groups of codes: the initial codes, and the group codes for one particular theory. It is possible to copy some initial codes into a group which may be called a tree. These selected codes become the subheadings under this tree. The use of trees is just a grouping device within the software. It is useful that the tree can be created at a late stage in the research. The tree is similar to making a pile of index cards consisting of two or three cards from each of several previous piles. The names of the previous piles are the subheadings of the tree. If there are less than 20 pages of text, you may not need a computer to do this work. Twenty pages is about 5000 words. Beyond this size, your database contents quickly become difficult to remember. Grounded theory helps produce a summary of the results.

The third kind of coding might be for discourse analysis. Here there are many options such as critical discourse analysis or the study of the internal rules that are intrinsically part of textual practices. In my experience it was useful to have a tree for each major discourse invoked by each speaker. In one study I had found six discourses about rural banking. There was a discourse of discipline, a prudence discourse, and four others. Initial codes naming the themes which people talked about, such as discipline, could be copied and moved into each discourse as the subheadings. Under each subheading the computer was aware of the text segments which I had highlighted in the beginning. Overall, the computerised method creates a complex database which is helpful when you are ready to write.

The backward impact of the coding plans on the data collection arises if the coding plans have implications for how you set up interviews or focus groups, and how you create the transcripts. Case coding is used if you want to relate multiple materials for each case together. Each case can be one code. *Casing* is the process of setting up a conceptual framework which separates the cases and gives them soft but clear boundaries (Ragin, 2009). After you have done the casing, you will be grouping the material about the cases and you may even splice the focus-group materials by identifying each speaker as a case. Each time you must highlight a segment of text (using click and drag with a mouse), then indicate which case it belongs to. In the case table, which summarises all the cases and their attributes, each case appears to be mutually exclusive, but in fact the computer programme has no objection to the multiple use of a particular text segment. A policy document might relate to all the cases, for instance, and small-group photos taken in bank offices, for example, could each be coded to several cases. In setting up case-study material you may want to have nested cases. In NVivo, you can have nested cases by using the tree structure again. For example, you might have six banks in your study. Within three of these banks, two branches have been approached. You list the various branches as sub-cases of banks. After interviewing managers, you code the textual material to the branches about which they are speaking and not simply to the branch in which they work.

So far I have shown that the specific purpose of the analytical coding stage will affect how you set up the initial retrieval codes. It is even useful to code the elements of discourse, such a metaphors and tropes, if you plan to do discourse analysis. In such ways, it is useful to be clever in planning a study so that it can be concluded within a reasonable time-frame. Therefore your coding method may have implications for the number of interviews which are feasible. More coding may imply fewer or shorter interviews.

On the other hand, a central idea in survey data collection is that coding makes the data highly efficient and can enable a large sample size. Coding here is the process of setting up numerical codes to represent themes or answers. Again, the plans for coding the data have some backward effect upon how you plan data collection (see 5.2 **measurement** and 5.4 **data cleaning**). Data coding thus applies within a variety of research contexts – qualitative, case-study and survey contexts.

2.4 Meaning

The search for meaning in human lives occurs both through introspection and through discussion. We sometimes reflect in very non-cognitive ways about the meaning of life (e.g. during religious worship). But finding meaning in 'data', and then planning how to collect more data in such a way that you can suck meaning out of it afterwards is a comparatively artificial and constructed activity. Still, there may be some connections between your personal search for meaning and your research about meanings. First of all, let me stipulate a meaning of meanings, and a context for them to be important. Then I will examine what hermeneutics (the study of meaning) has to offer to us, and finally turn to how different disciplines collect data when they are trying to study meanings. By approaching my subject this way I am refusing to go along with the in-depth, purely anthropological approach of total immersion. Instead I am advocating collecting data about meanings and allowing these data to be the subject of further reflexive consideration – that is, 'beyond the experience, can we spend time reviewing the experience?'. In other words, going native will not be enough. We have to be ready to discuss what happened during our ethnographic (or other) contact. Data facilitate these discussions.

Stipulating a meaning for 'meaning' is difficult. Try: 'the essential points that come to mind when a word or phrase is stated'. This is what dictionaries try to pinpoint. In searching for meaning, the context of a word or phrase is important. Meaning can vary, depending on the context. This implies that a single word or phrase does not necessarily carry a single meaning. In addition, notice that waving your hand, shaking your fist or clapping while using a certain word or construction of words also bears meaning – which can change meaning. And this idea of meanings 'coming to mind' – whose mind are we referring to?

Let us start, then, with an idea of meaning as a socially normal reference point for a communicative act. An act means what it is socially constructed by some group to refer to. It might refer to another event, to a rule, an emotion, a person or other agent, to an abstract concept, some mathematical law or other statement. For me, meanings are about reference. They help us refer to one thing by naming it or otherwise making an action.

So a book or a film can have an overall meaning; a word's meaning can change depending on its usage and who is listening; an answer to a question can mean many things all at once. Dictionary lengths of word meanings depend on the publishers' restrictions of page length. The *Oxford English Dictionary* is many volumes long and gives the historical meanings of words and phrases, as well as their current meanings. Most words also have a date and language of origin. By using words to give the meanings of words, dictionaries develop a web or network of meanings. The meanings borne by words often have negative or positive connotations, again in particular contexts. These connotations are very subtle and can include nuances of power relationships, thus referring to historically specific situations whose interpretation is going to change as decades pass by.

The context of discovering what others mean when they say or write things is always a contrast of cultures. Their culture and our culture come into contact. There is not just a single culture; we have many subgroups, including intellectuals, youth, classes, ethnic groups and language groups. Sometimes, when you attempt to define the meaning of something, you have to spend time describing the group or context to which you are referring. Perhaps in getting close to this group – even entering it temporarily – you as researcher place yourself in a boundary area where you are partly of that group and partly of your own group. Remember, too, that groups overlap. The following example might help illustrate this.

Compare the two extracts below. The first (from Olsen, 2007a) finds meaning in a case study of Yasmeen, a rural Indian woman, by interpreting the data in terms of a new theory. That theory builds on other theory, as is made explicit in the surrounding paper. So in a sense I force Yasmeen's interview responses to interact with the older theoretician and with myself.

> Strategies are in general defined as the orientation that an agent has towards future possibilities in which they declare one main aim and realise that several subsidiary events must or may occur, prior to that event, in order to make it come about. Explicitly stating or proposing a strategy requires some knowledge of what causes the outcome to occur, of what that outcome *is* or *would be*, and requires a willingness to engage in actions in the short-term which will – we think – lead to that outcome. Thus strategies have a visionary quality to them.
>
> > At the end of the interview, [Yasmeen] told us that she wants to see her grandsons in good positions and would not mind to leave the village to join them in a city. *(fieldnotes, WO, 2007)*
>
> Yasmeen's vision includes leaving the village some day. But in general, not everyone can or would be explicit about every strategy that they have: what to eat, where to buy food, how to get to work, and what type of cow to buy. Bourdieu's term *habitus* touches upon the habitual and socially normed nature of many social practices.

The second extract (Olsen and Neff, 2007) is a discussion of our perceptions of what Girija and Gopal, a rural couple, meant when they described the nature of unpaid labour that they perform for the landlord.

Dan Neff's notes following the interview stated that when they rented land: 'the landlord provides the land, the water and they share the yield half/half, but the owner decides what to cultivate. They do unpaid labour for the landowner like washing clothes, feeding water to his crops or collecting firewood.' In other words, Dan noticed, Girija was expected to do unpaid labour of various kinds, just as described in Tamil Nadu cases by Ramachandran (1990). ...

A: Six years back you rented in land you know; did you do any free work for the landlord?

Gopal: Yes I did. If we do that type of free work they will rent us their land.

A : What type of work? Please do explain?

Gopal: Visiting paddy fields, going to sugar cane fields at the time of sugar cane crushing while preparing *jaggery* [boiled sugar]. Doing work in the landlord farm, etc.

Girija: That means sweeping their houses, washing dishes and washing clothes. If we do all these type of work they will rent out land; otherwise they say that they will rent out land to some other person.

Gopal: We have to do these type of bonded labour otherwise they will rent out land to others. Under these circumstances we will stop and attend to other *kuulie* work.

... Sometimes the types of work being described as unpaid labour of a permanent servant are listed in a stylised way, as here. The man describes the male-stereotyped tasks, the woman describes the female-stereotyped tasks. Here, these are not tasks they are currently doing for their landlord, but which they did regularly up to six years ago.

In this second extract we first placed the quotation in context, giving some details about the family (making reference to other researchers, i.e. to our 'own' group), and then presented the selected quotations from both the woman and her husband with the interviewer's prompts, and finally we also presented an interpretive paragraph. We tried to explicate what obligations existed at that time since the phrase 'bonded labour' usually seems to imply a longer-term or even permanent bondage. In the present case, however, the bondage was in the past and did not currently exist. To explore the evolution of this relationship further would have required a revisit interview and more note-taking.

It takes a lot of space to explain the meaning of even short extracts like these from rural India. It is difficult to describe the context accurately, sufficiently, and in a sensitive and yet non-stereotypical way. I found it very challenging to write up these interviews from rural Indian villages. I worked in a team which had about nine members. Some did village-level interviewing, some did transcription work in Telugu then translated into English; some helped type the English text into the computer; one person worked hard on anonymising all the names; and I did a little of everything. We also had a photographer going around the village. Our database includes these photos as well as MP3 sound files for our reference when we are remembering the village scene.

The act of describing others' meanings is part of the art of being a good ethnographer. Good qualitative researchers write whole books explicating the meanings of what they hear during interviews. An example is Lamont's book *The Dignity of Working Men* (2000). Lamont used semi-structured telephone interviews and some face-to-face interviewing to study employed men in the north-eastern United States. Her work discovered certain types of racial and ethnic stereotyping which the men used habitually. She argues that there is racism there, but that much of it is non-intentional and – importantly – not meant to be harmful. Instead, she argued, the comments of a racist nature are aimed mainly at helping the man to construct an image of himself – an identity, if you like – as a wholesome, morally upright man. She argues that without this 'Other' personality's identity, it would be hard for the man to construct who his 'Good Me' is. It took an entire book to explicate a set of interviews.

Usefully for us as aspiring researchers, Lamont also describes her interview method and her sampling methods in a short appendix. While the context is different from my extracts from India, the data management issues are the same. There is the note-taking, the data on socio-demographic background; the process of anonymisation; the team-work involved – and then transcription, analysis, interpretation and writing up. Lamont also had to study the history and social composition of her selected states before she could write her book. For us as readers, it is an excellent introduction to the socio-economy and culture of part of the United States.

So far I have stipulated a meaning of the word 'meaning', and I have given three examples of how researchers explicate meanings. The study of meaning is also called 'hermeneutics'. Hermeneutics recognises that the meaning intended by a text's author may not be the one taken by a particular audience. Exegesis of the Bible or Koran would be key examples. Tracing the author and the translator are part of the work of deciphering the original meanings. Immersion in an old society through historical documents or oral history is useful as a way to comprehend the intended meanings. All the texts are likely to be contested. Contestation is an important part of what hermeneuticists (i.e. interpreters) do.

In hermeneutics we distinguish the etic meaning from the emic meaning of something. The etic approach is to take an outsider's view and explicate the meaning of something to other outsiders. This is very difficult. After all, it might not be accurate if we simply remain outsiders. On the other hand, the emic approach is to get inside a culture or a group and 'know' about meanings by doing, being, resting, talking and interacting with that group. One goes native.

Again, this has its problems. One's knowledge may then be hard to pass on to outsiders. It may become tacit knowledge; one may learn secrets – it may be in a new language. The act of translation is an act of linking emic (insiders') with etic (outsiders') meanings. Translation too is often contestable. Hermeneutics is the mess of human communication about human society.

A well-known theory of hermeneutics, known as the 'hermeneutic circle', has created fundamental doubt about the validity of the meanings that you explicate from a given communicative act. The hermeneutic circle begins with you interpreting the Other. You think you know what they mean. You hear them or see them; you do something cognitive in your mind; you speak. However, the cognitive step is cushioned, shaped, flavoured and heavily seasoned by your own past experience. This experience is highly social, as it is your socialisation. The past associations of this word are part of what you respond to when you hear this word. You may misinterpret the Other by interpreting it in your own terms. Look at the connections that are created in Figure 2.

We can present this in a circular form by recognising that both speaker and listener are actually making reference to what they consider normal meanings.

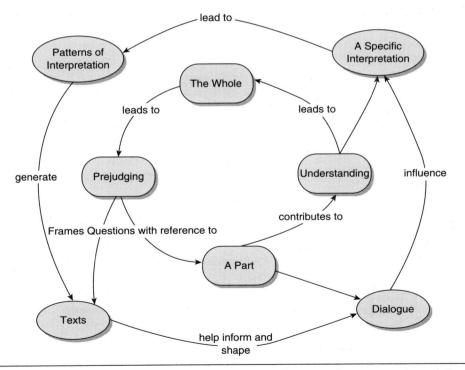

Figure 2 The hermeneutic circle: meanings in dialogue with agents (adapted from Danermark et al., 2002: 160)

But what I know about what they are making reference to may be too limited. Therefore my interpretation of their meaning is likely to be false compared with their real meaning. Figure 3 illustrates.

In anthropology there was once an attempt to gain valid (supposedly true) knowledge about others in places that are now known as post-colonial countries. But in recent decades anthropology has become much more respectful of the balanced recognition everyone should give to the knowledge of Others. 'Others' are not just indigenous people on tribal reserves in forests or other non-urban places. 'Others' are in our own house when we misunderstand people. Teenagers, for example. The mystery of what a boss means when they frown or smile is with us on a daily basis. Meanings are a mystery. Explicating them is an act of social intervention. We create the basis for tomorrow's society through our interpretations today.

In the management and health sciences, sociology and psychology, attempts to reach a valid interpretation of meanings have depended strongly on having good data. Grounded theory, discourse analysis, and other schools of interpretive research all require a capacity to recall, revisit, discuss and reanalyse the qualitative data. Experience is important, but so are discussion and reflection. Grounded theory, in particular, values having a detailed transcript. Some people even carry

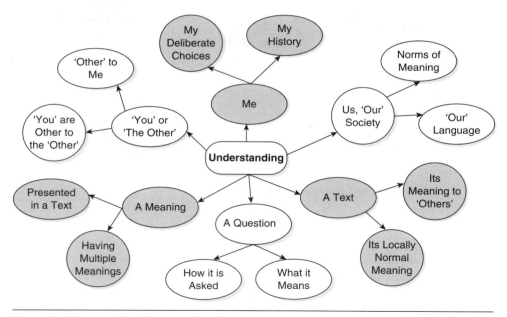

Figure 3   The complex elements of understanding

Key: The circles refer to units which are either knowers or items of meaning that can be known. Arrows indicate just some of the many inter-relationships which exist.

out content analysis to count up the number of times different themes appear in a piece of work. All these social research sub-schools differ from anthropology itself. They attempt to make the study of meanings more 'scientific'. I have argued that the hermeneutic circle itself makes it difficult to construe 'scientific' research as impersonal or asocial. Nor can hermeneutics be factual. Hermeneutics is a search for meaning without having a single simple constant meaning to which one can make reference. Like a scientist whose instrument disturbs the atom she's trying to study, the hermeneutic researcher has to make meaning. But they make something new which is neither emic nor etic – not what either insiders or outsiders actually meant – when they attempt an interpretation.

The communicative nature of knowledge is widely accepted in anthropology today. Indeed, in most social sciences the researcher is advised to be reflexive in their work of unearthing meanings. Their reflexivity is the very antithesis of the 'hard science' or factual empiricist approach. We do not talk about biases any more, because studying your own predilections is part of a good scientific method. Thus in the Olsen (2007a) extract I had to explain why I was so concerned to use a Bourdieuvian theoretical context to explain what people in the Indian context meant. Whether this was a good research strategy is in the eye of the beholder. For an empiricist, it might be considered biased. For a grounded theorist, there might be too much *a priori* theory; some advocate pure induction. But for me it was just right. The theory was transposed but not imposed upon the new situation that we came across.

In developing my theme I have arrived at a certain kind of knowledge that good qualitative data help us to develop. This knowledge is personal but also social; reflexive but also emotional and at times visceral. It is carefully constructed but still socially constructed. It is contextualised in a triple context: us, the audience(s), and the Other. We bring these three together during both the research and the writing-up stages. The data are a critical artefact mediating in this process. Normally data are passive but the respondents are very active. Most ethnographers now recommend revisiting the respondents to ensure that a dialogue takes place about the meanings you are attributing to agents. Nevertheless people do not have to agree with you. I have often disagreed with my respondents in the interpretation of their words! For example, I thought people were exploited by moneylenders even after people told me the lender was a charitable god-figure to them. We cannot reduce the world to a single viewpoint when doing qualitative research. Therefore contested meanings are a fine, healthy, normal situation.

2.5 Interpretation

Once you have some raw data or other qualitative evidence, you are ready to interpret the data. The act of interpretation can to some extent be planned. Therefore the way you hope to interpret the data will influence how you collect them. In this chapter I will explain how interpretation works first by discussing hermeneutics – the study of meaning – looking at some interview material as an example. Then I will go into two practical areas: how content analysis is usually done; and how discourse analysts would interpret qualitative data. In all three cases, the researcher may go back into the field, seek out other sources, discuss their nascent knowledge, perhaps do computerised coding, and generally hone the dataset before coming to the project's conclusion. Thus one does not simply collect data, interpret it and finish. One moves from acts of interpretation back to data collection from time to time, according to convenience.

Before defining hermeneutics, it is useful to try to define 'interpretation' itself. To interpret does not mean simply to describe what people said. If research just reproduced its sources, there would be little or no value added. In that case there would be no such thing as sociological knowledge or scientific expertise. The expert or sophisticated social researcher can probe the data in ways that lead to new conclusions, novel research findings, or policy proposals. Insight is an important part of the act of interpretation. Insight arises partly from getting an overview of clashing standpoints and views, and partly from reading history and comparing lay accounts with official accounts or social theory. There is also a nuanced sense of the underlying connotative meanings of phrases, which you develop in the field. To interpret is to re-present something is a way that delivers a new meaning. Interpreting art can be a model for interpreting social data. In various ways, interpretation is a complex and subtle way of processing your data. 'Mere description' is not enough for research findings (see 1.2 **findings**).

I have already discussed hermeneutics in the chapter on **meaning** (2.4), where I stressed that there is an internal meaning to each communicative act, but that outsiders may *take its meaning* rather differently according to their background. The idea of a socially normal or agreed meaning is highly contested in social science these days. Because of all the differences of background in complex societies, humans are very differentiated. We also have longer life spans than ever before. Therefore, we now have a chance to change ourselves considerably after taking great care over considering what kind of person we want to be. As a result, the very concept of a 'normal' meaning can be contested on the grounds that its applicability might be extremely narrow. Here are a couple of brief examples.

Would a mother and child interpret the word 'danger' in the same way? Would two adults agree on the meaning of the word 'marriage'? Later I will use the example of poverty to show three different, deeply divided social constructions of a common word. The idea of solving the hermeneutic problem by simply making reference to an external object does not often solve the problem (see 1.3 **data** and 6.3 **configurations**). Take the mother and child again. Suppose the word in question was 'daddy'. Would they have the same reference point, therefore the same meaning for the word? Maybe. But what about the mother's daddy? What about situations like a nursery where many daddies are present at the same time? And if daddy is not present, then the images conjured up by the word 'daddy' in the child certainly are not the same as those conjured up by the word 'daddy' in the mother. These images are important. They are not the same as a reference object. The richness of the images, as you may imagine, makes some people doubt that there is any reference object at all when we use language to 'refer' to things.

You may be thinking not of 'daddy' in the sense of a particular man, but 'the father' as an archetypical image or stereotype of adult masculinity. In this case, again one might argue that there is a normal reference point to which 'the father' refers. This reference point or norm is specific to a locality, to a time period such as a decade, and to smaller social groups such as a religious grouping or a cultural subgroup. The fact that iconic images or meanings of the phrase 'the father' are diverse does not imply that there is no reference point. It only implies that we cannot be simplistic about assessing what the phrase 'the father' refers to. Thus, in practice, when a woman says something about 'daddy', she may make reference either to a particular man or to a conception, and both of these can be real even though only one of them (the man) is material. The impact of having a conception of 'fathers' in a society is just as real as the impact of having a particular man in a society. Indeed, one quick proof that immaterial things can be real even though they are not physical objects is to note that if a man dies, and is a father, the word 'daddy' still refers to 'him'. This reference to our idea of him is to a real (but not physical) reference point. Interpretation of the phrase 'daddy' would need to pay attention to all these possibilities.

Whether there is an object to make reference to is a question in philosophy. On the whole, 'realists' might suggest that there is one (but still not say that the word 'daddy' has a single normal meaning in its context); 'idealists' might suggest there is not one; and some other schools of thought are agnostic about this question. The constructivist positions are sometimes confusing. (There is not space here to go into these positions, but see Sayer, 2000, for a discussion.) The idealist position is interesting. An 'idealist' might say we are only dealing with words and images anyway. We cannot prove that we are dealing with anything else. They say no one can prove the link between a phrase and its reference point(s). Unfortunately such an approach can lead rapidly to different types of relativism and a certain unwillingness to vouch for any true claims, or claims to truth, at all. One might call it nihilism about knowledge. It might not be polite to tell someone they are nihilistic about knowledge – they simply do not even accept that there can be any such thing as true knowledge. To them, there are only 'claims'. Some post-modernists take this general position where validity has no foundation. Yet it is sometimes true that a person's methodology – being perhaps post-modern or idea-based or too circular in its reasoning – leads them to not really believe anything at all. That is dangerous for the study of meaning. Hermeneutics need not lead to this morass. There are two ways out, and numerous procedures (such as content analysis and discourse analysis) for carrying out research using these avenues (see 2.2 **transcripts** and 2.1 **interviews** for examples of interpretation).

One can argue that claims can be tested, and that if they are not falsified, then they can rest for a while until further challenged. This is the Popperian viewpoint which is well established in America and some other countries' social science communities; see Popper (1963) or Fuller (2003) for a summary. Lamont (2005) has reviewed the different social science cultures of the USA, France and UK. Her work studied peer-review patterns to find out what was different about the generally accepted standards of published work. In the USA, facts are valued and peers help ascertain truths via falsification (Lamont, 2005). In France, theory is much more valued, and concretely grounded knowledge about a locality or a group of people using qualitative methods is highly respected (Lamont, 2005). The UK has a mixture of these two positions. In the UK a schism between qualitative and quantitative research is reflected in the various 'Economic and Social Research Council Training Guidelines' issued to postgraduate students (Economic and Social Research Council, 2005). The respected methods of research vary considerably from anthropology to economics or psychology, and this document simply lists the differing subject-specific areas of expertise that researchers require. There is no attempt to reconcile them. Table 5 summarises for convenience.

In this book I am arguing that they can be reconciled through realism, if the realism is carefully couched with respect for differing standpoints, for ethics, and for historical causes of difference. This leads to my second solution to the problem of 'knowledge nihilism' in hermeneutics. If you are looking for meaning, do something. That is, convert the search from a search for absolute meaning – insensitive to place and time – and make it a more conditioned search in which you respond to your audience's needs, to heuristic considerations, to what is possible in a given time limit, and to what you actually feel confident about knowing. Sometimes in this method, which broadly fits as a praxis method rather than a perfectionist approach to knowledge, and is more objectivist than

Table 5 Three standpoints about knowing interpretations validly

Polar extreme of hypothesis testing	A middle-way position	Polar extreme of multiple standpoint post-structuralism
Requires evidence; has procedural standards for evidence	Epistemologically accepts the need to recognise different standpoints, viewpoints, discourses and ways of construing things	Sees evidence as socially constructed
Needs objective agreement on adequate tests	Has ethical standards for research practice	Does not expect agreement on adequacy of tests or on interpretations
Runs test	Accepts that naturalism can only be highly coloured by real personal embodied involvement; sees researchers as agents	Avoids testing, tries to achieve 'naturalism' – a true representation without much observer involvement
Is prepared to reject claims if they are falsified	Creates new meaning through practices of disseminating research as well as through the acts of research themselves	Creates meaning through new texts
[May actually have some presuppositions that are never questioned]	[May actually have some presuppositions that are never questioned]	[May actually have some presuppositions that are never questioned]

Sources: For column 1 one might glance at the chapter on content analysis in Bauer and Gaskell (2000). Column 2 is supported by Blaikie (2003) and Sayer (2000). Column 3 is illustrated by Stanley and Wise (1993) or by Hammersley and Gomm (1997). It can be confusing to delve into this literature. For example, at one point Hammersley and Gomm (1997) seem to merge the meanings of 'realism' and 'naturalism', Realsim refers to having some reference point for knowledge about the world, while naturalism refers to trying to study the world as it really is, without influencing it; see Potter (1999).

subjectivist but does recognise your subjectivity as a researcher, the results will seem clear to you as they emerge (suddenly, unexpectedly or surprisingly, perhaps) from your subconscious to your consciousness. Discussions with others may galvanise a change in your outlook. Note these changes because they are meaningful; they reflect a move from an unknowing to a more knowing outlook on the *meaning* of what you have been studying. See also Flyvbjerg (2001) and Charmaz (2006).

An example will help with specific respect to the question of interpreting material from interviews. With support from the UK government's aid ministry and colleagues at the University of Manchester, I organised some field research in two villages in upland Sri Lanka near Colombo. From the interview component the two extracts below were translated and transcribed. I will discuss their meanings and how I approached interpreting them. (A full discussion can be found in Olsen, 2006.)

In the first extract (Olsen, 2006: 122–3) a male Sinhala Buddhist, unable to borrow from the bank, is interviewed:

> [Another] respondent expressed the discipline discourse as shown below. He is a Sinhala Buddhist man who works as a helper in stonemasonry. Previously his family were farmers but they have lost their land:
>
> | Respondent: | If we take any loan from the place where I work, they will deduct it from my pay. Therefore we don't take such loans. … when I have no work for three or four days I am short of money. Then we take goods on credit. As soon as I get money I pay up to the last cent. … they [the boutique shopkeepers] give me [goods on tick]. I owe to nobody. Therefore they give me at anytime. I am scared of continuing loans without paying. If we take too much, it's difficult to pay it back. Therefore we are used to live according to our income. When we go somewhere, if they ask about the money we feel shy and guilty. |

The second extract (Olsen, 2006: 121–2) begins with a Sinhala Buddhist woman of the worker class, married with four children, who designs decorative flowers and sews clothes:

> The dignity of saving:
>
> [Another] respondent used self-disciplining talk to describe the regular savings inputs which are compulsory in the Samurdhi (welfare benefit) scheme. Thus the sense of disciplining that emerges when interpreting the bank documents and passbooks (see below) is also echoed in the language used in interviews:
>
> | NF: | O.K., when you need some money, how do you obtain that? Do you borrow it from somebody? Or from your relations? Otherwise do you obtain it on loan basis? |
> | Respondent: | I borrow from the relations as a loan. |
> | NF: | You like very much to borrow from the relations. Is that correct? |
> | Respondent: | Yes. |
> | NF: | Normally do you give back that money at the stipulated time? |
> | Respondent: | Yes, indeed. Those people rely on us and give money. It is our duty to pay it back in the correct time. |
>
> A male respondent said:
>
> | Respondent: | I owe about Rs. 2000 to my uncle. But there's no problem in regard of that, as he won't force me to pay the money. Sometimes he asks whether I have money. That's also just like a joke. The bank is rather different from that. If we delay paying by one month or |

two months they tolerate. But in the third month they ask us to pay everything together.

NF: Even with the interest, no?

Respondent: Yes. Everything including the interest. Therefore I work very hard to earn more money or I take a loan from some other person and pay back that loan as soon as possible. Sometimes there may be nothing to eat for my wife and children, doesn't matter! Anyhow I pay the loan soon …

I interpreted the second extract in two ways. Firstly, there was an issue that the interviewer, who worked in the Singhala language and who was a Buddhist like the respondent, had got involved in making meaning and was notably affecting the statements by the respondent. The interviews had problems of 'leading questions'. If you belong to the falsifying hypotheses group, you might say the interview was therefore badly done and that responses should not be shaped by interviewers this way. In my view the interviewer cannot simply be like a glass bottle that we can see through to get a true picture of the respondent. The scene was this: Wendy sits quietly, a foreign white woman in charge of a group of six researchers. Some are out with questionnaires in the community. Some have already visited here. Nishara Fernando sits with the interview schedule asking questions in wording that he interprets from the written questions. He interprets things freely and helps the respondent get used to the interview. Her hut has a thatched roof, her pepper and banana garden is outside, the floor is tidied dried dung and mud, the walls are homemade brick. She is embarrassed by the situation as a whole. How can we *not* admit we are shaping the responses given? How would we imagine being an unbiased interviewer for a semi-structured interview in this situation? There may be some situations where one can do less biasing. Vox pop MP3 recordings in a large crowd of partying people might be an example. I had no doubt Nishara was influencing the respondents. The specific influence was to encourage them to express aspects of their dignity, and specifically if they could mention savings or loan repayments (in full) then this was praised or subtly seen as positive.

If you belong to the realist school of thought, then it is possible for dominant discourses to be real. But to find out about them, one needs to do research. In the Sri Lankan village research reported here, a clear set of dominant discourses emerged, and the resistance to them was muted. One of the discourses was a prudence discourse in which the speaker valued saving; another was a neoliberal discourse about banking in free markets being a commercial (not public service) activity. These discourses have internal rules and norms, which I had planned to study. However, in beginning the interviews I did not know either what particular rules, or what discourses, would be found.

In the study of social institutions the word 'rules' often implies contested or contestable norms, which are subject to change. Risseeuw's (1991) monograph on gender in Sri Lanka sets out clearly the common ground between Bourdieu and Foucault within which the 'rules' of discourse are malleable, i.e. subject to change. These rules, which Bourdieu called 'doxa', loosely translated as laws, are subject to empirical inquiry. Besides interviews, the study of graphic images, advertisements, legal documents, application forms and other documents – such as bank annual reports – can also reveal the dominant discourses. It is even harder to discover resistant, rare or minority discourses. An effort has to be made to generate texts which are not polluted by what is considered 'normal' in the wider society. Looking at marginalised people's discourses may require a research design that recognises the sensitivity of the people in that scene.

Foucault's (1977, 1980) own approach to discourse evolved through a descriptive phase, dating around 1970–2, and arrived at a stage of critical interpretation of contested discourses. The power relations surrounding contested discourses gradually came to the fore in his work. Most current discourse analysis is founded either directly or indirectly on Foucault's work. (His work, in turn, rests upon foundations set by Boudon and other French and European authors, and upon some primary texts.) When studying neoliberal discourse and the social factors underlying a tendency towards liberalisation, it is important to realise that the dominant discourses are contested. That helps the researcher to be open-minded even if some respondents are narrow-minded or, what amounts to the same thing, are accustomed to following their own habits which seem obviously normal and right to them.

Of all the social research methods, discourse analysis is one that tends strongly to make the researcher sensitive to breaches of 'normality' and to major social divisions. There are other methods which are less sensitive, whose users are often much more inclined to reach generalisation across a whole society or a whole set of texts. For example, content analysis tends to be quite descriptive and to make general statements rather than dividing up the texts into subgroups or attending to contestation. Content analysis (see the chapter by Bauer and Gaskell in Bauer and Gaskell, eds., 2000) measures the frequency of themes in a given set of texts. There is a strong methodical concentration on the question of selecting (or sampling) texts. After that, coding proceeds methodically and systematically. The frequency of appearance of each theme, which may change over time or vary over different genres of publication, is described as the findings of the research. Content analysis is usually very systematic and may take either published texts or documents – again in a published form – as its data sources. The use of content analysis with interview data is weakened by the rather arbitrary semi-structured way that time is spent on different topics. The interpretation of patterns in content analysis is grounded in the themes, topics, and phrases used in the texts. Thus it is almost a form of grounded theory, yet it does traditionally vary quite considerably away from the grounded theory school of interpretation (Charmaz, 2006).

An illustration of a discourse analysis is provided in Table 6. In this study, I examined a variety of documentary texts about development and poverty. I found a pattern that suggested three main discourses were present, and that if

Table 6 Discourse components for three typical poverty discourses

	Charity discourse	Social inclusion discourse	Economics of poverty discourse
Agents of technologisation	Non-governmental organisations	State and civil society	Economists, entrepreneurs
Agents	Givers, needy people, donors, orphans, refugees (the more oppressed the better)	Voters, citizens	Firms, workers, entrepreneurs
Assumptions about structure	Poor/rich relationship is one which creates a demand that rich donate to poor	Strong class awareness; strong awareness of ethnic, gender and other divisions	Nil, because atomistic. Each class role is one into which people can choose to join if they wish (e.g. via *Dragon's Den*)
Assumptions about human actualisation	Restricted for poor; enhanced by kind and altruistic giving of money, for non-poor	Stunting and deprivation are measurable effects of social exclusion	Money is a means to human happiness, important to measure money earnings
Role of states	State is not sufficient	State is an important actor	State role varies
Role of the UN	Assumes that UN fails	UN and EU may be important in setting up agreed frameworks of individual rights	UN role varies
Myths	'Giving helps'	'Human development' matters	'The invisible hand' of the market
Tropes*	Every little bit helps	Low level of development, 'backward'	Invest in human capital
Symbols	Cafe Direct logo	Country flags	Money logos on bills
Typical verbs	Contribute	Participate, voice	Earn, create wealth

Source: Olsen (2010b).

*A trope is a play on words. However, in sociology the word 'trope' has been used also to refer to performatively effective plays on words. That is, by saying something the speaker also achieves something.

one was present in a text then the other two would be muted in that text. The three were thus almost mutually exclusive in the published texts that I examined. (However, for that study, I did not have a systematic selection process for getting texts. Thus, if one did the same study using content analysis, the findings might be different.) Table 6 shows in column 1 the kinds of elements of discourse that I was looking for. In this column some *a priori* assumptions are revealed. I assume that discourses have assumptions embedded in them. These assumptions are of various kinds, and in practice the way column 1 was developed had to respond to the material I had in this study. Thus 'assumptions about human actualisation' was an important heading but it could not be generalised to other studies. The three discourses differed in how humans are assumed to actualise their own possibilities, i.e. how people develop in society. This is an important finding since it arises not from theory but from the empirical data. For example, advertisements by Oxfam were used as data for the project.

In this chapter I have discussed interpretation and some of the particular methods of interpretation. I have argued that planning a project includes planning the analysis stage, so I gave brief examples of interpretation and of discourse analysis as a well-structured yet empirically inductive form of interpretation. There was a strong contrast between the contestedness of discourse, assumed by those who follow Foucault or are post-structuralist and realist, and the content analysis method. I showed that there are extremes of methodology but that it is wiser to reside somewhere in the middle between extreme assumptions.

If you know that you intend to do content analysis or discourse analysis, that will influence the kinds of data you collect and how much data of different types you think you need. You cannot easily do both of these research methods well on the same dataset. The methods are poles apart in terms of their presuppositions, perhaps even typically lying in practice at the left and right poles of Table 5. Be decisive. Seek help with your method; either to find the usual social meaning for content analysis, so that your interpretation will be acceptable to its intended or actual audiences; or to find out about myths, tropes and symbols in their original context – not in your own mind which is a new import into the scene – by helping respondents delve into explaining what things mean to them and how they would interpret them. For discourse analysis, one almost needs evidence about the evidence, especially if the lay community one is researching has a range of rules about meanings that differ much from one's own starting points. Content analysis is more often applied to public, published documents, and discourse analysis to private talk and other communicative acts among specialist groups, because these methods are by their nature better suited to these two respective areas. Try to make sure the research design matches well to the nature of the thing(s) being studied.

2.6 Observer Bias

A useful definition of observer bias is that there is sometimes an essentially one-sided viewpoint or specifically grounded standpoint on a phenomenon. When conducting research, there can be observer bias in the researcher, individual interviews, focus-group facilitation and the observer during observation studies. There can even be biases in the framing of survey questions. Observer bias creates a mask over a scene, or puts a twist on what someone else might think from a different standpoint. Observer bias might also refer to the 'affect' or emotive aspects of a situation as they are seen or described by an observer (Olsen, 2007b).

In this chapter I will begin with a journalist's story about banking as an example of a topic about which there is observer bias. Then I will set out several grounded standpoints which exist both within and about this situation. Next I will analyse how interviewers would approach the issue if they were social scientists. Observer bias is less of a problem than one might initially think. I suggest that 'balance', tolerance and getting an overview are useful ways to off-set observer bias. The chapter concludes with a discussion of survey data and content analysis as 'unbiased' or 'biased' accounts. Both survey results and content analysis results are sometimes claimed to be unbiased, when in reality the findings are necessarily biased, or at least shaped by someone, but they should not be condemned merely for that reason. My normative approach towards observer bias is to have an accepting attitude but to be sceptical of all data and wary of each claim, rather than being dismissive of any biased argument. For me 'observer bias' does not have a negative connotation but is still a matter of concern.

Consider this example. In recent years the banking sector bonus culture has grown, and top managers and board executives in banks get huge payouts each year and upon their exit from a particular job. In Box 5, the *Sun* newspaper presents an account of change in the UK banking sector during 2008. This report appeared in the downmarket free-market-supporting tabloid which costs only 24p per copy. By contrast, we could list numerous articles about bonuses and bankers from the liberal intellectual broadsheet, the *Guardian*. This newspaper costs 90p daily or £1.90 for its Saturday edition. The first issue to consider is whether, if the *Sun*'s article is biased, the observer is 'the newspaper' or 'the journalist', whose name is Ian King.

One can practise locating observer bias in a broadsheet newspaper, where it may be harder to locate because of a more open-minded, plural, multiple standpoint mode of presentation of the situation. Reading newspapers critically is an excellent preparation for doing research because it forces the researcher to become aware of poorly supported or ill-considered ways of putting forward 'claims' in the research area.

Box 5   A Newspaper Account of a Banking Sector Event

RBS Chief Fred is Not Dead

Royal Bank of Scotland yesterday insisted chief executive Sir Fred Goodwin's job is safe – as it tapped shareholders for £12billion.

The record cash call is a humiliating U-turn for RBS, which only in February argued it did not need more capital.

Chairman Sir Tom McKillop admitted the RBS board was partly to blame for events leading to the cash call.

But he insisted Sir Fred – who had offered to quit, according to City whispers – would not be resigning.

He said: 'The board accepts responsibility for how it manages the business and you should be under no doubt about the degree of contrition. But there is no single individual responsible for these events and to look for a sacrificial lamb just misses the plot.'

Source: King (2008)

Based on past knowledge of UK newspapers we know that the *Sun* tends to support market-oriented or free-market values and the *Guardian* pro-state, liberal or left-wing values. So we might start off with two standpoints. (These are informally called the papers' 'biases', but inevitably a newspaper with an editorial team is going to have a general approach and several editorial stances. I will therefore call these the standpoint, not the bias, of the paper.) The journalist, King, appears to acknowledge and report unquestioningly the view that the bank is corporately responsible for its actions. He also seems to endorse the idea that no individual on the board is responsible for outcomes. The idea that these two claims can fit together coherently and can work for large corporations is more than just a standpoint or bias; it is a coherent moral or ethical approach to the corporate sector. For it to be applied to banks, another implicit premise has to be maintained: that whatever corporate board ethics apply to large corporations will also apply to banks. Each of the three ideas listed so far could be the subject of more detailed inquiry as well as more ethical thinking.

Instead of labouring particular points about the journalist's biases and the newspaper's standpoint, I want to identify a variety of other 'biased' observers that exist in the scene. The reason for doing this is to stress there are a number of different frames of reference from within, which each make this banking scenario look radically different. Frames of reference are the discursive lens through which people and other agents 'see' the scene. Here are some notes, which are inevitably incomplete to save space:

1. Shareholders in RBS. They are thought to have an economic interest in RBS's profits. They probably also have a stake in RBS not going bankrupt.

2. Goodwin. He was chief executive of a large bank, which was going bankrupt until the UK government stepped in and injected capital into it, taking partial ownership, during 2008. He had an interest in the bank's profitability and reputation, and in his own pay.

3. McKillop. As chair of the board, he was accustomed to regulating good practices of the bank with a view to survival, profits and making money for shareholders. Has an interest in ensuring that bank management is seen as a corporate, not personal, responsibility.

4. The Royal Bank of Scotland (RBS) board. The board of a bank is a corporate entity, also called an 'agent' in sociological terms. As such its interests and discursive frame are closely structured by the discourses within which it operates: the laws and regulations that apply to this bank, the accounting and profit discourses and the standard pay discourse as it is used differently for non-executive board members, executive board members and bank staff.

5. King. We do not know much about King without doing biographical research. We cannot be sure whether to apply what we know about the *Sun* to King personally. When studying frames of reference or observer bias it is important to distinguish a non-human agent – the newspaper and its tradition, management and culture – from a human agent such as King. There are perhaps standpoints 5a and 5b, the individual King and the corporate employee King. The latter is 'King playing a role' but also more than that – it is how the *Sun*, with King, creates images for readers. 5a is an individual standpoint, while 5b is a larger agent's standpoint.

6. The consumer of banking services. Consumers have material interests in efficiency and good retail service, as well as the costs of the service. Their subjective viewpoint about the bank may be tacit rather than explicit. If explicit, they may consider the survival of RBS important. Some will consider RBS the

holder of their financial savings, not just a bank which manages their day-to-day spending.

We might also explore the taxpayers of the UK as having a standpoint, but they have not been mentioned here by King. Altogether there are a lot of different standpoints.

These seven standpoints can each create biases and twists of interpretive focus when the agent looks at the changes in RBS from just one of these various viewpoints. After the article was published in 2008, Goodwin did lose his job. After he left, Stephen Hester was hired to replace him as chief executive with a salary of £1.2 million. Hester also received 10.4 million shares worth more than £6 million upon entering employment with this bank (data from November 2008; Treanor, 2008). Treanor reports that Hester 'gave the clearest acknowledgement yet that Goodwin and chairman Sir Tom McKillop were taking responsibility for the evaporation of confidence in RBS'. If this is the case, then the report by King (2008) might be said to have been biased in the sense of being wrong and misrepresenting the situation. However, we now arrive at a problem about who is responsible for a bias or error of fact appearing. There are not clear links between the statement that the board *does* take responsibility for outcomes, as stated by McKillop of the RBS board in 2008, and the claim that there is no use seeking a sacrificial lamb (also attributed to McKillop). Thus it may not be King or the *Sun* who introduced a bias, or error, but King's source, McKillop. In summary, the situation is confusing and accusations of bias may occur even where there were genuine good intentions to present facts in a reasonable way.

In a sense, every claim of 'bias' is a raising of knowledge issues (in this book, see also the chapters on 7.1 **facts**, 7.2 **reality** and 7.3 **retroduction**). The discussion of bias and error by Gomm et al. (2000) is a helpful discussion of some related issues. They distinguish different aspects and variants of being wrong or biased. For a researcher, it is important not to rest too much weight on a single quote from a single source. Instead we look for a series of points made by people from one standpoint, then visit agents of some other standpoint to get their point of view. It is rather obvious that this is best practice, and it may even apply to journalists.

The important thing is to learn lessons from the situation, as exemplified by the contested area of bankers' bonuses and corporate responsibility of chief executives. First, there are errors of fact, such as whether McKillop actually said what he is paraphrased as having said. Second, there are errors of judgement in interpreting a set of comments. Third, there is the advantage of understanding a viewpoint and presenting it coherently, even when King (or the *Sun*) may agree or disagree with it, simply because it is information for the public that this viewpoint is held. Fourth, there is a need to grasp that standpoints are not the same as viewpoints. Fifth, there is value in exploring ethical reasoning as exposed in how people present their 'interests' from their standpoint. And sixth, good research often involves bringing together the reasoning used from these different standpoints.

A standpoint is not quite the same as a viewpoint, because a standpoint is to some extent a social location rather than just being a subjective view that can be expressed in words. The default frame of reference for some standpoints is just a tacit, normal set of habits. Banks in the UK make profits, for example. The entry of government into capital ownership of some banks, even if temporary, has confused the standpoint of banks and caused quite some confusion and tension in public discourses about banking. At this time, then, the frame of reference used by banks to conduct banking is not stable and is undoubtedly in a state of tension or transformation. I want to stress that it is normal to have institutions underpinned by these frames of reference, which include idioms, word-sets, assumptions, implicit rules or guidelines and other aspects of discourse. For a serious treatment of management discourses, see Chiapello and Fairclough (2002). Like Fairclough, I would expect in specific text to see more than one discourse interacting – he calls this 'intertextuality'. But in society the grounded nature of each standpoint tends to cause coherent discourses to coalesce for certain periods of time, in different places of greater or lesser geographic extent. In some countries banks have for many decades been performing a public service and *not making a profit* (China, Sri Lanka, Burma for example in certain decades of the twentieth century). The profit discourse is not a necessary part of banking (Olsen, 2006). In general, standpoints are real starting-points for discursive norms, and viewpoints are more explicit statements of the approach or beliefs of an agent from a given standpoint.

Having cleared the ground like this, one must begin to realise that at the superficial or subjective level, and in texts like the two articles above by King and Treanor, there are bound to be multiple truths in a complex segmented society. The truth stated by one person from their standpoint may be found an untruth from the viewpoint held by another. I would suggest this multiplicity of truths is not only the case for normative statements – such as 'banks should make profits' – but also even for factual statements (see 7.1 **facts**). Thus, 'The RBS serves the public interest by providing banking services' sounds factual and, whether it is true or not, is a matter of the standpoint you take about the profit discourse and about service. If the truth of a factual statement is contestable, then inevitably at times the charge of 'bias' will be thrown at authors who try to write true accounts. One could find observer bias even in less emotively charged topics than this one – in the study of marriage, dementia and so on.

So far I have shown that numerous standpoints exist simultaneously *vis-à-vis* the banking changes described in the exemplar. It may be helpful to argue the case for balance, tolerance and getting an overview as useful ways to offset observer bias. A balanced presentation would try to offer different viewpoints in a coherent and understanding way without masking or silencing them. It might be quite time-consuming to develop a balanced knowledge and to write up a balanced account. It would be helpful in terms of cross-standpoint communication, though.

A tolerant approach would recognise that behind the claims, and embedded in the various discourses, people and other agents such as banks hold strong normative views. People are committed to rules of behaviour that they see as appropriate for particular situations. A tolerant scientist would acknowledge the *reasons why* each agent holds a certain type of view in a given situation. They would increase the understanding of their audience of how the reasons make sense for different agents. There is a communicative purpose here, just as in 'balance', but now we are communicating about values, not just about facts. In order to clearly explain someone else's values, in this instance why banks say they have to make a profit, or why boards tend to discourage blaming individuals, one has to go into the history of their norm. One would want to give a summary of how it aids sense-making within the small locality – here, of banking practices – in which the norm is commonly held dear. This work of explicating norms is hard if we as authors do not agree with the norms or think they are being misapplied. But a tolerant researcher will put their own views on hold while exploring the views of other agents. In a sense this is a strength of the 'grounded-theory' tradition (Charmaz, 2006) as reworked in recent years. A tolerant scientist cannot just make up stories but must instead have evidence with which to work. They can then make 'sense' of events, views, and processes just as the actors themselves make sense of them, without necessarily agreeing with the sense of things. They clearly understand the emic (insider) view or views, whilst taking an etic (outsider) view. The word 'grounded' in grounded theory usually means having evidence on which to base a statement. The word 'grounded' when applied to standpoints refers to the structural and historical location that intrinsically attaches to a standpoint. Standpoints are real starting-points for one's frame of reference: they are not just made-up fanciful sets of ideas.

We are now ready to assess why content analysis or grounded theory could at an earlier stage in the twentieth century claim to be factual and empirically value-neutral, but at a later stage in the twenty-first century can be revised to accept that observer bias is still inevitable. In the earlier period (e.g. Glaser, 1978; Glaser and Strauss, 1967), being a good scientist meant avoiding observer bias by having data to show others. Data, it was then thought, would enable replication of a study and help in the checking of validity.

In the new century many more social scientists recognise that good science is tolerant of observer bias. It is now commonly agreed that:

(a) we are all insiders to society as a whole;

(b) observers inside a situation know it very well;

(c) every agent has a set of terms and norms that help them make sense of the world;

(d) viewpoints often reflect standpoints;

(e) those standpoints are multiple.

The social world is so complex that no simpler reality can be claimed to exist. People still think that data enable replication in checking validity, but it is widely recognised that one person's valid fact is someone else's controversial misstatement. As a result social scientists often prefer qualitative research, in which competing voices are listened to very carefully and the observer tries to give a balanced, nuanced, carefully tolerant account.

Is it possible, then, that survey data are also 'biased' through observer bias? Remember (see 1.3 **data**) that survey data are just information, not knowledge. As information, the data could be true representations of what was said during an interview, but could still be biased by the frame of reference of the observer. Here the observer is the author of the survey, or the interviewer. It is easy to see that the information can be perceived as biased by others. The claims that are made *about and using* survey data could also be biased. My solution would be to try to get a balanced, nuanced, carefully tolerant account of what has been recorded in the survey data. In addition, I advocate getting qualitative data and carrying out an integrated mixed-methods study so that more is known about the history and context than can be placed in the survey data matrix. Survey data on their own are rather limited in several respects. Augmenting them with other data sources is often a good idea.

It is intriguing to notice that there is no 'emic' viewpoint for survey data. For closed-question surveys, the respondents in a sense have to conform to the discourses used by the survey. This may be an etic viewpoint for many respondents. The more mixed the sample is, the more likely it is that most respondents will find the survey language unfamiliar or uncomfortable. In small local situations, such as an evaluation survey, respondents may be more comfortable and the mixture of frames of reference more limited.

So, to summarise, I have defined observer bias as an essentially one-sided viewpoint or specifically grounded standpoint on a phenomenon. Since these kinds of bias are intrinsically present in many social situations, including the scientist as an observer, we are bound to expect bias to be a normal part of social descriptions. To overcome and challenge bias, to the extent that biases are limiting or problematic, it is helpful to try to develop a balanced, nuanced, carefully tolerant account. The scientist is now the agent who tries to allow for the reasons why certain beliefs are held, who forms their own views after carefully getting a deep understanding of a scene, with all its conflicts and internal viewpoints. The scientist recognises multiple standpoints as real.

2.7 Representations

Representations are a form of communication in which an agent portrays a situation to an audience. Four specialist terms contribute to explaining what representations do when they are used in the media and in policy statements. I briefly explain these four terms and then examine the use of representations in qualitative and quantitative data collection.

Firstly, representations take place through the use of discourse to portray an image of something. A discourse is a particular mode of communication which follows certain social norms, makes assumptions about the usual kind of agents and what they do and assigns certain terms to the world in such a way that some narratives make sense while others are seen as nonsense. The discourse of marriage, for example, has been changing in the UK and other Western countries. From being a religious seal of approval of heterosexual monogamy in earlier times, marriage has gradually been reinterpreted as a social and legal arrangement with some diversity. In the late twentieth century new laws allowed civil marriage to emerge as a civil institution reinforcing monogamy among homosexual people as well. Discourses within the marriage arrangements include the traditional Christian marriage vows and the Hindu practices of using flowers and jewellery to reinforce the marriage rites. There are many other variations. Thus, discourses of marriage portray the start of a couple's relationship in ways which carry meaning to a particular social audience.

The other three specialist terms which support the use of the concept of discourse to describe representations are the words 'narratives', 'texts' and 'meanings'. A narrative is a particular type of communicative act. Stories have narratives, but so do question-and-answer sequences. Narratives, then, are a subset of the wider range of communications known as discourses.

Text is an even narrower concept. A text is a particular set of symbols or movements which can carry some socially meaningful story. A text may be written in alphabetical letters or may involve using images as well. The meaning of a text may be contested. The meaning is – roughly speaking – the inherent conceptual content which is intended to be carried across to an audience by the author of the text. Discourses and narratives are considered to have meanings which are partly defined by their audience. Text, on the other hand, can exist independently of these meaning-making groups. However, as soon as we try to interpret the text, we have to invoke not only the intended discourses and narratives of the text-maker, but also some discourses and narratives of our own.

Hermeneutics is the study of meanings. Because meanings are sometimes contested, it is easy to begin a piece of qualitative research by asking what meaning was intended by a particular speaker or writer. It soon becomes apparent, though, that a listener or reader may also impute some other meaning to the communication. We now have two possible meanings in one phrase. Ricouer (2003) has suggested that a third meaning can be claimed for a given text. This third meaning is partially independent of both speaker and listener. The third meaning is the social meaning. Somehow, given the existing social norms in a particular place and time, one could claim that there is a socially normal meaning for a given communicative act. This norm can be breached by both the speaker and the listener. When breaching a norm one tries to create new meanings. If I claim the existence of a socially normal meaning I make an ontological claim. We now have three meanings: the speaker's, the socially normal meaning and the audience's. The difficulty of knowing these three meanings is called 'the epistemological difficulty of discerning representations'. The study of hermeneutics is a branch of social research which focuses on how people ascertain or derive meaning from communicative acts.

In collecting evidence we need to be ready to defend the claim that some particular meanings have been carried across by a given representation. Consider first the representations which are found in interviews. In qualitative research the interview is construed as a conversation. In this special conversation, one speaker is trying to elicit representations from another. The text of an interview may convey meanings which are good representations of events and mechanisms in the world. However, there are now four dimensions: the respondent's intended portrayal, the interviewer's interpretation, the socially normal meaning and the reality being portrayed. Finally, there are also audiences for the written or spoken research results and these audiences are large plural groups of people. Therefore there may be many different possible meanings for even one segment of one interview.

In a sense, there is also a circularity between reality and portrayal, because the interviewer is unable to describe the reality (about which the interview gives evidence) without utilising some discourses or narratives that existed prior to them learning to use their language and other signs. In other words, the interpretation cannot be original; it is not just created by this 'observer' but rests upon prior social norms of language. Giddens describes this problem as a hermeneutic circle (see Danermark et al., 2002, for a summary; an excellent resource for those who find this interesting is Outhwaite, 1987). Interpretation depends on social knowledge of social norms, and communication also utilises socially normative meanings in order to make its attempt at conveying meaning. Very little of 'qualitative data' is really personal at all, but rather social norms put into play. Perhaps, one could even suggest, the respondent in an interview is just a dupe. Some authors would therefore conclude that interviews are always fallible and cannot give factual evidence about the real world. Framed in discourses using particular narratives, qualitative evidence perverts our view of the world just as a mesh screen on a window perverts our view of the outdoors. No matter how carefully the text is deconstructed, it is biased by the people who created it.

For this reason critics of qualitative research have suggested that the findings from such research are always biased. Some of this scepticism arises from people defending particular interests such as those of hospital service deliverers or municipal decision-makers. In other words, people who do not want their world exposed to close scrutiny say that interviewers cannot construct truths about their world. Other sceptics are simply aware that a million meanings could be attributed to a single interaction.

Interviews can nevertheless be very useful for collecting evidence. In resolving this problem it may be useful to consider interviews as a source of fallible evidence, not truths. In this case, representations of the world are a purposive form of communication and the interview is just one means of developing interesting, useful knowledge claims about the world. The scientific side of interviewing is the use of systematic and rigorous approaches which allow us to reassess one person's interpretation by exposing the methods of the qualitative research to scrutiny.

Turning to the use of representations in survey data collection, in which the structured interview is more common than the semi-structured or unstructured interview, we again hit a snag regarding epistemology. This snag is that most interviewers collecting survey data claim to be neutral and are careful during the interview to repeat each question in exactly the same way for all respondents. This is widely considered to be a scientific method of administering a survey questionnaire. Quantitative data are often considered to be best constructed from this particular kind of interviewing procedure.

Would quantitative data then be a neutral and factual representation? Most scholars do not think so. The data themselves are not a very clear representation at all because they do not contain whole narratives, nor are they arguments. The data, consisting of marks in a matrix, tend to hold much smaller units of communication such as words or numbers. The reader of the data places these words or numbers into sentences which bear new meanings. The wording of the poll is likely to be repeated in the wording of the interpretation of the numbers that come from the survey data. However, it is also possible to interpret a survey in new ways not intended by the interviewers. Therefore, many representations can arise from a single set of survey data. In other words, surveys construct a set of information about society.

Post-empiricists argue that various representations can be developed in words. They would argue that this is so even when the raw materials are quantitative data. In Figure 4 the possible criteria for good arguments are set out using a Venn diagram. The left-hand side shows a typical post-empiricist approach to assessing the quality of some research. The research design should be adequate to its purposes, and the purposes are not merely fact-gathering but are derived from some purposive hunt for better knowledge arising from a project or a problem in society. (Scheyvens et al., 2003, and Brockington and Sullivan, 2003, illustrate this approach for development studies.) The criteria on the right-hand side show the typical criteria, such as having systematic data and having a rigorous method, which are more common among empiricist researchers. There is some overlap. The overlap is that both groups want us to achieve warranted arguments which any reasonable observer could understand and perhaps agree with. Thus one does not simply find that post-empiricist research rejects all the basic standards of empiricist research. They have some elements in common.

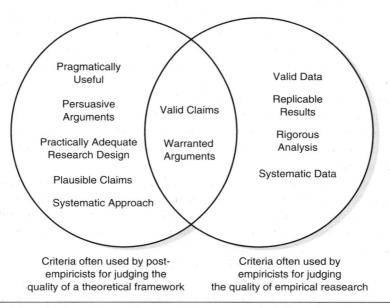

Figure 4   Selected criteria for good research from two methodological standpoints

Note: Sayer (1992) defines practical adequacy. Smith (1998) defines empiricist approaches. The phrase post-empiricist here combines post-structuralist epistemology with an interest in empirical observation.

The construction of good arguments is somewhat constrained by using survey data alone. On the bright side, one hopes that the representations we arrive at this way are also constrained away from being false by reality itself. Thus we might draw out good, warranted arguments using a mixture of survey data and other expertise. Through good piloting, a questionnaire can be made better so that by filtering and good question wording it can be made to represent a variety of realities (see **questionnaire design**).

Consider government censuses for a moment. Are these powerful, biased data sources or are they neutral, factual data sources? Government surveys can be powerful because the wording of the survey tends to be repeated in the wording of the reports derived from the data. An example would be the wording of descriptions of ethnicity. It is hard to argue that the government survey will be neutral when we know that the wording of questions is contested and debated among the various stakeholders. Questions about language, education and religion shape the ways in which people can officially be reported to speak, learn and worship. The questions also construe a wide range of behaviour, such as language switching and pidgin English, in particular categorised ways. For these two reasons government surveys are open to debate. They do not give a neutral or 'God's-eye' view of society.

It is interesting to note that some parts of life which were previously widely considered to be shameful are now being avidly recorded in official surveys. Examples relate to sexuality and health: gay sexual orientation and HIV infection in particular. These examples illustrate the way that socially acceptable representations are used and fostered by government. The people who collect data sometimes participate in progressive social change through innovating within data-collection bureaucracies. At other times the people who collect data can play a very conservative role. Whatever their wishes they may find it difficult to influence the workings of a bureaucracy. As the proverb from 1950s China under Mao put it: 'Let a hundred flowers bloom; let a hundred schools of thought contend.'

To summarise, then, I would portray social representation as an act of human interaction in which an agent (e.g. a person) makes some communicative efforts while trying to portray the world in a particular way. Values and preferences are sure to influence how we represent the world. In order to engage in serious discussion about representations, one needs to pay close attention to evidence about all the possible meanings which might be attributed to a given representation. These meanings will be embedded in discourses. The representations may play a part in particular types of narratives. In general, we can appreciate representations as a flowering of human attempts to convey meaning.

2.8 Focus Groups

A focus group can have from five to about twelve members, and it always includes a facilitator. The focus-group data-collection method can strengthen many studies which are more firmly based on other methods such as surveys and interviews. Focus groups are also useful as a part of participatory research (see 3.1 **participation** and 3.3 **action research**). Focus groups need tape-recording and transcription, so should be used within rather tight limits on the quantity of meetings in favour of a detailed analysis of the resulting data. For example, if a study had 25 personal interviews then the addition of six focus groups can contribute a lot of depth to the analysis, or if a study uses only secondary survey data then again six or at most ten focus groups based in just one or two locations will suffice to add a fresh qualitative dimension. As for other qualitative methods, the time allocated to the analysis of data should be at least equal to the time devoted to planning and conducting the focus groups and creating the data transcripts.

The use of video in focus groups is optional. On the one hand, it creates a historical artefact of some potential future value to museums or to local participants. On the other hand, getting the informed consent to use the video material in future in the research may be harder than for audio, because the speakers are easily recognised in the video. Even if faces are blurred out, clothes and local clues will tend to make the results non-anonymous. Thus for sensitive topics or with vulnerable subjects we may positively prefer to use audio over using video. However, in addition, enabling each participant to make a brief video diary may be a useful adjunct to the use of focus groups.

The analysis of focus-group data can use principles and concepts from the discourse analysis repertoire. Among the various sub-schools of discourse analysis, the more sociological kinds will tend to suggest that you supplement the focus-group data with visual images or other evidence from different genres if there is time. It will also urge that detailed and broad historical knowledge of the study topic be brought to bear on the transcript interpretation stage. There is a more linguistic form of discourse analysis (see Wodak and Meyer, 2009). Another variant is used among psychologists which makes clear reference to psychological theories (see Potter and Wetherell, 1987; and for practical help see Kendall and Wickham, 1999, on Foucauldian discourse analysis). It is harder to use conversation analysis because the turn-taking is so artificial in focus-group transcripts. A general method of interpretation can be applied (see 2.5 **interpretation**). Thus there are numerous choices which must be made to narrow down how the analysis stage will be carried out.

Finally, it is wise to code the focus-group data using a computer (see 2.9 **document analysis**). For a 40-minute group meeting there may be from 30 to 45 pages of double-spaced text. Holding 20 focus groups thus generates about 200,000 words of text. The computer can be used to simplify the job of coding such data. The transcriber needs to use unique identification (ID) codes for each speaker, and then automatic coding routines can easily be set up for spreading the auto-coding of each line in which the ID occurs to all of the following paragraph or section (Gibbs, 2002). To plan the auto-coding well, a pilot focus-group transcript should be auto-coded to ensure that the right editing markers are put into the transcript. Since the corpus is going to get very large, carry the pilot quite far before delegating the rest of the transcription work. The transcribers should have a list of detailed transcription guidelines (see 2.2 **transcripts**).

2.9 Document Analysis

Documents are accessed in workplaces, in internet sources, and in archives and libraries. When document analysis is proposed, the first two questions are whether a systematic analysis of variation is wanted and whether an in-depth qualitative analysis is feasible. To do the first, access to a large amount of text is advisable. To do the second, a background knowledge of language, history, the local milieu's norms, and idioms is required. If both are desired then in effect you have a mixed-methods approach to the study of documents. This chapter presents some guiding principles for a systematic analysis, then insights for the in-depth qualitative analysis.

In document gathering one either has all the relevant documents or takes a sample from a larger number (see 1.5 **sampling**). One can also take a sample of paragraphs, pages or phrases from within documents. Usually the systematic analysis will involve putting each extract into computer software. Software options include NVivo, MAXQDA, or ATLAS.ti (Lewins and Silver, 2007). A content analysis is possible. Here each theme is noted. Usually the themes are given short titles known as codes, and all texts are coded by linking up the codes to all relevant texts. Later the range of codes can be examined in itself as a shortcut to the themes in the data. Some codes are rare, some are frequent. A frequency count of all words in each text can be generated by the software. This is a first step towards developing a list of codes. Next, more complex theme names can be developed, covering topics such as 'opposition to government policy'. It has to be clear whether by this code, and for each one, you mean that the author took that position, or whether the code is simply what the text is about. This is one reason why the NVivo software allows trees of codes. A tree is like an umbrella code name. A tree called 'opinion of the authors' can have a set of codes indicating what the author sincerely believes and meant to say. A separate tree can have a code 'what text is about', and here the topics are listed. Some coding for content is easy and straightforward. Some take much more thought. A simple word-processor will not be much use because it will be hard to see an overview of the frequency and reoccurrence of major and minor themes. In summary, specialist computer software is useful for the more systematic forms of content analysis.

Another possibility for systematic document analysis is case-based analysis. The cases could be students, and the evidence their essays and report cards since there is a one-to-one relationship between students and report cards, the cases have these documents nested within them (see 6.1 **case-study research**). With a larger number of essays, the database can quickly get large. Suppose we have 50 students and 6 essays per student. Suddenly there are 300,000 words in the database, if each essay averages 1000 words. This sudden mushrooming of data is easily handled through a mixture of sampling and computerised case-based coding. (Byrne, 2009, gives advice on analysing such data. See Gibbs, 2002, for computer-assisted coding.)

In the managements of documents, various file types can be converted into simple text. If multiple languages are involved, it is strongly urged that some documents be kept in the original language, even if translations are to be introduced. Translation itself is extremely difficult and time-consuming. The first step in coding is usually to decide on the size of text segments to be coded (e.g. sentences). Then it is useful to develop a list of codes for basic retrieval. Each document, for example, can be coded as a whole under its title. Next, further codes for detailed retrieval can be chosen from among the words in the word count list. Then groups of two or three words can be chosen, within limits set by the research question. Naturally the research question of the study gives guidance and narrowness to the research coding acts. An exhaustive coding is usually not necessary unless the texts are supposed to become a searchable corpus. Finally, you are ready for the most interesting part.

The search for meaning (see 2.4 **meaning**) is an adventure with document analysis. We move now into qualitative research proper where your background knowledge influences your interpretation. You go through the text searching for units or phrases that bear meaning which is not explicitly named in the text. For examples, see 2.5 **interpretation**. For instance, opposition to government policy might be expressed elliptically using satire. Sarcasm and humour also bear complex meanings. Within reason each meaning-unit can be coded. This implies that some paragraphs of your text will have overlapping multiple codes. That is normal.

In content analysis your work could be completed by noting the texts with greater or lesser occurrence frequencies of these important codes from among your exhaustive list. A project might have 120 codes, but the written report would only discuss ten or so of these in detail. Content analysis is especially useful for comparing the frequency of themes across different groups or over time. It gives a balanced, reliable analysis. Here, reliability means that even if another observer took up the database and analysed it, coding it afresh, they would come up with similar findings.

When a more in-depth qualitative analysis is being done, we take a smaller amount of the text and look into the purposes and intentions of the speaker or writer in much more depth. Now the argument within each text is summarised in a code, and the hermeneutics of these arguments is studied. By hermeneutics we mean that the intended meaning of a speaker might differ from how different readers would actually interpret the implications or meaning of this text. The classic example is a proclamation signboard during wartime. The army producing the sign has one intention and one meaning. The sign may instruct people in how to register their names. But the reader from a supportive social group may interpret this very differently from someone in a different social group. Examples from occupied countries where there are sympathisers to the occupation and there is a secret resistance would illustrate this. One group may be 'reading into the text' what punishments are really likely due to the implications of this text. A different picture is painted in their mind from the explicit statement about punishment which may be contained in the text as a literal statement 'if ... then this punishment ... will occur' (e.g. 'failure to register will be punished with ...'). The interplay of these varied interpretations is known as hermeneutics. Most analysis methods depend at least a little on hermeneutics.

So when explicating what a text means, we break it up into phrases or parts, examine what they meant to different groups of people, and generally interpret the text. In the above example, future scenarios bear contested meanings. More detailed analysis methods such as critical discourse analysis and discourse analysis depend heavily on the ability of the researcher to do the interpretations. Multiple interpretations must be contemplated. A kind of pluralism can be considered possible before the final argument is written up. Most qualitative analyses are fallible in the sense that a different observer, given the same dataset, would not derive the same conclusions. The particular background of each interpreter affects how they work with and understand the text. In this methodological area, reliability is much less of a value in its own right than one might expect.

2.10 Accuracy

In this chapter I look at two kinds of accuracy. Firstly, I consider what is meant by harmonisation of a questionnaire over different countries or language groups. I give examples of excellent international datasets that have been harmonised. I note the linkages between the concepts of accuracy and measurement – the latter ranging in type from categorisation through to index scales. As a second topic, I discuss the debates about scientific method, in which accuracy has been seen as an advantage by some and as an ideological tool of empiricist supremacy by others. In other words, I look first at practical issues and then at deeper philosophical issues of accuracy in data collection.

Accuracy involves mapping the features of the human or social world into a specific method of data collection. There may be many ways to do this. The idea of mapping is a useful place to start when thinking about accuracy. Suppose a questionnaire is intended to cover the region, county, locality (city or town) and ward of the respondent. How can you be sure that they will give accurate information in answering these three questions? Numerous problems could crop up. First of all they might live in the border area of a region, near another region, and they may prefer to name the second region instead of the first. In the UK a number of large regions are separated by watersheds which meander along following the highest point between two major river systems. As a result someone living in a high place might consider themselves to be in the North East when technically – according to experts – they might be living in the North West. The borders of these regions also changed historically. For example, the county called 'Cumbria' has had different boundaries over the centuries. In Europe, too, numerous countries have also experienced changes in their boundaries over periods of decades. Respondents may make a mental reference to an older border than the current one. A good system of questionnaire interviewing will allow the enumerator to make checks and correct the data on region and county if it is simply wrong. Similarly, one needs to refer correctly to the city or town in which someone lives. There may be two or three contiguous towns all making up one urban agglomeration. As a result people may cite the larger city name (e.g. Greater Manchester) without naming their actual town (e.g. Oldham or Salford). Normally respondents are sitting in four or five regional 'places' (town, city, region, country) simultaneously. They need to be given clear directions or a drop-down menu to select the right kind of geographic place name in answer to a direct question about where they are. One way to increase accuracy is to use showcards. A showcard will list the reasonable options in a large font. After seeing the showcard the respondent can choose which of the appropriate options fits their case best. The interviewer can pause the survey to check if they think this is a false choice.

Geographic examples get harder at the smallest levels of accuracy, such as electoral wards, neighbourhoods and postcode zones. People often do not know which of the various local wards they live in. In face-to-face interviewing, the interviewer can use a Geographic Positioning System to get accurate latitude and longitude data and include this in the questionnaire answers. By Geographic Information System techniques, these GPS coordinates can later be mapped to give each respondent a ward, neighbourhood and postcode. If a survey is set up this way, there is no need to ask the question directly of respondents – that only tends to create an opportunity for error. There are some areas of life in which accuracy is so important that we try to avoid allowing errors to creep in.

The larger grey area of 'fact' includes the person's whole life history, their attitudes and beliefs and their reports about their own and other household members' incomes, employment, industrial sector and other activities. It is common in surveys to let one respondent answer straightforward questions on behalf of other people from the same household. The method known as 'proxying' invites them to fill in the survey form for each household member (age, sex, employment status, etc.) without directly approaching every person. The reason for using proxy answers is mainly down to efficiency. A single interview can cover the respondent in full and their household (in a rough factual way). Ironically, what are usually called 'facts' about people are subject to a lot of estimation and there is plenty of scope for error:

- Is the tenure of the household social housing or privately rented? The respondent may not know.

- Is the employment status of the absent head of household self-employed or employed? Again the respondent may not know.

- Are the weekly working hours of the absent son below or above 30 hours a week? The respondent may not know accurately.

Due to our tendency to try to satisfy a questioner, people often give answers even if they are not exactly correct. Misclassification can result. We need to be absolutely accurate, so here are three rules of thumb when carrying out this particular line of questioning:

- Ask the person who knows the situation best.

- Stick to a very short recall period, not long ones.

- Get them to gather supporting paperwork, such as pay slips, and use this to prompt their answer.

Surveys with long recall periods are known to develop inaccuracies and inconsistencies in the data.

Harmonisation of survey questions involves carefully working out the wording in different languages so that they can be considered to cover the same range of answers, with the same meanings, even across large geographic distances. Harmonisation is very challenging. Even within a single country there may be multiple languages, dialects and local idioms. These are important to respondents as they usually couch their daily activities in the local lay language. There are also real differences in legal and regulatory institutions, which creates a difference in the answer options that should be given for each region, country or language group. The showcards will in general expand in length while the options specific to each local area are included in the list of possibilities. Agreed showcards in each language can be developed by the survey administrators. Back-translation is used to check and recheck the content of questions for large surveys such as polls and censuses. To do a back-translation, write the questions in the first language and get that translated. Then give this new document to a second person to translate back to the first language without knowledge of the original question. If the result is similar to the original, then consistency may have been achieved. If there are differences then further clarification and refinement are needed. Back-translation can continue with each revised version of a survey.

Piloting is also crucial for good survey writing across diverse language groups. The piloting should not be done in a single city or area. It needs to be sensitive to outlying areas, small distant regions and minority language groups. An extended piloting period may be needed to get an accurate survey in the sense of a close fit between what was meant to be asked, how it is understood and what the answers mean over a wide range of types of people in different places, to increase accuracy further, give the enumerator or interviewer an opportunity to write down details of any difficulties they come across. At least half a page is needed per survey for their comments. For surveys that respondents fill in themselves allow half a page at the end for them to express any doubts. Read the survey documents as they come in. Do not wait for them to pile up as they bear clues about how you could hone the survey while it is being carried out. All improvements are worthwhile even if some of the data collected early on cannot be improved. As data collectors our goal is to try continually to improve the accuracy of our survey and lower the number of selectively missing or wrong responses.

The idea of accuracy is derided by some qualitative researchers who are critical of the survey method itself. In the history of science, the debate about qualitative and quantitative research has been dogged by a schism between two camps.

The first camp is usually called the positivists, but its followers are also known as empiricists or standard empiricists.[1] They have focused on getting facts as if the information gained were impersonal and could be separated from the relationship between the knower and the object which is known. For researchers from this camp the respondent is objectified; they try to use people to get facts. They may see the survey 'instrumentally' – that is, as a way to increase efficiency or improve tax targeting or preventive health care. They have depersonalised the researcher process in the interests of good science. The positivist camp may be thought of as objectivists if they assert that the data simply 'tell us things' or can be 'true' without recognising the softness around the edges which arises from the social and human basis of social findings. The softness, as I describe elsewhere in this book, arises from the deep human ingenuity that leads to continual invention and difference; from the breadth of human personality and diversity of our bodies which makes it hard to make consistent comparisons even for biological events such as cancerous growths, asthma, achievement of muscle growth, speed of bone development or height to weight ratios. One rather obvious attack on the objectivist universalism of biological research is that it requires 'normal' human bodies, and thus the datasets should – if one seeks facts – omit people with physical and mental disabilities and any other relevant abnormality. But by omitting these abnormalities the scientist has set up a normative world in which the facts are sought. The norms are implicit and hidden and unfortunately make the research rather exclusive. The positivist camp, if it really exists, seeks refuge in accuracy as a way to defend surveys and keep building up their reputation as 'scientific'. However, at the edges of critique, the positivists have been found to be unable to respond creatively to human difference and diversity. See Harding (1993a, 1993b) for details of one critique of positivist biological and medical research.

There are two types of researchers in the other camp. There are subjectivists and there are post-structuralists. There is some overlap between these two groups. Subjectivism is the notion that truth (as a feature of a claim) can only be assessed using other claims, and is therefore relative to speakers' starting positions. The interplay of subjectivities, they say, generates shifting grounds for truth; there is no foundation for truth. Post-structuralists are more concerned about determinism in social science, which is perhaps one form of foundationalism but is not the same as the objectivism (commitment to objectivity of truth) which subjectivists use as a foil and resist. Post-structuralists have developed a wide variety of ways to analyse society without resting heavily on the notion that social structures influence the present and shape social change. They resist the concept of the human as a 'dupe'. Instead they see people as malleable and as reflexively able to focus upon themselves and each other.

These branches of social science generate researchers who can confidently analyse qualitative data. They simply do not care about surveys and they get on with other types of research: discourse-theoretic, theoretical, macro-sociological, theological, literary and other modes, some of which lie in the humanities and are rather different from the fact-finding part of the social sciences. For this group accuracy is important in terms of citing other texts and sources, but there is no attempt to generalise about large concrete populations with reference to what these populations actually say about themselves. Iconic authors, art styles, moral trends and change over historical time are the main subjects of this research. For this group, accuracy is usually left on one side, and questions of epistemology are taken to refer to much deeper and more philosophical questions. The issue of 'how we can know about someone else's experience', for example, raises not only issues of accuracy but of perception and the nature of being itself.

Although in practice many university social science departments divide into two camps of staff, there is a middle way between these two opposing outposts of social science. With regard to 'accuracy', a middle way approach appreciates accuracy as one among a variety of epistemological values.

Note

1. Regarding positivism in its three variants, these categories should not be used pejoratively because they each refer to a whole set of basic research assumptions. One would want to agree with some but disagree with others of these assumptions. Smith (1998) offers a balanced summary of the three styles of positivism. These could be thought of as schools of thought, but if a reader finds one or more of them incoherent then it is a specialist activity to work out exactly why by noticing where their inconsistencies are, or where one decides to disagree with a basic premise such as naturalism or nominalism. For a discussion of the implications for statistical inference, see Olsen and Morgan (2005); for commentaries about the critical realist approach, which clarifies several of the relevant issues, see Potter (1999); for practical advice, see Blaikie (2003); and from a qualitative perspective, see especially Outhwaite (1987).

2.11 Ethical Clearance

The ethical clearance process for university and hospital research projects is often lengthy. It varies from place to place too, which can be confusing. The ethical procedures document that advises researchers about what they need to do may be long and complex because the ethics committee or ethical assessment board has to take into account a whole variety of possible ethical and legal problems.

In this chapter my main focus is on what implications ethics has for data collection. First I describe the ethical clearance process in a university environment, then take up some of the linked legal and data protection issues, and finally comment on what ethics really means and the impact ethics has on data collection generally.

The ethical clearance process usually starts with a proposer examining which parts of the ethical clearance guidelines apply to this particular project. If the project has no volunteers or subjects (i.e. if it is not experimental) then there may be a simpler process. If the project involves interventions such as paying the participants or providing them with certain chemicals, then it will be a lengthy and complex process. The statement on ethics will need to cover the following areas:

- an assessment of the risks to the physical and psychological health and well-being of all subjects in the proposed study, including interviewees and informants;

- whether and how insurance will be obtained for particular aspects of the project, if any;

- a summary of the whole research design of the project, so that the ethics board can consider the validity of the scientific proposal and understand what positive contribution to knowledge is being sought;

- a list of all acts of recruitment of volunteers or participants, especially noting whether and what vulnerable groups might be contacted or involved;

- the screening and precautionary actions to be taken to minimise risks to health and well-being;

- a commitment that the data will be lodged in the department and that the university will have full access to the data on request, and that the data will be kept in conformity with data protection legislation and regulations;

- how volunteers will be warned of any threat to their confidentiality or any sensitivity that might be touched upon by the research, attaching the forms to be used to get written informed consent from each volunteer;

- the informed-consent form must state that the volunteer or participant is not required to take part and that they may withdraw at any time, and this should be shown to every participant.

This process can work well for encapsulated projects. For participatory processes on longer time-scales, however, ethical clearance is difficult to achieve. Annual reviews may be necessary (see 3.1 **participation**).

The underlying assumption of this sort of ethical process is that the volunteers and participants are fundamentally equal in status to the researchers and have rights which cannot be abrogated. Covert research is never approved by university ethics committees. Research done covertly has little formal scientific status because of the lies involved in setting it up. Covert research usually involves a breach of trust, whereas good scientific research often involves the building up of trust. It is often a good idea to offer a newsletter or other summary of the research to the participants as an offshoot of their participation. Remember to tell participants that it will take up to 2 years for the results to be ready.

After putting in the ethical clearance request form, there may be an interview in which the details of the research design and methodology are discussed. It is crucial for some evident potential benefit from the research to be proposed and explained convincingly. Otherwise why would a university agree to trouble volunteers, participants or interviewees to take part in the research? Only afterwards will it become clear whether there is any potential benefit. Some projects do not succeed for a wide range of reasons.

The committee will approve the project or ask for more information. It can take months to complete the ethical clearance process. All co-researchers must agree and then conform with their own ethical statement. Having a co-researcher or participant from outside the university environment can make the ethical statement more difficult to complete. There may be two reasons for this. Firstly, they work under different regulations so the risks may be different or even increased. Secondly, they are not made to conform to all the university procedures. There may need to be an explicit statement within the ethical clearance statement that they will conform to particular policies or guidelines (e.g. equal opportunities policies or child protection guidelines). Outside university environments, some enterprises encourage their staff to conform to the ethics guidelines of professional associations. Whether it is the Social Research Association or a nationwide sociological or management association, nearly all the larger professional associations offer standardised documents giving guidance on ethics to their members. These guidance documents can help to handle real ethical issues even if they do not provide the insurance cover and legal protection that a university ethics committee is able to provide.

The university may ask for a short memo after a year to update their records on the success of the project. They use this memo to review the practical aspects of ethics across a wide range of disciplines.

Research involving people who commit crimes is a particularly problematic area. In general, the university research ethics committee will advise researchers that if they hear of a crime being committed, or one which is soon to be committed, they should report the matter to the police. Researchers in this area tend to advise their informants of this rule and dissuade them from passing on key information about specific crimes. Conversations and interviews can then happen with this prior rule being known to both parties. Informed consent, and indeed signed paper forms showing this consent, need to be obtained before and not after any data-collection meeting.

Some exceptions are made to the rules in specific local circumstances. If people are not literate then a pre-agreed exceptional form of verbal or other assurance of informed consent can be accepted. If risks are inevitable then insurance cover for a high-risk area can be obtained, and the ethics statement can have a protocol for the handling of health and safety and risk. An example of such a protocol is included in the Appendix as Document A1. The protocol is a helpful guide that can be used for training all staff in the project. It can be used to support the induction of each new staff member no matter how casual or temporary their contract may be. A sample informed-consent participant permission form is also included in the Appendix as Document A2.

The legal issues arising from a study include:

(a) The risk to health of participants, following which they might decide to sue the university or the researchers involved.

(b) The risk to the reputation of the university, which can be protected in part by a cautious ethics committee making sure each researcher takes their role as a knowledge-seeker seriously and is prepared to present the research in a clear and readable way that can be understood by any intelligent audience.

(c) The risk that the staff doing the research might get injured and then claim that the university is negligent. As a result, the university may decide to take care of all insurance arrangements. After dealing with the insurer they can inform staff of the risk management and precautions needed in each specific area of health and safety. Whilst one might argue that the ethics committee should not interfere in routine health and safety matters, it is important that the ethics committee does not approve a project if it shows in any way a risk to health or well-being that is an avoidable or unnecessary risk. It would be unethical to approve the project. It is generally necessary for the ethics committee or board to approve projects before the standard legal cover and insurance is valid for scientific experiments as much as for social science fieldwork.

The data-protection issues arising from a study involve following both the laws of the country where the fieldwork is taking place and the country in which the funder and researchers are located. In the UK the Data Protection Act offers clear guidance that the respondents must be informed about data being held about them, and that they must agree to such data being held. It is even the rule in the UK that each person must be aware they can review and alter the data held about them. Research must promise to conform to the Data Protection Act before it can pass its ethical clearance stage.

Examples of non-conformity would include:

- having data about the interviewers in an appointment process, including actual names, held on a computer to do the sampling before getting these interviewers' written approval to hold such data;

- typing in a lot of questionnaire data with the actual names on them without assigning a serial number to each questionnaire, unless the respondents have explicitly agreed to their names being typed into the computer;

- loading MP3 sound data into a computer without having the explicit consent of the people who were recorded.

Consent needs to be obtained in advance, but in reality it is always best to go ahead and get consent afterward if a procedural mistake has been made. The likelihood of conviction is low but the impact of being convicted is high, because under the Data Protection Act it is not a single researcher who is accused, but the whole organisation.

Video records of public events are particularly problematic. Here the law is vague and case law would, in the UK, have to be searched to find out exactly what rules apply. Good sense and practical ethics (i.e. being respectful to people) suggest that research videos of public events should not show identifiable faces unless the identifiable people have given informed consent to be recorded (Alfonso et al., 2004; Pink, 2007).

Taking pictures of children is another problem area. It is usually tricky to get the consent of children for a research process that applies to them. Asking the parents is also awkward since that implies that perhaps the child has not been consulted. A good route through this mess is to avoid taking any full frontal pictures of children at all. Pictures taken from the back and pictures of bodies without heads are more useful in social research even if they may not be aesthetically pleasing. The standard of a photo being 'pleasing' is almost irrelevant in social research, where the well-being and legal standing of each participant is of prime importance.

In all these interactions with participants the researcher needs to keep in mind that they are not working alone. They are acting as a representative of their university, their department and – more broadly – their discipline. If they are accused of any illicit practice, a public fuss could be made. Even if the accusation is false, bringing the university into disrepute is a serious matter. Risks of accusations need to be foreseen as far as possible in order that they can be avoided. Laws about data protection and the rights of ordinary people in public places and in research projects will vary from country to country. It is wise to do your homework and find out the laws applying to the country or countries you are working in, then adhere to all the laws of all the people involved. Thus if you work with migrants from an African country you should look into what laws apply to them in their own country and try to conform to those laws too. If you find you cannot conform, then there is a risk of you breaking the law, and you should inform your university. By spotting this problem, you can make it a collective issue for investigation. Do not ignore awkward issues: they can grow and become very serious in an unexpected way. Make a written note of the difficulties you have raised verbally with the legal, ethics, line management or research support officers of your university. Your written notes can be used to track the issue over time.

An illustration to show that multi-country legal issues really matter is research about distance learning. Suppose you wanted to evaluate a distance learning programme. Your participants in the evaluation will live in a variety of countries. You can quickly see that from their standpoint it is obvious that you need to conform to their laws, since you are effectively doing the research on their terrain even if it is done via post, Skype or email.

Having seen that the legal and ethical issues are wide-ranging and involve a lot of preparation and guesswork about risks, you can now see that ethical clearance has direct links with the development of the research design. You can only do things that will work, and for your project to be valid you need to get ethical clearance. So make a list of activities and data types you want to collect, and work through any potential difficulties. Then drop the ones that look too difficult or unworkable or which raise hazards that are scary or severe.

As a research team accumulates experience it gets easier to manage the ethical clearance 'process'. The substantive ethics of research are a different matter. At a deeper evaluative level, one needs to be sure that the research offers value to society in some way. It can be very indirect or long-term, but you have to be able to track that value added or potential extra knowledge. There are likely to be trade-offs and all kinds of difficulties in the research. It may be awkward for somebody, interviews may embarrass someone, legal implications may crop up, and the researcher cannot guarantee that everyone will benefit. The study of ethics is interesting because ethics are so complex. A primer on ethics suggests that looking at procedures alone is rarely sufficient (MacIntyre, 1985). Indeed, serious social science interview research with American respondents showed that lay ethics among ordinary people in American cities was also quite complex. People consider a whole variety of factors before they make a decision (Wolfe, 1989). In the same way, the researcher sets up a research programme that is aimed at an overall gain in knowledge. They then set out specific research designs for each component or each project, which they argue will offer value for money and contribute to the wider programme. The hope is that any discomfort for the participants is somehow outweighed by the social benefits of the results.

Further Reading for Part 2

For the qualitative researcher, Fairclough (2001) – or any other work by Fairclough – is an extremely easy way to gain insight into the study of social power through hermeneutics. However, it is also easy to gain concrete knowledge of how to set up and interpret interviews through the much more constructivist book by Kvale (1996). In a nutshell, the difference of perspective between these two works represents a division of entire schools of thought. Fairclough is openly realist about the workings of power pre-existing the social construction or deconstruction of the text; but Kvale tends to focus more on the epistemological problems rather than on the world's 'real' features. Kvale encourages researchers to undertake acts of interpretation, but it is not quite clear whether there is any truth to be found using the qualitative method as he describes it. With Fairclough's realism, by way of contrast, there are truths to be found because discourses and power relations have a pre-extant nature and we come upon them ready to discover whatever we can, using innovative methods such as text analysis.

According to Fairclough – and I agree – we cannot just make up any story freely to interpret the texts that we have gathered. The range of interpretations is constrained by the reality of the world from which the texts have emerged. Discourse analysis is ultimately about reality not just about language. Many books on qualitative method leave this issue unresolved – notably Wetherell et al. (2001) and the excellent work by Charmaz (2006) on *Constructing Grounded Theory*. Mason's (2002) introduction to *Qualitative Researching* helps with both practical and theoretical aspects of interpretation.

Part 3

Observation and Involved Methods

3.1 Participation

Participation in research makes the teamwork more complex. By 'participation' we usually mean the involvement of active agents such as people or organisations in a process facilitated by the researcher(s). The research may be fostered by an agency, by enterprise or by government. Participation has been lauded by those who notice the marginalisation of voices from the edges of society. For example, homeless people, minority ethnic groups, immigrants and refugees would typically be unable to access all the usual rights and privileges of other citizens. Research might, among other things, help them to help themselves. In this chapter I first review what it means to have a marginalised voice, then describe how participation can work in research. Finally, I briefly review some criticisms of participation in research. This gives a balanced view of the possibility of participation in social research.

'A marginalised voice can hardly be heard.' The meaning of such a claim is not just metaphorical, nor is it about the literal 'loudness' of a voice. It is more a statement that certain kinds of people are not accepted into the social milieu of dominant and powerful elites. The main aspects of marginalisation are three: low social power, lack of involvement in elite planning, and exclusion from corporate society. Two examples will introduce a description of these aspects. The first example is the female gender.

Research on management and labour markets was for many years (the 1950s and 1960s) focused almost entirely on men and male managers because it was considered somehow 'additional' or 'not normal' for women to do paid work or become senior managers. The more research there was about senior managers, the more likely it was that there was a presumption that the manager was male. In the 1950s the ideology prevalent in many Western countries was that women should not do paid work, although they had played important productive roles in past societies. In the agrarian society of the Middle Ages women milked cows or worked on the farm. In industrial society they had jobs in factories and in post-industrial society they were service workers or employed in retail, health or education. One common theme has been that all the roles played by women were classified as marginal to the core labour market. In recent decades it has been widely recognised that this is unfair to women and that women's earnings are not just 'pin money' to supplement the core household income.

In studies of gender it has been pointed out that the marginalisation occurs through linguistic classifications and typical stereotypes of the roles men and women play. Stereotypes operate by suggesting that the roles *commonly* played are the ones that *should be* played. There is a merger of the descriptive and normative tones of the description of the roles. Men and women themselves will tend to help contribute to this pattern because they also think it would be odd to be abnormal, and therefore that what is 'usual' is good. Marginalisation is then compounded when the oppressed, sidelined or silenced group is politically weak. Women – who were present in labour markets but mainly in part-time or low-status jobs – were excluded from core political roles. The ratio of women to men in parliaments in democratic countries was and is low. In undemocratic systems, too, the number of women in power-wielding roles was also low. Women were silenced from public life but very active in 'private lives'. A critique of the role of public science in such environments was clearly voiced by Haraway (1988) who argued that the silenced voices could not be heard because they would not even be talking the same language or using the same idioms as the dominant masculinised groups – such as hard-science 'hypothesis-testing' language or the discourse of 'fact-finding'.

Stanley and Wise (1993) also explored this phenomenon, through which the gender dimension of science itself has made Western science very masculine in its orientation to knowledge. Stanley and Wise suggest that a more women-oriented or 'unmasculine' science would pay attention to profound axes of difference in a population, listen to rare and creative voices giving new ideas and be unwilling to 'harmonise' and generalise to a universal norm because it would have to recognise local norms and genuine differences. Cultural difference within a population – specifically about gender roles but also the autonomy of children or beliefs about medical interventions – are examples raised by feminists to illustrate their critique of universalist law-seeking science (Alcoff and Potter, 1993). The marginalisation is thus partly about a circuit of powerful elites using science to reproduce power and – necessarily – exclude the powerless from this scene unless they are co-opted into the ideology and discourses of the powerful.

In the gender example, we can see that the women themselves may be unable to rescue themselves from low social power. They are liable to become disengaged from national and international planning because of their gender-assigned family roles. As a result women are often excluded *en masse* from the large-scale corporate society. Social inclusion research tries to explore ways to break this impasse, and studies of social exclusion have repeatedly advocated participation at the local and grassroots level in democratic and budget processes as a way to raise the 'volume' of local marginalised voices.

A second example is that of immigrants and refugees. Some immigrants have a clear citizenship status while others are not accepted as citizens of their new country of residence. The terms 'refugee' and 'asylum seeker' have evolved as ways of summarising a legal status different from a legal immigrant. Meanwhile, the social norms and affective overtones of the words used have evolved too. Someone who is an 'immigrant', 'refugee' or 'asylum seeker' may have difficulty being accepted into the everyday, normal group activities of social life. They might be shunned in a parent–toddler group or treated with diffidence at their local sports centre. Confusion over the legal and regulatory status of the immigrant group may – simply through ignorance or an unwillingness to explore the complexity of the situation – spread into negative reactions towards people of visible ethnic minorities or those whose first language is not the home language. The dominant ethnic group population may actually act in a racist way without meaning to.

In the UK, where I live, a group of workers deciding to arrange a typical 'British' social occasion – a visit to 'the pub', or public house, where they would chat, relax and have several rounds of alcoholic drinks – could be an example of institutionalised racism. Any Muslim friends would be excluded from this social occasion, without intention. The planning of the pub visit may ignore the cultural reality that some Muslims in the group do not drink alcohol or go to the pub.

People can cause social exclusion simply by being more comfortable with people of their own type either visibly or audibly – that is, they speak the same language or dialect. The marginalisation that results can be profound. The country's political system will tend not to include the migrants. The ability of migrants to express their political demands or engage in tension-reducing confrontations or negotiations may be limited. The impact on research data is multi-faceted. For example, the addresses of migrants may change rapidly and they may not have voting rights, so using an electoral register to do sampling would tend to exclude them. If the research is about voting or civic rights and the migrant does not have any, then it may be felt acceptable simply to omit them from the sampling frame for this reason. If the migrant is asked whether they (subjectively) care to participate in research, it is more likely that they – rather than the dominant ethnic groups of indigenous people – will decline. They will be aware of their own real difference. They will know that it may be hard to be understood or heard and that they will be perceived as not conforming in certain ways from a supposed norm, such as in their basic religious or cultural views, household structure, language and historical knowledge. Self-exclusion is an important part of social exclusion.

Research on migrants has to take account of these risks of exclusion. Migrants in general are less likely to have same-ethnicity role models in politics, often have lower local social power than others do, and – by virtue of their newness and difference – cannot participate in the civil society groups that the local indigenous people do. An example in the UK would be that some Catholic schools are publicly funded but migrants cannot gain access to them unless they are either Catholic or have a stable local address, or both. Also, a newer non-Catholic migrant may not even think of joining a Catholic (or other) faith-based school. Thus, in general, those migrants who are 'different' – in this case those who are not Catholic – are excluded from important opportunities for getting the benefits of corporate life. Yet the regulations state clearly that these Catholic schools should accept a specified number of non-Catholic children. The UK government also makes an effort to include all social groups in education by ensuring that there are 'comprehensive' non-selective schools to educate every child needing schooling. However, the elite schools are more selective and less likely to have – or hear – migrants than the non-elite schools. As a result the school system participates in the reproduction of class power and social power hierarchies.

In research terms it may be easy to get access to migrants but hard to get them to express in explicit terms the problem that the researcher may see in this system. People are often not aware of the systemic properties of the society they are living in. They may not want to talk about it. Most lay people do not have the vocabulary to articulate their feelings of social exclusion or frustration. Instead they focus their daily routines on aspects of life they are more comfortable with, which may be holidays, mobile phones or other consumer practices. Social exclusion thus tends to reproduce itself in a divided society. There is the public sphere, and separately there are smaller and narrower social circles in which people often feel comfortable. In the smaller groups, people can discuss at length the daily routines they focus on (religious worship, managing pets, etc.). Lay people may not often discuss the biggest issues that are problematic for them, especially if these issues are seen as impossible to resolve.

This segmented social scene is the context for participation in research. A research process that is participatory can come under one of several subheadings. Participatory action research (PAR) is an important type. PAR uses the action-research method to engage people in processes that enable their participation and personal growth – see Heron (2000), Reason and Bradbury (2009) and Reason and Rowan (1981); and Fals-Borda and Rahman (1991) write about PAR in developing country contexts. Fals-Borda (1988), like more theoretical works by Freire (1993), argues that the power relations in society are underpinned by social structures and the distribution of resources in ways which typically silence the voices of marginalised people. Anthropological and social research can be a form of participation, but it is up against these barriers. Other forms of public participation might engage citizens in feedback processes or social partnership arrangements which are influenced by large governmental or quasi-governmental organisations (Hickey and Mohan, 2004). In most participation processes there is a paid facilitator whose organisational sponsor is very influential in the research process (Heron, 1999). The research may follow a standardised process. A typical research protocol is described in Box 6. This kind of process is described by Mikkelson (1995, 2005) as including a variety of creative data-creation processes in the middle stages. Danermark et al. (2002) also stress that the stages of research can be visited in any order.

Box 6   Research Protocol for Participatory Research

- Identify a problem or topic.

- Engage stakeholders and select some methods of participation.

- Facilitate and record the participation, staggered with the next activity.

- Share the records of statements or productions by different groups or individuals.

- Draw the process to a close with democratic or facilitative larger-scale meetings.

- Write up the findings of the process in a document or produce a video with multiple voices. Return to earlier steps and iterate.

Among the participation processes commonly used are:

- participatory mapping, using images to represent issues like inequality or hunger;

- focus groups, identifying and defining differing perspectives (see 2.8 **focus groups**);

- discussion groups, bringing stakeholders together to achieve a deeper understanding of other standpoints;

- facilitators, bringing processes to an agreed moment of closure or conclusion.

The question for data collection is whether any of these stages is going to be recorded in ways that would count as 'data'. Clearly, from all the stages memoranda or field notebooks could be written up. Would they be private or public? Would they be individual or group products? Researchers differ in their views about these two questions. In recent years it has become easier to put multimedia materials into computers. Therefore the diagrams, maps and creative products (such as a short drama production) produced during participatory research can be represented in a data format.

It is important for informed consent to be obtained before data are gathered (see 2.11 **ethical clearance**). In the ethics of participatory research informed consent is just part of the broader process of gathering consent and fair involvement over time. For legal reasons – notably the data protection laws – the official step of getting informed consent for data gathering has to precede each data-gathering activity. If you are not sure about whether informed consent will work perfectly, it is still important to get some informed consent. The consent arrangements can be revised later, but there does need to be an explicit permission or agreement – preferably signed – at an early stage.

The agreement is likely to give participants access to their own and perhaps to all the data. It is not always clear whether all the participants can actually use the data later. It may not be practical and they may not be motivated to use data at all. In addition, one cannot assume away the digital divide. The digital divide refers to difficulties with access to computers, internet and software among poor and socially excluded people. In addition, some people will not have enough free time to look at or use the data. There is also a strong danger that the research sponsor, facilitator or end-user will dominate the interpretation stage. This leads me to my next set of observations about participatory research, which consider the 'critiques of participation'.

There are three main lines of critique. The first is that the participatory materials have a low factual content and have not been checked for their accuracy as representations. Someone might make a statement about an ethnic group. However authentic their belief in that statement, there might still be a need to challenge it and seek further evidence – perhaps scientifically, systematically or without observer bias – to give some legitimacy to the use of that statement in later reports. For a post-structuralist this critique does not have much weight because the voices in themselves are valued for what they can tell us about how it 'really is' to be in the marginalised place. Even the people in advantaged positions have a right to hold their views. The whole purpose is to listen to the logic of how social life is constructed by the people who are participating. Challenging their beliefs as not 'being true' or not being factual enough imposes on them the elite structure of knowledge that is being fundamentally questioned in participatory research. In general, PAR processes are very tolerant of different views.

The second critique is that the oppressed will find it difficult to give voice to their real needs and instead may express very short-term demands or even use the process instrumentally to achieve some networking or publicity aim. This critique notices that the social-ethical nature of the facilitator's approach may not be matched by a social-ethical response. Instead the whole process may get fragmented, especially when there is government funding at stake or a powerful sponsor. The facilitator's job of deriving a closure or conclusion may be extremely challenging precisely in situations where real conflicts of interest are brought together and made to interact. This critique has been questioned by those who want to respect everyone's views, of whatever kind, without pre-judging what views or demands people can be allowed to have. The idea that a person from a marginalised standpoint cannot know their own real needs is sometimes called the 'false consciousness' problem. False consciousness could arise if, for example, a migrant group wanted to have a special school rather than put their children into a mainstream school. It might be argued that they do not realise the benefits of mainstreaming and inclusion. They 'prefer' to be separate, finding it easier, but their preference is not in their best interests.

I have tried to summarise this argument briefly here. It is a controversial argument, very much about knowledge and validity and who is authorised to say which views or proposals are more valid. In social science the whole issue of false consciousness raises a wider question of how to discern truth when conducting qualitative research. Is the researcher authorised to claim something as true which the research participants do not agree with? Participatory research is riddled with issues about truth and knowledge and power (Babbitt, 1993). Some researchers avoid participatory research for this reason. Others find ways to do it in carefully structured contexts, floating through the controversies as one among many participants.

A third critique is that even in participatory processes, which try to be democratic and advocate 'good listening' to excluded social groups, there is a tendency for well-educated or ambitious types to come to the front. Worse still, bringing the excluded types of people in as 'participants' can often objectify them or co-opt them into the dominant group's discourses. Cooke and Kothari (2001) argue along these lines, stating that participation in research in developing countries is sometimes a form of tyranny. Participation is now routinely required by some research funders they suggest it is often adhered to in name only, but actually reproduces social power and hierarchies by giving apparent democratic approval to policy development processes.

As a researcher you have to decide what aspects of a research process to document, what ethics to follow and what kinds of achievement (praxis) to attempt during a research process. If participation works for you, use it.

Here is an example to consider. I experienced local participatory research in Salford, Manchester, between 2000 and 2001. I was brought in to facilitate a process in which 12 local community development workers were trained and then engaged in interviewing people locally about poverty in Salford. I was also asked to bring secondary data on house values, poverty levels, social and economic deprivation and incomes to bear on the issue. All the researchers looked closely at detailed ward-wise deprivation data from 2001 (see 5.5 **data extraction**).

The whole activity was sponsored and funded by the Community Network, which is a partnership of the local council, a regeneration board and some community groups. The Community Network also allowed private individuals to be members and people could come to meetings whether 'members' or not. The research process over a 12-month period followed most of the steps described earlier. The results were summarised in the final – much revised – claims shown below:

Hypothesis 1: In Salford, relative income-poverty of households is persistent and affects people's daily behaviour. About one-fifth of households are poor in this sense.

Hypothesis 2: The subjective fear of poverty and of degradation in Salford causes many people to defend themselves against the label 'poor' and to struggle for a sense of decency and self-worth.

Hypothesis 3: The deprivation associated with the locality of Salford makes it all the more important for local people to be able to establish healthy, rich lifestyles.

A summary document of around 20,000 words brought both quantitative and qualitative data to a public viewing. This document contained important state-ments by local people, illustrated by the following vivid commentary on poverty:

> A. People who are individually poor are, ummm. There are neighbourhoods within neighbourhoods ummm that are poor. So perhaps ummm, particular groups of people, maybe people with unemploy (sic), who are unemployed and don't have enough money coming in, or if we're talking about a different aspect, say health. Then it'll be people who can't access some health services.
>
> Q. So you'd consider that as being poor?
>
> A. Yeah I think it's a deprivation problem. So we're poorer because we can't get certain things. We're poorer because we can't put food on the table.

> (Olsen, 2005)

The geographic issue of neighbourhoods was an important one for local people. Deprivation data at a very low geographic level were used to clarify which areas were most deprived, leaving the qualitative research to focus on why and what the experience of inequality is like. To some extent, the research concluded that poverty is not so much an individual income problem as a locality-based deprivation problem. As a result, one might argue, the use of civic amenities and social assets such as community centres could perhaps offset income poverty by offering communal assets and new ways to engage publicly. In recent years Salford has introduced community committees to increase local grassroots par-ticipation in the way the council makes its decisions. The participatory research method is very close to action research when it is done this way.

The three claims listed as 'hypotheses' summarised the findings, not the *a priori* or *tested* hypotheses. In participatory research, 'testing' is not usually an important part of the process. Instead, voicing views, learning and listening, hearing and engaging in face-to-face dialogue are very important. Some call this a dialogical process (Freire, 1996). A dialogue contrasts with the usual scientific monologue. The Salford research process was used to develop and inform the city's strategy for local development and regeneration, and most of the community development workers soon moved on to other jobs and activities. In Salford, other participatory processes of research are currently happening. They are all controversial for the kinds of reasons I have listed. Many of the participants found the creation and reanalysis of the data fascinating. The data for this study have been retained for future use.

3.2 Praxis

You may have had the experience of filling in a questionnaire and wondering what the results would be used for. Perhaps it was while you were evaluating some teaching that you received, or filling in a market-research survey form. You wonder what the data will be used for because you assume that the author of the survey has praxis in mind. Their praxis – purposive action – cannot easily be read off from the questionnaire content, but sometimes it can be. Your research will benefit from having an explicitly planned and strategic approach to your own praxis.

In this chapter I explain the context and origin of the word praxis, and then explore why practices are considered so important these days in research contexts. There is a wider movement towards studying people's *practices* which looks closely at the underlying values, norms and expertise which make practices run smoothly. The most ordinary activity is full of practices – sports and games have referees, coaches, players and ticket-takers who all play their roles in routine ways. Practices involve people following 'usual' routines, but praxis means people doing things that may surprise other people *for a good reason*. Practices are pre-ethical, automatic, habitual ways of acting but praxis is the special kind of calculative or planned behaviour that is strategic and can cause change.

The word praxis was used by Marx and Lenin to refer to the actions of revolutionary party activists or the 'vanguard' of the people (Marx and Engels, 1998). In Marx's view, the way social change occurs had been dominated all too often by a single set of elite ideas. He called these 'bourgeois' ideas in order to label the elite with a scientific class label. He named the other classes the 'workers' and the 'petit bourgeoisie' or small traders. According to Marx, praxis is more important than ideas. A strike or other visible collective action is more powerful than any speech or written set of demands. A strike would be the praxis of the working class. Marx did work in the realm of ideas, but he said the ideas were only suitable if they led to right action. The testing ground for ideas, according to Marx and many other modern writers, is how they help to guide right action. Praxis refers to the action as part of the consequences of research. According to this view, new theories, new concepts and innovative diagrams are simply not meaningful unless they influence somebody's actions.

The word praxis helps to focus our attention on what the strategic implications or impacts of research are going to be. If we have a clear idea of a problem but do not know the solution, then research can seek out and test different alternative solutions. Much health research works like this, and the praxis arises when medical, dietary or other advice and treatments are given to the patients.

Another example of praxis arising from research is when management culture is changed by the actions of researchers who critique a particular management orientation. Marx critiqued some ideas in political economy precisely because they were stale, unhelpful ideas that worked only in a purely conceptual metaphorical space. Marx, and later Lenin and others, advocated social action rather than just musing about society (Lenin, 1964). For them, criticising ideas was one form of action.

These days the advice of Marx and Lenin has a mixed reputation because of the difficulties that the Soviet Union and some other socialist republics have had with democratic rights and public justice. It is often forgotten that both Marx and Lenin were serious researchers in their own right. Marx studied philosophy in a very serious way and reached the conclusion that *materialism* needed to replace *idealism* and that this would be a helpful way forward for society generally. A widespread scepticism about superstitions and luck arises from this tradition. According to the materialist tradition, it is important to look at actual lives and livelihoods and to assess the progress of a country by its citizens' lives, not by beliefs. Marx tried to be very scientific, although his empirical work was controversial. Lenin, in turn, writing slightly later (between 1898 and 1917; see Lenin, 1964) did serious historical and social research on the transformation of working-class peasant lives during the industrial revolution in Russia. Lenin was also a follower of Engels (see Engels and Kelley, 1892; Marx, 1969) who did materialist research on the industrial sector in Manchester and the rest of England – and both of them in turn were adherents of most of the political economy framework set up by Marx.

All in all, praxis has a reputation arising out of this tradition of struggle and activism. Praxis also has a place in the ideas of Freire (1993), who thought learners should be able to influence or even control their learning situation, and Heron (2000), who thinks people should work together collaboratively rather than being placed in strict hierarchies.

Praxis implies taking responsibility for an action strategy. Flyvbjerg (2001) has written that social science research could be invigorated and avoid staleness by a strong reference back to concepts of praxis that date as far back as Aristotle. Flyvbjerg, like myself, is a follower of some ideas of Aristotle that are materialist and realist. Realists are critical of socially conventional idea systems that cause or underpin inequality and suffering. Flyvbjerg reintroduces the concept of *phronesis* – prudent action – to refer to the use of knowledge to change society. Flyvbjerg uses a word like *phronesis* because no other word will do: social science is transformative, information is part of human strategies of transformation, and knowledge is important mainly in so far as it aids *phronesis*.

Here is an example of how *phronesis* as proposed by Flyvbjerg (2001) might work in applied situations. If the marriage system seems to be breaking down, and the deinstitutionalisation of marriage is causing suffering and disappoint-ment along with divorce, then research into marriage could look at alternatives to marriage as well as alternative lifestyles within marriage. The research might be expected to conclude by advocating some particular solution as a strategy of action both for the 'bride and groom' and also for advice agencies like Relate (www.relate.org.uk) that advise people about marriages.

A key element of a praxis approach is that it is not enough to learn about the world. As Marx (1969) said: 'The philosophers have only interpreted the world, in various ways. The point, however, is to change it.' Perhaps you can develop your own example now. Take a moment to consider the research topic you like best. Why do you like that topic? Is it just a hobby or is there some seri-ous purpose vaguely in your mind? Someone studying alcohol abuse might, for example, be concerned that 'innocent' habits of socialising are causing health problems and anti-social behaviour. They may wish to change the situation – but how? Research can help you work out how to change whole systems of habits. Research is not just about redescribing the habits.

If you succeed in working out what your broad purpose is, in your chosen research topic, you can then explore (as a mental exercise, or with a pad and pen) what data are needed in order to move towards a new strategy for improving changes. Do you already know what to do? Why has this not already been done? How can things be changed so that these obstacles to improvement are removed?

Retroduce backward, exploring these issues and questions, and keep notes of what kinds of data, information or new theories you might need. Retroduction is explained by Blaikie (2000, 2003), Sayer (1992), and Potter (1999). You can't actually 'do' research this way, but it is a useful way to guide your planning. You can keep these notes in your research diary, and return to them later.

For praxis, taking a problematising approach acts as the starting point of research. The researcher does not just do research on whatever they fancy. They start with a pressing problem, trying to reduce suffering or lessen the confusion and tensions of daily life. They investigate the system in order to try to change it, not just for the sake of writing books to earn money or generate a good career. Praxis raises our horizon of interest beyond the personal, artistic or merely plea-surable. Praxis follows Aristotle's advice that the good life is not just a life of pleasure but a life that has good effects and is virtuous (Aristotle, 1925, 1988).

Flyvbjerg says we have to study where society is going then look at how we want to change the direction things are taking. Research fits in because it can help people to know more accurately and consciously what is happening and what might be possible. Flyvbjerg's recommended form of research would also consider very carefully what the valued outcomes are for society (see also MacIntyre, 1985, for a discussion). Whilst MacIntyre is mainly a social theorist, Flyvbjerg's advice is to get out and start doing things.

So the evaluation form that a teacher gives out is intended to help them improve their teaching, and the market researcher's survey aims to help a company improve its products – or at least its marketing of those products. These intentions are clear and rather narrow.

When we move towards management research, medical or health research and social science research, we are moving towards broader and broader social objectives. We are not meant to look at just sectional intentions – that is, working in someone's private interests, against others' interests. According to the praxis method, we are aiming to look at the broader social good. Research is just the special word for how we proceed to look at that good in a dispassionate, active, interested but cautious way. Data collection has deeper intentions which may be obvious to the respondents – that is not a problem. No secrets need to be kept and covert research is not necessary because if the research is aimed at the 'public good' then it can generally be done publicly.

The praxis approach affects research and data collection in many practical ways. One obvious impact is that the research should not generally harm anybody along the way since it would be hard to justify doing harm in the public interest. If harm occurs, it should be unintended.

A second impact is that qualitative research can be respected as a very important method in helping reframe old social problems. The more persistent a problem, the more we need qualitative research to readdress it and look more closely at the barriers to change.

The praxis method works best in the context of a slightly disinterested ethics. A third impact of praxis is to question your personal and individual interests and hobbies and allow them to become part of wider social movements or collective interests. The very definition of 'ethics' might be that we are considering what is 'good' while taking into account not only our *own* personal wants or needs but a wider set of competing wants and needs. Therefore, the praxis researcher may not want to work entirely alone but instead affiliate themselves to non-governmental organisations, international organisations or other enterprises – even government departments – where the aims are generally consistent with approved purposes. The researcher tries to work in the public interest, bring harmony where there is discord and misunderstanding and find new solutions to old problems.

The praxis method informs action research and some forms of participatory research. However it can also be used as an ethical and purposive basis for secondary data analysis, primary survey research and many forms of qualitative research. Praxis is not really a 'method', more of a methodological framework. Indeed, it reflects a whole philosophical position, similar to 'critical social science' but with a more activist orientation. It is good to underpin data collection with a conscious set of methodological principles. Praxis might be one of the principles you choose.

3.3 Action Research

Doing action research is an exciting departure from the usual hypothesis-testing methodology used in scientific contexts (Olsen, 2010a). Action research can take several forms because the degree of involvement of lay actors in the research can vary from minimal commentaries to total control. The edited collection of essays by Carroll (2004) explains the linkages between shadowing in organisations, critical social science, praxis as I described it earlier and action research. A step-by-step guide to action research is offered by McNiff and Whitehead (2009). This useful guide can be complemented by the in-depth chapters found in Reason and Bradbury (2009).

Whether action research is scientific or not is an important question if the researcher is based in an academic setting. For some disciplines, in some contexts such as a final degree project in social science, action research will be a strategically difficult method to choose because it challenges so many traditional assumptions of scientific research. For example, it gives credence and authority to the voices of ordinary people or to an organisation's management. These voices are said to offer examples of 'lay' discourse by Sayer (1992), who contrasts academic discourse with lay discourse in general. Discourse analysts have noted strong differences in the style and meaning of phrases used by academics, journalists, teachers, young people and those untrained in social science. If lay discourse is so different from academic discourse, then to include these voices as authoritative or as co-authors is likely to be highly problematic. In addition, the question of control arises in action research. I will set out what action researchers usually do, then conclude by commenting on the way that action researchers collect and retain their data.

Generally, action researchers are critical of those power relations in society which often go unnoticed. I find that it is rather challenging to talk about social power and power relations among ordinary – or non-academic – people, because it sometimes goes against the grain. A typical phrase from this genre of research is 'the fish don't talk about the water' (Risseeuw, 1991).

There are two aspects to the problem. The first is that to preserve your own dignity, you try to develop a sense of belonging and place which precludes feeling directly indignant about social power oppressing you (Olsen, 2010b). Instead, even if you are in an oppressed group or position – for example, out of work – you develop a gang of friends or a hobby or a customary defence of your current position. For example, instead of saying you are unemployed you might say that you are caring for a relative or learning a new trade. Some unemployed people feel depressed and then say that they are depressed rather than unemployed. It is very common for lay people to confuse the causality. It might actually be that unemployment has caused their depression, but workers might say that the depression is the cause of the current unemployment. When the social scientist comes into the scene and wants to label the person as oppressed and identify structural causes of the unemployment, it breaks into habitual discursive habits and makes things feel awkward. People often do not know how to respond: some would prefer to avoid such a conversation.

A second problem arises if the analysis is meant to be less personal and more 'about the world'. The social scientist feels well prepared for making general, abstract or concrete statements about large groups or trends in the world. Take this example: 'The recession has caused a lot of unemployment.' When the researcher involves lay people in a discussion about this, they may feel less well prepared to comment, and may simply make comments about concrete things in their locality, such as 'I didn't lose my job' or 'I don't see any shops shut around here yet'. Subtle differences in the whole type and purpose of the discourse become problematic: Are we talking about society or about us? Are we making normative or descriptive commentaries? What are we talking about anyway, and how do you define things? In my research into poverty – especially in Salford in North West England, where there is plenty of it – it proved almost impossible to get poor people to talk about their experience of poverty. They always depersonalised it and even insisted on talking about poverty in other countries rather than in their own community. Overall it can be a challenge to get people to talk about power, poverty or society as it relates to them or as it exists in a broad sweeping general scene.

As a result action research creates difficulties for itself. It normally starts off with a problem and a set of stakeholders. These are approached to get their agreement to participate in the research. The ethics of consent are not simply 'informed consent' but 'process consent' (McNiff and Whitehead, 2009), i.e. they agree not only to someone else 'using' data they create, but also to participate in the whole process of data creation and use.

The problem arises that the person who wants to write up or conclude the research will eventually have to limit the agenda. They will need to facilitate drawing up a list of concluding points, or get to the point where a sense of closure is reached. This can be challenging. One useful argument about these social processes of research is the idea that a 'catalytic event' or 'cathartic moment' may occur about midway through the process (Heron, 1999). The facilitator wisely prepares people for a face-to-face event around the time when this cathartic moment might be expected to occur. Then the facilitator will, if they are kind and cautious, try to ensure that any hurt feelings are dealt with and any surprises treated with care and consideration. For example, someone may discover – when they did not previously realise it – that they are, technically, poor. This may cause them to want to start maximising their income, and the facilitator may provide the phone number of a community centre which has staff who can help them, either by advising them on how to claim all the benefits they are entitled to, or by offering job-hunting support.

In general, human social small-group processes go through predictable stages of development. An action research project is no exception. No doubt in each cultural context these stages will differ slightly. In general, there will be an initiation stage, a stage of getting to know the other researchers and participants, during which labels and typical phrases are batted around and discussed, then an in-depth period of inquiry and mutual investigation (this is when secondary data or new information can be very useful, and the researcher may play a data-providing role). This will lead to a cathartic meeting when different interests are expressed or conflictive discussions occur. Finally, while the researcher or participants are trying to get to a stage of closure, there may be resolution-seeking processes such as writing memos, giving feedback, circulating posters that present the views of different voices from their varying standpoints, performing a skit or making a video, and finally someone may decide to write up the research.

McNiff and Whitehead (2009) assume that all action research gets written up neatly by an academic. Their book is useful for those who are doing a thesis or dissertation by action research. A concrete example where ethnographers worked closely with local non-governmental agencies in eight American cities to tackle homelessness over a long period is Snow and Cress (2000). Snow and Cress continued their research after doing a rather systematic write-up of the early stage. Their next stage after 2000 was to use statistical evidence, and they thus moved away somewhat from the action research method. Not all ethnographers would engage in action research, but there are some close linkages between the methods used by ethnographers and action researchers.

On the other hand, it is possible to do action research without writing it up. This is the ultimate departure from scientific practice. In science today, written accounts are used to ensure that replication is possible, duplication is avoided, and dissemination to a wide audience can take place. Some people say that if it is not written up then 'it did not happen'. In a sense, research is only research if a written or otherwise conclusive account (e.g. a video) is made as a product of the research. Action researchers realise that the product is not the process and that the process has huge spin-off effects on participants. Most action researchers follow a Freire-allied line about learning. Freire (1993, 1996) argued that learning takes place in face-to-face settings and is best facilitated when the learner is able to set the agenda. The learning is not embodied in the written products or the exam results but in the changes that take place in each person involved. For Freire, non-traditional education can successfully help people to learn; they help themselves. Facilitation is crucial. Similarly, in action research one is only a 'researcher' in the sense of facilitating a variety of processes over time, not controlling them. This kind of research is an activity that is gentle and not rigidly structured. In this way, it is rather different from most academic science. The scientific write-up – if one is done – may not be the most important result of the process of action research.

McNiff and Whitehead (2009) argue that data collection occurs mainly through the researcher writing up a description of the process and findings of the research. I would add that a good academic researcher can – through the use of secondary data – considerably enrich an action research process. As shown elsewhere in this book, it is easy enough to download relevant statistical data and present it in simplified collapsed tables and produce a nearly self-explanatory memo. The action research facilitator can then explain the relevant findings to a varied audience. The facilitator can also make transcripts of discussions and enable people to comment on what was said. Action research with social data can be a rich and vigorous process that critiques and falsifies hypotheses, moves to new claims, develops an explanatory theory and describes conflict where no one had previously acknowledged the existence of a problem. However, it does need careful facilitation and clear goal-setting at each stage. For these reasons I tend to advocate action research mainly in adult contexts and not for final degree dissertations.

3.4 Observation Methods

The main differences between casual observation and scientific observational research relate to keeping systematic records and the ethics of getting permission for access. In many cases the former also requires the latter. In addition, the sophisticated analysis of data is a third distinguishing feature. I will discuss each of these briefly.

Observational methods of research usually involve people watching people doing things (see Frankfort-Nachmias and Nachmias, 2000: 203). Often when people are in a public place doing things in full view of many other people, it can be considered that they are accessible for live observation without getting any permission. The delicate issues arise when a record is going to be kept of their facial image, their figure or actions, their name, or what they say. In order for the records to be retained, if there are any identifying features, you must have their permission to keep data about them under the terms of that country's data protection laws. In short, surreptitious casual observation of visitors as they go to and around a hospital or museum is not going to enable you to do research on the resulting videos or photos unless permission has been gained. To get permission, consent must be in writing and after being informed about the purpose of the research and how the data will be used. As clarified in the chapter on 2.11 **ethical clearance**, surreptitious methods are not generally used in scientific research. Covert methods are unacceptable in this context, too. Consent must be given in advance of the records of observation being made. In some countries there is an additional legal requirement that if the data are to be kept for a certain time then the subject should also be given the possibility of checking the validity of the data and, if necessary, making corrections. People are surprisingly sensitive about their photos being taken and their names being attached to their speech on cassette tape or computer-based audio. On the other hand, if you decide to show a photo 'anonymously' and not attach any name, all faces must be blurred out using special graphics software, because otherwise the person would be identifiable anyway. Indeed, it may also be considered offensive to print someone's photo without their name in the caption, and great care should be taken about this matter.

Three examples of reasons for the sensitivity of photographic and video material are as follows: first, the person may be part of a religious group which requires that images of people's faces not be made or shown; second, although they are in a public place, that does not mean that people want others knowing that they were there; and third, people at times want to control or shape how they appear in print and not leave this to someone else to decide. They may feel that their appearance in a casually taken photo is untidy or that they are grimacing. These sensitivities must be taken seriously by each social researcher. If they are not respected, it tends to give all social researchers a bad reputation.

The excitement of visual research is greater if, having got permissions, we think in terms of systematically gathering a range of images and artefacts, then conducting an innovative and in-depth analysis of the data. Advice on the process of visual-based research is given by Banks (2007) and Pink (2006, 2007). The findings should take our knowledge into unforeseen areas, giving us new knowledge. In the broad area of observational methods we need not be restricted to the visual. New research methods for analysing sounds, smells and even the touch sensations are described by Pink (2009). The use of touch and voice in research furthermore can encompass several ways in which the researcher enables a group of respondents to create objects, say what they represent, manipulate the objects or comment on groups of objects (Prosser, 1998). Such methods are potentially highly creative. They can tap into the non-cognitive as well as cognitive elements of human minds. Since computers can now easily retain and archive records of objects, as well as audio and video of people discussing what objects mean to them, the range of research methods involving observation has widened in recent years.

The use of the visual and audio records can also contribute to the later development of museum exhibitions and to the teaching of history. Oral history has been enriched by the capacity to link artefacts to sound in complex databases. The long interview is now not the only way to conduct an oral history. Gathering photos of photos, photos of rooms and objects, and then gathering commentaries on these objects, creates further layers of data.

While developing a research design based on specific observational methods, keep in mind that in general the methods of analysis will be ethnographic. The literature on visual ethnography can guide you between different aspects of the history of visual design, the role of art and art evaluation, and the possibility of creativity of interpretation (Alfonso et al., 2004). Reflexivity of interpretation is also usually taken for granted in ethnography because the viewer or listener, who is developing an interpretation, is influenced by their own background as well as by the observations. There is no blank slate for observation. What we really mean by observation is perception and interpretation (see 2.5 **interpretation**). A fieldwork notebook is a worthwhile part of the project (see 7.2 **reality**). If a team is working on the project, then members may want to consider and discuss their initial biases and prior commitments, such as intense belief in one theory. For research to be scientific or innovative, it is useful to take existing theories as fallible and open to reinterpretation or amendment. Otherwise ethnographic research could turn into stale quasi-factual description.

3.5 Online Data Collection

Research using online methods takes advantage of the speed and vast networking of the internet world. The computers of users in many countries are connected up through cabling and wireless radio signals, and new software enables data about users of all these personal computers to be gathered and sent to a central point, almost without the user being aware of it. The speed and subtlety of the internet software raise new ethical issues about confidentiality and privacy. The principle of informed consent still applies for social research using online sources. This principle, combined with detailed methods of analysis, makes online research a growing area of fascination quite distinct from the market research and user surveys carried out by internet software companies (Burnham et al., 2008: ch. 8).

Three models of online research can be described here. First, there are online surveys. Firms offer a quick and easy survey-writing service. Thus for a small fee you can write your online questionnaire, filling in blank elements in a proforma provided by experts which is then easily filled in by online users. These online surveys can be made anonymous, which reduces the complications of data protection, or can involve an initial consent stage and then the inclusion of names and addresses with each row of data. Some providers of online survey software include in their pricing the provision of a statistical data table once the sampling quotas have been filled up. Email can be used to encourage relevant or sampled individuals to participate. Surveys still need to be piloted so that the risk of partial completion or dropping out can be reduced. Both qualitative comments and simplified precoded numerical answers can be gathered (see Lobe, 2008).

A second form of online research is netnography (Kozinets, 2010), involving ethnographic processes of investigation in an online community. Ethnography can explore the meanings and social implications of attitudes and events online, as well as the deeper human conditions underlying the entry and (to a lesser) exit of users from the virtual computer-based community. The virtual worlds of Facebook, online dating groups, and interest-based clubs are new social phenomena which now form a key part of how some people spend part of their leisure time. Studies of work practices, too, have to recognise the role that computers now play in many working lives and careers. Even family life is beginning to be mediated by the internet. Carers, in particular, are being encouraged to use bleepers and sensors so that a problem in one room or building can be rapidly if not instantly reported to a carer or the emergency services – often in the form of a warden service in a different part of town – without waiting for human intervention. The possibilities for technical development of such services are many, and one role of social research is to ensure that a good understanding of the interpersonal and human–machine dynamics accompanies the development of technology.

Thirdly, online research can lead to the creation of case-based longitudinal data. A longitudinal (time-based) panel of data can be created for several purposes. One might be to develop summary measures, such as the total spending of certain kinds of member or customer. Another might be to conduct a statistical analysis, perhaps comparing groups (see 4.2 **handling treatment data**). Or one may want to look at the structure and evolution of social networks. Apart from elegant descriptive graphics, social network analysis can also involve the use of qualitative investigative methods and hermeneutic analysis. Thus even when panel data are collected, mixing methods is still feasible. The bounds are set by how one can communicate with members of a network or community and what consent has been given for the research activities. A discussion of the analysis of panel data from observing online games players can be found in Kirkpatrick (2009). A reanalysis of longitudinal studies of families can be found in May (2009). May calls for more mixed-methods research because the attrition found in longitudinal surveys can lead to poor-quality generalisations, and because qualitative methods are intrinsically a good adjunct to systematic data collection.

The golden rule with online data analysis is that users or data providers still have to be consulted and thus informed about any procedure that is going to involve their personal data being moved around and used in research. It is wise to gather consistent written permissions for the specific research activities that are planned. One cannot just convert a bunch of existing online friendships into a project. Instead the usual procedures must all be applied: plan a research design, select a research question that is feasible, conduct a pilot, gather informed-consent forms, and then gather the actual data. Even in the pilot stage it must be made clear that research is being conducted and that permission is sought, in writing, for the involvement of those who are being consulted.

Online research is no panacea, though. The digital divide is the ongoing exclusion of those without access to the technology from the whole online 'scene'. The digital divide can be partly overcome in random sample surveys if the personal computer and internet technology can be brought to those selected for participation. In the past, the cost of such acts of inclusion was simply too high, but in recent years the computer has become more analogous to the mobile phone, and simple programmes can be set up to mediate the communication and thus cut out the steep learning curve that applies to Microsoft Windows and other complex software packages. The digital divide applies not only to hardware but also to the cable connections that make virtual gaming worlds possible, and to proprietary (usually expensive) software. The boundaries of representativeness are usually described as follows: the population that can be represented by a given online research project is the kinds of users who are already involved in a particular set of online activities. The sampling of users from that population can then be either random or non-random, as usual in social research (see 1.5 **sampling**).

Further Reading for Part 3

For fieldwork that is sensitive to the need for wider social participation, see Mikkelsen (2005). An excellent source on action research is McNiff and Whitehead (2009). In addition, the research team may want to get training as facilitators using Heron (1999). Additional help with liaising between the visions held by respondents (or participants) and the research team can be found in Heron (2000, 2001). Here Heron describes how cooperative research might work. There is less of a superior attitude on the part of researchers in this approach; see also Reason and Rowan (1981) or Reason and Bradbury (2009). MacIntyre (1985) covered some issues of praxis in an interesting way. Part of his message is that an agent's praxis does not necessarily cause its intended outcome. The praxis which makes sense to you as a researcher may have an internal logic, but it may not initially make sense to external actors. MacIntyre (1985) discusses the internal values and external values (or valuations) that can be applied – differentially – to the real outcomes that result from some activity. The implications for research ethics are several, since one then needs to be aware of slippage, difficulties with mutual agenda-setting, reasoning used by different actors during participatory research, and the important knowledge that can come from apparent 'mistakes'. Surprises and 'mistakes' need to be taken rather seriously during the fieldwork stage. Discussions of this problem for international research can be found among the examples in Scheyvens and Storey (2003) and in Holland and Campbell (2005).

Part 4

Experimental and Systematic Data Collection

Parts 2 and 3 covered qualitative forms of data collection, but for many research-ers the basic purpose of data collection is to create a systematically organised set of materials that can be used either to test or generate hypotheses. These tend to be called 'quantitative' data, yet there are also some qualitative studies that benefit from applying relatively systematic methods. In this part of the book I handle survey- and non-survey-based systematically held records and how to start the record-keeping process. I begin with some basic advice on designing a questionnaire (there is more on this in Part 5). Then I turn to the experi-mental research process, looking first at how the control groups are set up and then at the ethics of recruiting volunteers. An experimental dataset has compar-able measurements for contrasting groups of cases. Some special record-keeping issues arise when there are complex control groups and blind experimentation. In some ways, experimental data have aspects in common with case-study meth-ods (which are covered in Part 6). The last two chapters of Part 4 cover methods of research that can be used in marketing, business and management research (and elsewhere) to create a multi-method dataset. First I consider marketing research. Research methods for marketing often combine different approaches to data collection to achieve their desired outcomes, so I survey three of these. Then I conclude Part 4 by introducing ways of starting up and improving the systematic gathering of raw data by invoking a spreadsheet to identify the gaps in the data. Whilst this is written using examples from the sociology of labour, the lessons can be applied more widely. The whole of Part 6 offers more general suggestions about data collection for case-study research.

4.1 Questionnaire Design

The order of questions in a questionnaire should appear logical to the respondent. How this is achieved may depend in part on whether you administer the questionnaire verbally or in writing. I first suggest what the questionnaire should contain, and then briefly cover the layout issues. Further detailed advice on developing the content of surveys can be found in Part 5.

Your questionnaire is going to create data, and it can be thought of as a data-generation process. Deciding on the order of questions opens up several strategic issues. You need to be very clear about the concepts you use in the questions. Closed questions make a questionnaire work much more quickly than open questions. A closed question provides only a few possible answers and usually has pre-coding and a showcard to indicate what these answers are. If you want to include an open question in a questionnaire, then you may want to enter the whole text of all its answers into your database. Alternatively, for open questions you may scan all the answers and develop a set of codes *ex post*, i.e. after the whole survey has been delivered. This would be more efficient than full text entry, but also gives less data. Double-barrelled questions are usually too long for respondents to answer in a straightforward way. Try to make the questions rather short and simple.

Next you may decide whether to have sensitive questions in a questionnaire. If you need to include some sensitive questions then you may think strategically about putting some innocuous questions before them, and making sure that the respondent is clear about why it is worthwhile for them to offer their sensitive information to you. It may be helpful to ask a concrete question before you move into an attitudinal area or a sensitive question. Many respondents find questionnaires challenging to answer. Therefore it is important to navigate the respondent clearly through the survey and to motivate them throughout. The worst questionnaires offer huge blocks of similarly worded questions or are too long overall in a self-evident way. It is useful to refer to your own research question during the piloting phase so that you can restrict the questions to relevant areas. Advice on the wording of questions is offered in Part 5.

The layout of the questionnaire should be attractive and easy to read. The background questions on demographics which are included in all questionnaires need to be placed at the end rather than at the beginning because many respondents actually find them relatively challenging. For example, household income is typically a sensitive question. Age is felt to be rather private. Limit the background questions to those which really are needed in your survey.

You can use computer software to generate a questionnaire and thus obtain direct access to easy data entry. There are both online services and offline methods of using a statistical software package to generate a questionnaire. The IBM SPSS Data Collection Author software, for example, is an offline package.[1] The cost attached to using such a service may be worthwhile in generating a smooth, easily understood questionnaire document. The document needs to be easy to revise. After piloting occurs, the document needs to have the flow management shown using a mixture of words and diagrams. Questions which are not relevant to some types of people need to be preceded by a filter or skip instruction. Always include space on page 1 for the date of the survey, and for an indication of the identity of the interviewer, a questionnaire number (or case ID number), page numbers, and a location identifier. Have clear question numbers and put the phrase 'Thank you' in a large font at the end of the questionnaire.

Note

1. Note that the IBM SPSS Author software can be purchased in either a Desktop or a server based (online) version. See http://www.spss.com/software/data-collection/author/index. htm (accessed December 2010) for more details.

4.2 Handling Treatment Data

The collection of data from experiments is a potentially controversial part of social research. Experimental data are characterised by having cases lying in groups which are treated differently from each other (for an introduction, see Payne and Payne, 2004: 84–9; Frankfort-Nachmias and Nachmias, 2000: chs 5 and 6). The selection of cases into the treatment group is sometimes random, as in randomised controlled trials (RCTs) of drugs. But in some situations non-random sampling schemes are used. Some experiments rely on an assumption of universal homogeneity of the cases. For example, in medical experiments it may be assumed that to take several hundred volunteers and select the treated group as a random subgroup from among the whole population will adequately represent the much wider population of the same age and sex. This universalism could be questioned. Taking volunteers is not the same as random sampling itself (see **sampling**). Non-randomly selected volunteer subjects might work if all subjects were identical to the whole population on all key variables. However, the universalism involved here might not transfer easily to a different treatment context, such as treating cases of criminal offenders who are undergoing probation treatments. Overall, creating RCT trial subgroups is a sophisticated process involving overt assumptions about representativeness as well as cautious attempts to avoid making an inappropriate assumption. By selecting the treatment group randomly from among the volunteers, some RCTs succeed in making a valid scientific test of a hypothesis without having had the resources to create a simple random sample of cases of a given disease.

Another sort of treatment data arises in the reuse of hospital records. The patient data can be anonymised after analysis to simplify the ethical issues involved, and a quasi-experimental method involves *ex post* placement of cases into two groups – a group of treated cases and a comparable group of untreated cases. Clearly for experimental data collection the definition of the 'case' is also going to be critical. If there is a suspicion that the proper unit for the analysis of probation outcomes is not the ex-prisoner, but the probation officer, then the data can be organised at two levels. The first level of cases is the person released from jail and the second level is the probation officer. Multi-level statistics or complex case analysis will be needed. The informed consent then has to come from both sets of respondents.

Experimental treatment data also arise when researchers do social or psychological experiments in a laboratory setting. Individuals agree not only to participate but also to accept treatments which will be handed out or explained to each individual according to some grouping plan which may be kept a secret from them. In both medical trials and in lab experiments, all possible outcomes, including side effects, should be explained to all participants, and each person needs either to opt out or agree to participate. Each participant needs to give their permission in writing.

In general, in collecting experimental data there is much attention to avoiding non-random sources of bias. Statistical methods are often needed to tease out the patterns in the treatment group data versus the non-treatment group data. In non-experimental data, among the cases there are assumed to be diverse backgrounds and recent experiences as well as a wide variety of experience in people's exposure to current events. The defining characteristic of treatment data, on the other hand, is that the treatment is the key factor distinguishing all of the treated group from all of the untreated group. Other factors go into the background in conducting statistical tests, and these are called 'controlled factors' or are considered irrelevant.

In handling the treatment data there is one row of data per case per period, and one column indicates simply whether or not the subject had a treatment, or which treatment, at that time point. There is also one column for recording the time period. In this column one indicates the date and time of each record that is kept. Usually at a minimum this involves a pre and a post date, but in many cases the data will also extend over time to include multiple tests and visits over time. Thus, for two visits to a lab, there would be two rows for a single person. Another column indicates the identity of the subject, and a third column represents the operative identifier. Next a column indicates the location of the test site (or the lab identifier). Each identifier has to be unique, and thus when subjects are signed up into the experiment they each need to be assigned a unique serial number. Note carefully that when data are collected over time, the initial records may be kept with one time-period per row, and that means that for one case there will be two or more rows. These rows are sometimes called records. A case with four records has four rows, reflecting one initial visit (or episode, such as release from jail) and three treatment or post-treatment visits. The data can later be fluently converted to other formats for data analysis. For instance, there is a 'wide format' in which there is simply one case per line. To create this format, the records for one case are placed side by side in one row with all the identifiers at the left.

In a drug trial the records are usually kept in an anonymised format with numerical subject identifiers rather than names. Among the reasons for this are the avoidance of any name-related bias, the way that data-protection laws apply to anonymised data (as they are more complex for datasets that contain actual names), and finally the advantage that even the data analyst can have the treatment status hidden from them. A data subset can be made, removing the key column indicating what treatment the subject had. Similarly, hospital scans can have all other data removed from them, such as previous diagnoses, and then be sent to experts via post or email for fresh, blind assessment. Methods like these reduce the likelihood of measurement error due to attempts by the analyst to cut corners or make inferences across the data for a case. Instead they have only to look at relevant outcome data and then create a summary – usually statistical, and possibly added into the database as a new column indicating 'post-test status overall' for each case.

The data for each point in time need to consistently record the background characteristics of each subject and full details of the mixture of treatments they have had. A wide variety of analysis methods can be used for such data. In the details of statistical methods are possibilities which may affect how data are collected. To give a flavour of these options, which are usually not used in tandem with each other, I briefly describe three methods.

If a non-random sample is being produced, then propensity score matching might be used to create a carefully weighted batch of cases exactly comparable with the treated group. Propensity scores for each case arise from a mathematical function that is developed (as a latent variable), based upon background differentiating variables such as age, sex, ethnicity, occupation, and level of education. An internet-based sample used for psychological testing might have propensity score matching applied to it. The untreated group is developed to give a common base of support, i.e. matching types of cases in a balanced distribution across types to the treated group.

If random samples are used then a panel data model for longitudinal data could be developed. Here two sub-options are survival modelling, which requires measures of how much time has passed between case treatments, and fixed-effects modelling, which can gauge how far the change over time is common to the whole treatment group and how much is specific to other factors which also changed over time, such as age or blood pressure. In the fixed-effects model, some control variables that are fixed over time drop into the background because only changes in values are taken into account. An example would be gender or ethnicity. These models are not as good at looking at gender effects because gender is fixed over time. A critic of medical treatment science has pointed out that ethnicity and gender are not handled particularly well from within the 'medical model' of health, both because of the diversity of how gender and ethnicity operate in society, and because of the tendency to drop them out or ignore them as they are control variables (Harding, 1993b). Some neurological studies call them 'nuisance' variables.

Finally, there is a special difference-in-differences model which builds upon the basic panel data model (for discussion, see Olweus and Alsaker, 1994). For growth and learning processes, we are trying to look at how the process of change is actually enhanced or inhibited by the treatment. The slope showing the response of the outcome, such as tumour size or test score, is compared for the treatment group versus the untreated group. A confidence interval is estimated that allows us to say with 95% confidence whether the difference of the change rate (over time) for the treated group versus the untreated group is at all significantly different from zero. This method relies on random sampling and a low or zero refusal rate. Attrition for any reason, where cases are lost from the study, can be adjusted for, but attrition becomes a potential source of bias in the conclusion that will be reached.

4.3 The Ethics of Volunteers

Three aspects of the ethical clearance process for treated individuals in experiments need attention. The core question about ethics which is specific to randomised experimental data is whether a given subject is going to be allowed to know whether they will be in the placebo group or given the actual treatment. Usually the trial works by going through the same motions with all patients, whether this involves giving a placebo pill or a real pill. Managing the treatment substances is tricky because the best trials are double-blind. The first blind stage is that a subject does not know what they are being given. Yet any injection has to be labelled in such a way that there is zero risk of error and a certainty that a given subject will consistently be treated with the right material (pill or injection). In psychology the treatment may involve a training session and a test session, with subjects blind to what the other subjects are experiencing. The second stage of blindness (as it is called) is that the researcher or technician does not really need to know the name of the people being treated. In order to be fair and to avoid bias, avatars on computer screens are sometimes now used to deliver psychological tests to avoid the personal intervention of the researchers. Another trick is to have three or more operatives who do treatments, and to randomise the choice of the operatives who will meet each patient. Code numbers identify the operatives and the patients in the data, so the researcher can test to ensure *ex post* that there was no operator bias in the results. These record-keeping issues affect the data gathering stage.

Background data may be needed from the patient's own medical records. The production or reuse and sharing of these case documents is subject to data-protection laws and the ethical clearance system. If research is done across country boundaries the laws of both countries can be assumed to apply. The reason for this assumption is that a case for abuse of personal data or breach of privacy can probably be brought in either the country of the subject or in the country in which the data are held. Whenever multiple-country teams are formed to study experimental data, the teams have to understand the regulations relating to patient confidentiality and data management of all the concerned countries. Otherwise there is a risk that when data are sent in an email attachment the researcher may be in breach of a law of a different country than their own.

When pharmaceutical companies fund experimental research they sometimes deliberately form a team across three or more countries since the data analysis expertise may be located in one place and easy-to-access cases (i.e. individuals) in another. In a globalising world these considerations are receiving more attention in government-funded research.

The second aspect of ethics for experimental data collectors is getting informed consent from all participating subjects. The people involved need to know in outline form what will happen to them and what uses will be made of the data. Open-ended statements about what might happen are not very useful in the consent process because the subject really needs to know what they are being asked to agree to (see the Appendix and the more general chapter on 2.11 **ethical clearance**). Otherwise they are not well informed; and, in addition, the ambiguity can increase the risk of people refusing to participate. In random sampling contexts, every refusal causes a deterioration in the final sample. Most externally funded studies have to report the response rate after all refusals, so mid-experiment refusals are considered most undesirable.

No matter how much one might wish, it is not possible to use data on health-care patients without consent. In other words, involuntary participation is not possible on live subjects. An exception may arise in the use of post-mortem brain scans. Reassessing brain scans after death may be seen as not affecting the patient in any way. However, to link these to a patient's database records, the complex ethics protocol again must be invoked. There are two aspects here: firstly, the care agency's responsibility for legal and responsible data management, following the guidelines they originally set up when they gathered those data; and secondly, the researchers' responsibility to living relatives and caregivers. The use of health-care patient records is carefully monitored by ethics boards and ethics committees.

For voluntary participants, a fee may need to be paid. Generally these fees do not exceed local hourly wage rates. The fee should usually include some coverage of transport costs as well as any necessary food costs and baby-sitting costs.

4.4 Market-Research Techniques

In planning a treatment study or experiment, it may be fruitful to consider market-research methods. Marketing itself has been a rich source of research methods because cost-effective innovation has been promoted by companies acting as funders (Kent, 2007). Market-research methods are to some extent defined by their audience, which is likely to be a company or all the companies of a sector. Some market research is consumption research – about who buys which product, who uses the product and how, and how tastes are affected by advertising. To a business, accurate information about consumption can mean making more money. Some market research is provided as a public service for the whole business community. Many large datasets on consumption patterns fall into this category. Both at the national government and international level there are attempts to bring about external benefits to commercial users from the public sector production of statistical data. In addition there are huge time-use datasets in each country which offer excellent free opportunities for relatively easy analysis of consumer behaviour patterns (Gershuny, 2000; http://www.esds. ac.uk/government/timeuse/ for UK time-use datasets). Although the secondary data are free, detailed cost estimates should be made of the time and expertise needed to conduct the secondary data analysis. Many businesses also build up a picture of demand by conducting primary data collection in local streets or by commissioning consultants to do market research. An enumerator is a person hired on a piecework basis or hourly-paid basis to carry out the survey or interview in the street. Businesses also use 2.8 **focus groups**.

A variety of statistical methods are routinely used in market research (examples from business contexts are found in Hair et al., 2005). One example is that a battery of taste tests can be run. Then a treatment is conducted, which consists of letting the subjects try, taste or use the product that is being studied. Treatment group differences can be introduced by allowing different subjects to use different variants or prototypes of a broad product range. A series of identical taste tests, or a short self-completion survey giving the customer's views, is then recorded after the testing has been carried out. There is both a qualitative and a quantitative aspect to the analysis of data in these market-research situations. Verbal commentaries and body language can be interpreted qualitatively. Data patterns can be studied statistically. Market researchers can either study the distribution of taste, the average taste, or the change in taste as a result of the test (change over time). The difference between a market researcher (who studies the whole market, including context and institutional factors) and marketing researchers lies mainly in their aims. Whilst the market researcher aims to learn more about all aspects of a given market, the marketing researcher aims to increase sales by changing the marketing approach. A skilled social scientist can easily adapt to working in either a market-research environment, or in marketing.

Using a slightly different tactic, some management researchers and those interested in marketing or other business topics may choose to use qualitative methods. They can use interviews and focus groups, for example (see 2.1 **interviews**, 2.8 **focus groups**). Bryman and Bell (2007) describe how ethnography and mixed methods can also be used in business research.

Adding to the standard range of methods, the concept of co-generating knowledge is offered by Greenwood and Levin (2004) as a way for insiders to relate to the rest of the community as well as to an organisation. The co-generation of knowledge can be useful for marketing and market research. Greenwood and Levin (2004) argue that, by knowledge co-generation, one can generate knowledge while recognising that knowledge plays different roles in different arenas. For example, costs may play a role in efficiency discourse among staff, but a role in some other domain for customers. Here it may be felt that the research is moving into pure storytelling by allowing for each actor to speak about a situation from their own point of view. One seems to move away from any possibility of systematic record-keeping. But having multiple stories about one reality is quite normal (as I argue throughout this book). One way forward would be to recognise that stakeholders have voices and that they all matter. Stakeholder research could offer new gains by voicing concerns from outside each actor's usual milieu. Each speaker or voice in a research output may have originated in either a dominant or a marginalised position within the broad context. They may be more or less aware of what others think and say. The social context could be the company and its surroundings, or it might simply be the complex internal milieu of a large company. In recent years management research has shifted towards recognising that questions of fairness and equity do arise in the conduct of business-oriented research. A strict separation of facts from values cannot be imposed on the data at the interpretation stage, but a stakeholder approach can be used to try to understand what different agents think about a situation (Harrison and Freeman, 1999). Making reference to the stakeholders is now a widely used way to help identify the various agents related to a particular research problem (Harrison and Freeman, 1999). In market research, the identification of the case might now include not only the product or service, but also the producers and consumers as stakeholders for that product. More details on the case-study research method are offered in Part 6.

4.5 Creating Systematic Case-Study Data

Part 6 of this book is devoted to research via case studies, but researchers who usually use some other approaches can also benefit from the systematisation of the evidence that they have. Here I would include interviews, stakeholder research, action research, and those who cull evidence from cases held in existing files, such as court cases. Again this is like generating data from a large body of other evidence. Sometimes after generating a partial dataset one needs to revisit each case in order to try to fill in gaps.

Two examples from spreadsheet-based records illustrate. In a fieldwork-based study of rural labour markets, I placed the survey data for each household in rows of a spreadsheet and then created separate tabs for individuals (much greater in number, hence sitting on many more rows of the spreadsheet), and for attitudes and other special commentaries noted by the various interviewers, who were four in number. Using this spreadsheet, we could compare what the commentaries held and identify whether an additional visit should fill in gaps on particular headings for any particular respondents. A sample segment of that spreadsheet is shown in Table 7. Just three households are shown from among 39 in the dataset.

The work of typing all these data into a spreadsheet is useful if it brings a gap to light. For example, the data here may make someone realise that the occupation of the household differs considerably from the occupation of each individual.[1] Systematising the data in a spreadsheet also reminds us that the education need not be recorded for children below a certain age, perhaps age 6. So making a systematic table can help identify gaps or omissions in the data. Since the fieldwork included interviewing, there were opportunities to correct gaps. A separate table held the pseudonyms for publication purposes. Again, though, a one-page summary was useful because it showed that some pseudonyms chosen by respondents matched the names of other respondents. Some pseudonyms also had to be changed to completely avoid similarities and repetition among the pseudonyms. For 39 households we needed up to 200 pseudonyms for individuals (household size averaging 5 in southern India). Systematically managing data helps make errors less frequent in large datasets like this.

Table 7   Systematically organised household data

ID	Hamlet	Occupation code	Age	Sex	Relationship	Education	Main Work
1	Main village	Cultivator	90	1 Male	Father	Illiterate	Old age
			60	1 Male	Household head	Up to Primary School	own
			35	1 Male	Son	Illiterate	Agricultural labourer
			55	1 Male	Son	Illiterate	Agricultural labourer
			40	1 Male	Son	Illiterate	Agricultural labourer
			48	1 Male	Son	Illiterate	Agricultural labourer
			45	1 Male	Son	Illiterate	Agricultural labourer
			42	2 Female	Daughter	Illiterate	Agricultural labourer
			40	2 Female	Daughter	Illiterate	Agricultural labourer
2	Main village	Cultivator & own flower business; tractor service	60	1 Male	Household head	Up to Primary School	Own cultivation
			55	2 Female	Mother	Illiterate	Flower business
			30	1 Male	Son	Middle Level	Own cultivation
			23	2 Female	Wife	Illiterate	Flower business
			9	1 Male	Child		
			7	2 Female	Child		
3	Main village	Small and marginal farmer	43	1 Male	Household head	High School	Own cultivation
			35	2 Female	Wife	Middle Level	Own cultivation
			22	1 Male	Son	Diploma course	Student
			18	1 Male	Son	Above High School	Student
			15	1 Male	Son	High School	Student

Next consider Table 8. This table has been finalised and there are no gaps in the data. Interview data were used to obtain the last column, whereas a questionnaire survey was used to obtain the first seven columns. This spreadsheet reflects the possibilities within mixed-methods research for systematising the interview material. On the one hand, its strength is consistency and comparability. On the other hand, its weakness is that interviews are with individuals and involve personal voices, but this spreadsheet organised by household numbers seems to assume that each individual speaks on behalf of the whole household. This would have to be clarified at the interpretation stage.

If the data collection is not based on fieldwork, then you may have partial and incomplete data. For example, if you use client records or some historical evidence then your data may have gaps, as shown in Table 9. This table is derived from reading case histories prepared by a set of seven interviewers in southern

Table 8   Mixed-methods spreadsheet records

Hhid	Assets	Education	Caste	dalit	oc	rentinwet	havecows	Resist
1	0.87	0.17	BC	0	0	2	1	0
	0.5		M	0	0	0		
2		0.5					1	0
3	0.5	1	OC	0	1	0	1	1
29	1	0.87	OC	0	1	0	1	1
30	0.87	0.17	SC	1	0	1	1	0
31	0	0.5	SC	1	0	0	0	0

Table 9   Data from *post-hoc* analysis of case studies

Education	Land Owned	Housing Situation
n.d.	2 acres	
n.d.	5 acres dryland	
None	2 acres dryland	Own thatched house (not
None (man)	1 acre dry land (In Father's name)	sufficient for all family members)
		Pukka house
n.d.	3 acres dry land	Thatched house
Studied up to 3rd standard (man)	11 acres	Pukka house
n.d.	2 acres	No house (stay in migrant brother's property)

Note: n.d. = no data. This coding arose from recording each column systematically long after the case material had been gathered during long interviews and translated as texts. It illustrates the diversity of the case materials. Key: *Dry land* has no irrigation source. *Thatched* roofs involve the use of hay. *Pukka* houses are made of brick or stone with a metal or wooden and perhaps tiled roof.

India. Since education has been omitted from several of these case histories, we cannot make reasonable comparisons between the cases about the impact of education. Overall this table indicates some areas of weakness in this dataset. One has to either revisit the respondents, or avoid making statements that suggest that the data are more complete. Interview data should be more systematically organised, as described earlier in Part 2, to ensure that there are not gaps in the resulting dataset. Sometimes a spreadsheet is a useful way to check where the gaps are. Another alternative is qualitative data-handling software.

Note

1. To some researchers, this is obvious. Those who study household consumption behaviour might find it more problematic, and they can study the distribution of occupations by individuals before deciding whether to look more closely at individual employment rather than the 'dominant' or highest-paying household member's occupation.

Further Reading for Part 4

For more details about marketing research see Kent (2007). Business research methods in general are covered by Bryman and Bell (2007). More details allowing the application of discourse analysis to the texts obtained in management research are offered by Alvesson and Deetz (2000). Some methods that can support a stakeholder analysis are covered in parts of Carroll (2004) and Holland and Campbell (2005). You can see samples of questionnaires at official, free websites for different countries rather easily by searching the internet using a country name and the word 'Census'. Census questionnaires are sometimes rather short to keep them easy for respondents. For longer questionnaires, there are two types of sources. The UK Question Bank is a useful source for questions covering every topic under the sun (http://surveynet.ac.uk/sqb/). Secondly, detailed survey questionnaires can be obtained from www.esds.ac.uk for many hundreds of surveys. A similar site for India is http://mospi.gov.in/nsso.

Part 5

Survey Methods for Data Collection

5.1 Operationalisation

To operationalise something usually means to measure it, and more generally to make it easy to examine and discuss. In surveys, operationalisation is carefully separated into measuring the experience of an event, measuring attitudes, measuring activities such as earning money or spending time, and the many other aspects of life that lend themselves to measurement. There is a surprising amount of complexity to measurement. It is useful to run through an example of the experience of bribery to give a sense of the differences between the operationalisation of attitudes and the recording of experiences. I conclude this chapter by revisiting some issues of validity and causality, since measurement affects the validity of research.

In a broader social science context, operationalisation refers not just to survey measurement, but rather to any attempt to make an abstract or general concept usable in practical research contexts. For example in qualitative research, if we were exploring bribery and corruption we might make a short list of the concrete kinds of bribery and corruption that we can look at in a given city, such as police taking a payment from a criminal whom they protect, teacher corruption in the appointments process, bribery of judges, and bribery of restaurant owners to allow an illegal activity to occur at the site. Qualitative researchers would then set up site visits, observation, or interviews that refer to these kinds of things. In a social survey context, operationalising this set of concepts might mean several slightly different things, such as measuring the amount of police corruption, measuring the prevalence of the experience of being made to bribe someone, measuring attitudes to police corruption, or measuring attitudes to bribery. One has to carefully tease out all the possibilities and then specify which particular ones can be looked at in a given situation. At the end of the research one may try to comment on the broader picture. It is very important to be precise when operationalising the central topic of research so that there is no exaggeration of what has been achieved in the research.

Measuring the experience of something in a survey requires a specific reference period. The reference period might be 1 month, 1 year or 5 years. A question about bribery in the International Social Survey Programme (ISSP, 2006) uses a five-year reference period as shown below.

Variable V62: Public officials wanted bribe

Q19 In the last five years, how often have you or a member of your immediate family come across a public official who hinted they wanted, or asked for, a bribe or favour in return for a service?

The question wording is interesting because it opens up the possibility that bribery is not only done by money, but also by return favours. I find the wording vague in that to 'come across' something might mean either a direct personal experience of it, or something much less direct. One might have read about it in a paper, heard about it at work, or had a family member experience it. Depending on how the question is interpreted, people in different countries might answer very differently. If response variation is not sensitive to bribery experiences, but to the tightness of networks and how people hear and remember rumours of bribery, then the operationalisation may not be ideal. It may give non-comparable measures of the frequency of bribery in different countries. Later the results for two countries are given.

Consider whether the measure of experience using the following possible answers (ISSP, 2006) has any validity:

1 Never

2 Seldom

3 Occasionally

4 Quite often

5 Very often

8 Can't choose

9 No answer

Do you think it is very clear what 'quite often' means? It might mean annually, or in certain years at a particular festival season. On the other hand, one might select this answer after getting free from punishment for car speeding tickets more than once a month. We cannot be sure how the respondents will interpret these options. The question appears to have a certain degree of vagueness in the measure of frequency. In such cases, users of the data will be wise to collapse the categories into a smaller number of groups whose meaning is more clear. For example, one could group together 2, 3, 4 and 5 to give 'ever experienced bribery in 5 years' and leave 1 and 8 and 9 to reflect 'reported no experience of bribery in 5 years'. Thus even when the survey is a little imperfect, good usage can improve the reliability and comparability of the findings from secondary data analysis.

Consider, for a moment, the differences between measuring attitudes and measuring these experiences. Attitudes are quite tricky to measure. Some experts separate the general area of attitudinal research into three parts: attitudes, beliefs and values. Beliefs are background knowledge of a more factual, taken-for-granted type that is less normative than attitudes and values. Values are deeply held, often tacit, norms about how things should work. An attitude, then, is a more practical and more immediate orientation to a particular situation or thing. Measuring values is difficult because of their tacit, implicit nature. It is not easy for people to express their values. They can also hold conflicting values. Values are rather general. An attitude, by contrast, is more explicit and makes reference to a particular thing or situation. Thus the value 'corrupt government is bad' might lead towards the specific attitude 'bribery among criminals and police is disapproved of'.

For attitudes, we often use a five-point Likert scale to measure the extent of the disapproval or approval, with strong approval coded 5, approval 4, a neutral position 3, disapproval 2, and strong disapproval 1. An alternative is to use codes 2 to −2, giving a midpoint of 0 and thus the welcome property that positive values reflect approving attitudes.

Likert scaling does not necessarily give an accurate measure of an attitude because there are numerous possible ways to have ambiguity in answering the question. For example, the 'neutral' category may be more popular among certain groups, and give a bias away from approval because it is numerically lower than the approval ratings. If men answered willingly, but women hesitated to answer, and said they were neutral, but actually dislike bribery of police, then we would have an upward bias in the disapproval that we were expecting! Sometimes it is preferable to have a missing value, say −9, covering not only those who are neutral but also those who are not comfortable answering the question. The scoring options should be printed on a showcard and shown to every respondent while asking the question.

The causes of attitudes might include the kind of structural factors that I listed earlier. A simple model might look like this:

S3: Attitude to police bribery is affected by ... caste group, and whether in a minority tribe.

I have not included in this statement causes which seem irrelevant to attitudes to bribery. In Western countries, it is often found that some basic structural variables affect attitudes to most public issues. The different age cohorts have differing views; the two genders may have differing views; and social class may be associated with specific sets of social attitudes. Furthermore, reading a newspaper regularly might also tend to affect one's view about bribery; all these claims fit in with the following revised claim.

S4: Attitude to police bribery is affected by ... age, gender, newspaper recently read, social class of origin, current social class, minority group membership.

If you want to address this question about attitudes using statistical methods, you need one survey that covers all these factors. An example of such a survey might be the British Household Panel Survey (Taylor, 2001).

A basic difference between measuring experiences and measuring attitudes is that the former refer to an individual's own life, whereas the latter also refer to the social context. When measuring attitudes, we are sometimes using the person as an information point to try to gauge general socially normal, or usual, attitudes. We take the average of the responses to estimate this social norm. (It is also interesting to measure and study those who deviate from broad norms. Multiple correspondence analysis or factor analysis can be useful for this purpose.) If you ask people what they think others' norms are, they may end up confused and unsure what you mean. The wording of the question may need to differ, depending on whether we are trying to gauge the person's own (perhaps unique) view, or a social norm, or their assessment of the general norm.

To practise using the concept of operationalisation, consider how a few questions about bribery and corruption are worded in ISSP (2006):

Variable V50: Trust in civil servants

Q11f Most civil servants can be trusted to do what is best for the country.

1 Strongly agree

2 Agree

3 Neither agree nor disagree

4 Disagree

5 Strongly disagree

In particular, notice here how implicit reference is made to the respondent's country. If you live in a small country like Belgium, which in itself has three main geographical-political parts working in a confederation, it may not be quite clear which 'country' is being referred to. The survey presumes that the whole of each person's country is going to be their reference point. In Germany, where, by 2007, 10% of employees were from some other country, which country are people likely to have as their reference point for question V50? These are difficulties with keeping the survey text short. If all these possibilities were dealt with, the questionnaire would become much longer.

In the following question (ISSP, 2006) the country is specifically named by the interviewer:

Variable V59: Treatment by officials depends on contacts

Q16 Do you think that the treatment people get from public officials in [respondent's country] depends on who they know?

1   Definitely does

2   Probably does

3   Probably does not

4   Definitely does not

8   Can't choose

9   No answer

The problem is that questions like this do not measure attitudes at all. Instead they seem to measure a broad public experience of something. We do not find out whether the respondent approves or disapproves of using contacts from this question 16. The measurement of attitudes is more time-consuming and complicated than it perhaps appears when you start.

A true attitude question is framed more like the following (ISSP, 2006):

Variable V4: Obey laws without exception

Q1 In general, would you say that people should obey the law without exception, or are there exceptional occasions on which people should follow their consciences even if it means breaking the law?

I find it interesting that this attitude question does not specify the country location. By not doing so, the question presumes that the respondent is going to give their attitude about people universally, which might mean country-wide or world-wide. Yet some people might argue that in one kind of country you should obey the law without exception, while in a different kind of country you should, at times, break the law. These nuances are not permitted by the wording of the question. One simply has to locate oneself on a scale, choosing one of four options:

1 Obey the law without exception

2 Follow conscience on occasions

8 Can't choose

9 No answer

This scale is not a Likert scale. Instead, one expresses a view either for or against this attitude statement, or backs away to the response 'can't choose' if one finds the reality too complex to fit the statement.

Now consider the validity of the measurement of the experience of 'public officials wanting bribes'. In the case of the two countries South African and Australia, the range of answers can be summarised into a simple table as shown in Table 10. After downloading the data, a rather simple programme constructed the summary measure found in the columns in this table. The answers 'occasionally', 'quite often' and 'very often' were combined to give the summary of whether they experienced substantial exposure to bribery. The country estimates are significantly different. For example, the estimate in Australia that 4% of people experienced substantial exposure to bribery has upper and lower 95% confidence interval limits of 4.5% and 3.1%. The programme to create this result, written for STATA software, is shown in Box 7.

Table 10   Exposure to bribery in Australia and South Africa, 2006

Country	Exposure to bribery		Total percent and total sample size	
	Low	Substantial	Total	N
Australia	96%	4%	100%	2781
South Africa	80%	20%	100%	2939

Source: International Social Survey Programme (2006). Whilst the 'raw sample size is given as N, the weighted averages are presented here. 'Substantial' exposure to bribery is recorded if in the last 5 years the respondent or a member of their immediate family has come across a public official who hinted they wanted, or asked for, a bribe or favour in return for a service, 'occasionally', 'quite often' or 'very often'. The alternatives are 'seldom' and 'never', coded here as a low exposure.

Box 7   Programme to Take a Groupwise Weighted Average

```
drop if V62= =.              *Drops a case if this variable is missing.
drop if V62>10               *Drops some incomplete cases.
svyset [pweight=WEIGHT]      *Sets up weights for South Africa.
gen propoqv=0                *Generates a new variable for
                             *the proportion having occasionally,
                             *quite often, or very often been exposed
                             *to corruption.
replace propoqv=1 if V62= =
3|V62= =4|V62= =5            *Sets value 1 for yes.
tab propoqv V3               *Checks results by tabulating
                             *within countries.
svy: mean propoqv if V3= =710 *Produces averages for South Africa
svy: mean propoqv if V3= =36  *and for Australia.
svy: mean propoqv             *Produces an average across all the cases.

Key: Note that | is a symbol that means 'or' in STATA.
```

Whether these results are valid depends on two sets of factors under the broad headings of internal and external validity. Internal validity is concerned with whether the question corresponds to what it seems to refer to. If it makes sense in each country – notably, in South Africa, after some translation into local languages in some areas – and if it measures the experience that it says it measures, then it can be considered valid in this sense. On the other hand, when we move from the South African context to the Australian one, there is a risk that the things that count as bribery or offering favours might be rather different. We are now beginning to assess external validity. In general, external validity of measurement and operationalisation asks the question whether the data refer to what the user thinks the concepts should refer to. We now need to ask whether bribery and favours mean the same thing in Tokyo or Manchester as they do in South Africa or Australia. There is a real problem with external validity in large-scale surveys, since not only do the concepts refer to some different events in Australia (compared with South Africa), but also what readers expect may also be different. These are all aspects of external validity. Are the underlying central constructs transferable to all these different contexts, and are the questions specified carefully enough that they can be restricted to comparable sets of events? It is possible, but not easy. The ISSP has been piloted, tested and honed so that it is as valid as possible. The ISSP researchers work in in-country teams which communicate with each other over time. This process, which involves harmonisation of question wording, is meant to increase validity. A high level of expertise is applied. It is valid to say that in 2006 exposure to bribery was more common in South Africa than in Australia. I would be careful not to make a statement about corruption, which is a much broader concept. If question V62 does not cover all aspects of corruption, then I cannot make a valid statement about corruption based on these data. I would need to make more effort to operationalise corruption. I would also be wary of making timeless statements such as 'South Africa is a corrupt country' because the society is changing over time.

From this example you may have noticed that concepts can be wide or narrow in scope, and can mean different things in different contexts. As a result, operationalisation is inevitably difficult. Someone can contest the validity of your measurements. The survey method can be redefined now, in more detail, as the development of a set of measures harmonised across a group of respondent units and the use of these measures to record the ways in which the respondents experienced things (or have attitudes to and about things), along with measures of the geographical and other units in which these respondents are grouped or share common aggregate characteristics. Thus the survey method is consistent with harmonised measurement across a wide space and time, although it may be challenging to get consistent and harmonised operationalisation over that wide scope.

5.2 Measurement

The concept of measurement automatically brings to mind the use of a survey instrument or the survey method. Measurement links the theoretical framework of a survey-based study to its data-gathering instrument. There are a few instances where the social researcher wants to measure physical properties of things (e.g. the age, height and weight of children in a study of the prevalence of malnutrition), but there are many more instances where the measurement of intangible social and personal qualities raises a variety of issues. In this chapter I focus on the preparation for measurement in the writing of a questionnaire, using the 2001 Census for England as an example to illustrate (see Office for National Statistics (ONS), 2005). In the United Kingdom, separate questionnaires are set out for England, Wales, Scotland and Northern Ireland. The questionnaire for England is used here throughout.

Four levels of measurement are usually distinguished. These are referred to as nominal, ordinal, interval and ratio levels of measurement. The word 'nominal' refers to naming something, or indeed making one symbol represent something else. Nominal measures simply give alternative options for something. Usually the nominal measure has mutually exclusive categories.

The Census asked about household facilities using several nominal variables. One question was: 'Do you have a bath/shower *and* toilet for use only by your household?' It had the answer options 'Yes' and 'No' (ONS, 2005). This is a very simple question, and the measurement here is also called a dichotomy (yes or no). If one has only one of the three items (bath, shower, private toilet) one should answer 'no'. If one has two of them, including a toilet for private use, then one should answer 'yes'.

Another nominal variable was: 'Does your household own or rent the accommodation?' There are five possibilities: owns outright; owns with a mortgage or loan; pays part rent and part mortgage (shared ownership); rents; lives here rent free. Measurement in each of the constituent nations of the UK has been improved in its accuracy and comparability through detailed piloting of the questionnaires over the period up to 2001. Some categories exist in the 'nominal' variables which may not apply in a particular nation within the UK. For example, the methods used by the social housing sector to arrange part-rental vary from nation to nation. Nevertheless the final questionnaire, as an end-product of detailed testing, covers the topic of social housing part-rentals in an adequate way across all four nations.

Now consider the ordinal level of measurement. Ordinal measures give ranked outcomes to a closed question. Here is an example of an ordinal variable from the 2001 Census (ONS, 2005):

H5 What is the lowest floor level of your household's living accommodation?

The answer options are:

Basement or semi-basement

Ground floor (street level)

First floor (floor above street level)

Second floor

Third or fourth floor

Fifth floor or higher

In setting up an ordinal variable the options are ranked from lowest to highest. Crucially, there is not an exactly parallel distance between the different pairs of categories. For example there is a one-floor level distance between some pairs, and a one- or two-floor distance between the fourth and fifth categories. The distance is not set rigidly in the latter case.

The last category is a catch-all. An open-ended category like this, which comes at the end of an ordinal set, is known as a 'truncated category'. It is the sixth of the options but refers to a wide range of possibilities. The respondent could live on the 15th, 28th or 30th floor if they live in a large tower block.

'Censored data' is a technical term which does not mean the same thing as truncation (see Breen, 1996). Censoring occurs when the case could not report any figure for a given variable, and is thus missing from the data in that column. Truncation refers to the data at the top end being squeezed into a particular cell or value.

Ordinal variables are very common, even when exact measurement seems to be taking place. We distinguish the exactness of 'cardinal measurement' from ordinal measurement. In cardinal measurement the scale allows for comparable intervals across the whole scale, while ordinal measurement involves only rankings. If any part of a scale is ordinal then the whole variable is considered ordinal. Exceptions would require recoding, adjustment or analysis to make the ordinal variable a valid cardinal variable.

A second ordinal variable from the 2001 Census is about caring (ONS, 2005):

12 Do you look after, or give any help or support to family members, friends, neighbours or others because of:

- long-term physical, mental ill-health or disability, or
- problems related to old age?

  No

  Yes, 1–19 hours a week

  Yes, 20–49 hours a week

  Yes, 50+ hours a week

In a sense, the variable does not measure hours worked as a family carer very accurately. In another sense, though, the ordinal variable captures the key qualities of yes or no and the options of 'little, some, lots' very well. Through collapsing categories some variants can be reported upon. For example, one could inquire whether men more frequently 'do no caring' for old or disabled people than women, by collapsing the yes responses into a single one.

The third level of measurement is the interval level. Here, each unit rise in the variable has the same meaning across the whole range of the variable. Many interval variables start at zero and go up. Here is one measured in integers, where you can see that the division of the number by some other factors (e.g. 'rooms per person') will result in a number that has decimals of accuracy but does not refer to a real possibility (e.g. 1.7 rooms per person):

H3 How many rooms do you have for use only by your household?

Number of rooms □□

Notice at this point that the higher level of measurement subsumes and includes the lower; thus the interval variable 'number of rooms' is also nominal and ordinal as well as interval. However, the converse is not true. Nominal variables can never also be ordinal or interval. Ordinal variables cannot be interval: if they were we would just call them interval variables.

Finally, here is a ratio variable in the 2001 Census (ONS, 2005):

35 How many hours a week do you usually work in your *main* job?

Answer to nearest whole hour.

Give average for last four weeks.

Number of hours worked a week □□

The ratio level of measurement has a property that the other levels usually lack. The zero in the scale has a meaning (which for example is not the case for the measurement of rooms in a house, since a house with zero rooms is not a house). The existence of 0 working hours (non-employed), 0° temperature, and 0 on an income scale (for a non-earner) suggest that these are not only interval variables, they are also at the ratio level of measurement.

Two terms for the 'range' of the variable are useful here to help researchers discern aspects of the measurement: the 'domain' and the 'potential scope' of the variable. The domain is the part of the scale that the variable's values fall on. A positive integer runs from zero to infinity as its domain. Its range is the distance from the maximum to the minimum value observed. The biggest house may have 25 rooms, and the range is 25 since some people have 0 private rooms. The number of rooms cannot be negative.

'Hours worked per week' also has a domain restriction in that the number of hours cannot be negative. But the variables potential scope is also restricted. Since there are 168 hours in a week, hours range from 0 to 168 potentially. It is useful to consider the range, domain and potential scope of each variable before implementing a questionnaire with a large sample. That way the reasonable range can be known in advance and outliers can be easily caught by a simple checking routine.

The potential scope also lets the scientist know how wide the column that holds the measurement needs to be. The rounding-off of 'hours worked per week' (see above) is useful because it restricts the measurement to two simple digits. It is thought that the accuracy of the measurement in minutes would not be as important as simply getting a rounded-off record of hours worked.

So far we have analysed and illustrated four levels of measurement. Many variables resulting from surveys can undergo transformations of the level of measurement. Two general rules apply. Firstly, you can always simplify measurement to a weaker level of measurement:

- Interval and ratio variables can be made into ordinal ranked variables.
- Interval, ratio and ordinal variables can be made into nominal variables.
- Ordinal variables can be made into nominal variables.

We call these conversions 'data transformations'. Computers are used to make these transformations from the original data. One never deletes the more detailed original variable! From 'Hours' for example one may create a nominal variable 'Part time'. This would take the values 0 for not part-time and 1 for part-time work of 30 hours a week or less.

The second rule is that if something is inherently ratio or interval level in reality, then a survey recording it at a weaker level of measurement loses some information. However, it may be easier or more cost-effective (perhaps in being quicker) to ask the respondents a question at a lower level of measurement than the one that is most accurate in reality. These are issues that can be solved pragmatically.

Words like 'imprecise', 'fuzzy' and 'less detailed' seem to apply at the 'low' levels of measurement. Words like 'specific', 'accurate' and 'precise' seem to apply at the 'high' levels of measurement. Statistics can sometimes be misleadingly precise, though. The concept of 'spurious accuracy' can sometimes be applied. For example, if you ask a poorly worded question about the respondent's attitude to racism and put the response onto an interval scale from 0 to 10, you are likely to get spurious accuracy. There is a measurement issue here. Of course there may also be deeper theoretical and conceptual issues in the measurement of attitudes to racism such as 'What is an attitude?' and 'What do you mean to refer to as racism?'. Do not confuse measurement issues with conceptual issues. Work out the concepts that you want to use first, then work through the evidence methodically from the piloting stage so you deal with each measurement issue.

It would be fallacious (i.e. a poor argument) to say in general that a higher level of measurement is better than a low level of measurement. In other parts of this book I take up some related issues of viewpoints, standpoints and imputation. Viewpoints refer to the orientation of the person who perceives or describes something. Standpoints refer to differences of perspective that give interesting angles on the same events or situation. Imputation refers to the process of having to estimate a value for a variable from indirect evidence. Clearly measurement issues arise from all of these three angles. The level of measurement is not the only measurement issue.

5.3 Causality

It is easiest to organise a questionnaire survey if you have a causal hypothesis or an explanatory theory in mind. In this chapter I set out the nature of causality as it relates to the measurement of variables in a questionnaire survey. This helps set up the overall content of your questionnaire survey (see also 5.2 **measurement** and 5.1 **operationalisation**).

Causality in a questionnaire survey refers to getting evidence about both the dependent variable and the independent variables. The dependent variable is the outcome; for example, in studies of poverty it might be a simple zero–one indicator of poverty. The independent variables are the things that you expect are causing the outcome to be higher or lower, or to be 'present' (Olsen, 2010b).

To illustrate causality, here are two simple causal statements that might derive from the same income survey. The context here is India, where poverty is very common among certain minority ethnic groups and castes.

1. Income is affected by education of the members of the household, hours worked per week, caste group, and whether in a minority tribe.

2. Poverty is affected by education of the members of the household, hours worked per week, caste group, and whether in a minority tribe.

The two statements are very similar because they have the same four sets of independent variables. Education might be the number of years of formal schooling, summed up over all adults. Hours worked per week would have to include all adults doing both employment and self-employment work. Caste group is a four-way set of indicators (see the next chapter for how to set these up), referred to as a multinomial, since a person can only be in one of the four caste groups. Multinomial indicators both imply and presume that the person cannot be in two of the groups – that is, caste groups are mutually exclusive. Of course you can marry someone of another caste group, so for households a tricky choice would have to be made to get 'household caste'. But data on income are typically analysed for each individual. Finally, the fourth indicator shows whether you are in one of the dominant 'Hindu' groups or in the broad, minority 'Scheduled Tribe' ethnic group.

The two causal statements have different kinds of outcome indicator. The first one is a continuous measure. My causal statement refers to income, but instead we often measure it using expenditure in rupees per person per month. Expenditure is close to income but not quite the same thing. The income measure is usually developed through painstaking questionnaire coverage of each and every item of expenditure, grouped into about 40 main headings. It may take several pages of questionnaire to cover all the headings of expenditure. It is easiest to record expenditure for the whole household, but then after dividing it by household size we can record 'per capita expenditure' for each and every individual. We have theories about the causes of income which we can apply, with care, to the measurement of expenditure even though there are some minor differences. Saving and borrowing are one of the major sources of difference. But the theories can be tested, developed and worked on even if we do not have direct measures of income. Income proves to be very difficult to measure accurately. There are many issues with measuring income, such as tax, illicit earnings, the difference between profit and turnover for small businesses, and bonus earnings. Our measure of expenditure will suit the theory of income fairly well. The expenditure measure is a proxy.

In the second causal statement, we have poverty instead of income as the outcome. Poverty is measured as 1 if they are poor, and 0 if they are not poor. Money is generally shared out among household members. If it were not, all dependent children would be poor and few employed workers would appear to be poor. Instead, we add up all the income and divide it by the total household membership, reflecting how the earners share funds to feed and clothe (etc.) the whole household. Now it is more obvious why we do the study at the 'person unit of analysis' – the person is only poor if they lack at least one earner in the family earning enough to bring the whole family over the poverty line. Using a computer, we can set a poverty line and simply create a poverty variable after doing the questionnaire, like this:

```
poverty=0
replace poverty=1 if expendpc< 360
mean poverty
```

The second statement here refers to expenditure per capita being less than 360 rupees per person per month. The three statements together form a simple transformation routine that creates a new variable, poverty. This variable could be seen in a spreadsheet as a whole column of 0s and 1s. The mean of the variable is the proportion or percentage who are poor. For instance, if 80 are poor and 120 are not, then the mean of the variable is 0.40, which is 40%. It is very easy to do this transformation once you have an income variable. You would not want to ask the respondent whether they are poor. That would be inquiring about something else altogether. You would be asking about their subjective view of whether they are poor. Our causal statements were not about that; they were about objective, measured poverty. In this way, with great precision and care, we go through our theory or hypotheses and we measure and develop each indicator that we need in the questionnaire survey. See Blaikie (2000) for more examples.

These issues are complex and you can return to this task later. For the moment, consider how economists actually do study income. They find income, proxied by expenditure per capita, strongly skewed, and this is not a good situation for our analysis even though it is an accurate portrayal of an unequal income distribution. The skewness shows that many people are on low incomes (estimated by expenditure per capita) but a few people, perhaps 2% or 5%, are on extremely high incomes relative to the poor. This skewness can be removed for the purpose of statistical study and graphing by taking the logarithm of the per capita expenditure. This gives the same ranking of all the people, but uses a different scale for measurement. 10,000 has a log of just 9, 1000 has a log of 7, 100 has a log of 4.6, and 10 has a log of 2.3. The log brings the very high numbers down to a reasonable comparative scale. Our first causal statement now looks like this:

---

1. The log of expenditure per capita ... is affected by education of the members of the household, hours worked per week, the caste group, and whether in a minority tribe.

This works very well for a questionnaire survey about poverty.

Statements 1 and 2 should give consistent results. Notice that income rises as hours worked rises, so we expect these to be positively associated. However, poverty works the other way. Poverty is less likely as hours worked rises. We expect an inverse relationship in statement 2, in contrast to a positive relationship in statement 1. All these detailed expectations are usually worked out before a questionnaire survey is set up.

Make sure your questionnaire survey covers all the topics that are included in all your causal statements, theories and hypotheses. That creates a basic guide to the coverage, scope, and level of detail of the survey. This helpful guidance, when combined with your pilot survey, will lead to a cutting-down of the questionnaire (and the hypotheses) if the study seems to be too ambitious. A lot of planning is involved. Costs and timings need to be worked out in detail. Questionnaires are known to be a cost-effective method, but only if the underlying survey instrument (the questionnaire) and the sampling are carefully worked out. In the rest of this part of the book, I'll explain more about the details of surveys and sampling. You can also use a good research design book (e.g. Hakim, 2000; De Vaus, 2001).

If you are given some data that others have set up, then you still have to work out your causal statements in detail, as shown above or in some similar way, before you start working with the data. You can then make a sensible subset of data by extracting only the desired variables from among the hundreds or thousands that you receive in the main dataset (see 5.7 **subsetting of data**).

5.4 Data Cleaning

The phrase 'data cleaning' implies that dirty data are bad data, but this thought applies mainly in a survey context and not in a qualitative context. After cleaning some survey data, the dataset as a whole should be in a more usable form than before cleaning. But according to qualitative researchers, something important may get lost during cleaning, and the pilot stages are fundamentally qualitative and only gradually involve more quantification. If you would like to read about the values implicit in the survey measurement method, see Williams (2000). These are relevant to decisions one makes during the data-cleaning stage. In particular, Williams argues that interval data impose a valuation upon high- and low-ranked values of a scale. If you have doubts about a scale in a dataset, and this scale appears to be at the interval level of measurement, you have several options to weaken the assumption and thus avoid making a false premise in the research. One option is to code the variable as a multinomial (i.e. multi-category) variable, giving up its ranked measurements. Another option is to move from cardinal scaling to ordinal scaling. In any case you will want to clean the data too.

To clean the data you need a well-developed codebook. The codebook contains each question's number and wording, the variable name that arises from that, the variable labels, and perhaps some basic tabulations. It should indicate the kinds of reasons for selectively missing data. You might see three of these amongst other options for answering a single question. Here is an example, from the British Household Panel Survey (BHPS) (Taylor, 2001), for a question about the person's savings:

3.16. Purpose of Saving

Purpose of Savings (wSAVEY1)

01 Holidays

02 Old age/retirement specifically mentioned (include pension schemes/plans)

03 Car

04 Child(ren) (include children's education, and if buying shares to invest in children's education)

05 Housing/property purchase inc. land purchase

06 Home improvements

07 Household bills (eg TV license, etc.; also include motor maintenance such as car/bike insurance, tax, servicing)

08 Special events (eg weddings, burials, Christmas)

09 No particular reason specified (eg just saving for a rainy day, to be safe, emergencies, just in case)

10 Shares schemes

11 Own education

12 Grandchild

96 Other (include shares not elsewhere specified)

98 Don't know

99 Refused / Not available

The values are all numbered as well as labelled. Developing the codebook is a gradual process. It starts when you plan the questionnaire, and the bulk of the codebook should be typed during the piloting of the basic questionnaire. As you hone the questions, you also modify the codebook. Only at the very end would you add basic tabulations, since they will only be accurate once all the data are entered. The codebook pre-dates most of the data entry.

During piloting and data entry, you may want to keep a diary of decisions. For each date, record which variables you have changed, why, and what exceptions arose that caused you to modify the codebook. This is a tedious job, but will pay off because you then do not have to remember these steps but can recover them later if you need to. Annotations can go directly into the codebook if you are working alone. If you work in a team, you need to find ways to discuss and agree on a master codebook. Thus if each team member keeps a diary, then at periodic meetings you can agree on one member to type the agreed revisions into the master codebook document.

During piloting, the data cleaning has two parts. First there is a review of the question wording. Perhaps instead of cleaning up the result, you need to clean up the question itself. Avoid double-barrelled or complex attitude questions, in particular. Compare these two questions, which arose from the self-completion questionnaire and the youth questionnaire of BHPS, respectively (see Taylor, 2001, for the documentation):

Q2. Here are some questions about family life.

Do you personally agree or disagree that. . .

a) A pre-school child is likely to suffer if his or her mother works

Strongly agree	1
Agree	2
Neither agree nor disagree	3
Disagree	4
Strongly disagree	5

(Varname QOPFAMA)

Q3. How interested are you in politics?

Very interested	1
Fairly interested	2
Not interested	3

(Varname QYPVTE6)

The first one is fairly complex. It presumes a certain model of family life, perhaps with a couple and with children or the possibility of children. If you were piloting this questionnaire, you might decide to simplify the question by revising it as follows:

> Do you personally agree or disagree that a pre-school child is likely to suffer if his or her mother works?

The revised question does not have a prefix clause. The BHPS has a complex framing of the prefix clause because the respondent is asked a whole series of ten or more attitude questions. This is a calculated risk. The complexity may be off-putting, but on the other hand once the reader gets the idea, it is easy for them to put all their answers on the same basic Likert scale as shown. This scale is repeated for each question, and the respondent just ticks an option. The BHPS assumes that respondents can read and tick rather easily. No options for missing data are visible here. We would then have just one category for missing data, −1 (not answered). However, because the BHPS is rather complex and does allow for the imputation of data, either by getting a proxy response from another household member or by imputation during the data-cleaning stage (by BHPS staff), numerous codes for missing data are actually found in the BHPS data. Some of them are shown here.

We find in the BHPS codebook the cleaned, final tabulation shown in Table 11. The raw valid percentage who agree with the statement is 33% (i.e. (849+3542/13,447).

Data cleaning involves setting up the missing values and all the other codes, ensuring that each datum entered matches correctly just one of these values, checking the coding to be sure the typing is done correctly, and checking for any values that are out of the valid range for each variable. In summary, here is a data cleaning checklist:

- Are the missing values for individual variables coded consistently? For example, −1 for not answered, and −9 for any other missing or wild value. Refusal would get a different value, perhaps −7.

- Are the lists of value labels in the codebook adequate?

- Have you checked that the number coded on each sheet by hand is the right number?

Table 11   Tabulation of attitudes in the UK about whether a pre-school child suffers if the mother works

Value Label	Code	Frequency	Raw Percentage
Missing or wild	−9	490	3.3%
Proxy respondent	−7	954	6.4%
Not answered	−1	19	0.1%
Strongly agree	1	849	5.7%
Agree	2	3,542	23.8%
Neither agree nor disagree	3	4,643	31.1%
Disagree	4	3,578	24.0%
Strongly disagree	5	835	5.6%
Total		14,910	100%

Source: BHPS 2008, Wave Q. There are 1 3,447 valid raw cases.

Reprinted with permission from the Institute for Social Economic Research

- Is the typing of the data from hand-written numeric to typed numeric format correct?

The last of these is the classic data-cleaning task. Many teams agree to have two typists enter all the numbers independently. There is very simply one grid of numbers per typist, and most errors will pop up as inconsistencies between these two grids if the typing has been done twice. If it is only done once, it is almost impossible to identify typing errors.

Table 12 gives a sample of a data entry grid. The first variable is a personal identifier; the second is the opinion (labelled OPFAMA for the Opinion about Families, Part A) about children suffering. The third is a social class indicator associated with the respondent's current job, and the last is a detailed social class indicator for their most recent job. Such a grid can be typed very efficiently and quickly. Compare it with Table 13, which shows the statistical meaning of the same grid with value labels. Obviously it is much faster to type the numerical codes. There is a risk of error which we handle by *ex post* data cleaning. Value labels are also much longer than those shown here. They can have varying lengths and quite a lot of detail, as we saw earlier. The computer applies all this detail to the numbers in the data grid. The 'data' are thus the code numbers. The codebook shows a master code for matching the numbers to the labels.

Table 12   A data entry grid

PID	QOPFAMA	QJBGOLD	QMRJSEC
130001104	−7	3	72
10017933	4	2	91
10017992	4	2	41
10023526	4	3	60
10048219	−7	4	72
10048308	−7	3	71
10049304	−7	4	91
10055266	3	3	41
10055339	4	−8	−3
10067213	−7	1	33
10067248	4	1	31
20045018	4	−8	−3
10076166	3	−8	−9
10078401	3	−8	−9
10079556	3	1	81

Table 13   Data grid showing value labels

PID	QOPFAMA	QJBGOLD	QMRJSECD
130001104	proxy re	routine	intermd
10017933	disagree	service	own acct
10017992	disagree	service	lower pr
10023526	disagree	routine	hgher su
10048219	proxy re	personal	intermd
10048308	proxy re	routine	intrmd c
10049304	proxy re	personal	own acct
10055266	neithr a	routine	lower pr
10055339	disagree	inapplic	never ha
10067213	proxy re	service	high pro
10067248	disagree	service	higher p
20045018	disagree	inapplic	never ha
10076166	neithr a	inapplic	missing

Key: proxy re = Proxy Respondent. Neithr = Neither Agree Nor Disagree.

5.5 Data Extraction

It is cheap and easy to extract a survey dataset from an online source. As data 'collection', this method is dependent on the provision of data by other institutional sources, large and small. A large number of government and international organisations offer data for free use by the public. Examples of data sources include the following:

- the World Values Survey (http://www.worldvaluessurvey.org/);

- census tables (many countries);

- Indices of Multiple Deprivation (UK; www.communities.gov.uk/communities/neighbourhoodrenewal/deprivation);

- Labour Force Survey (see http://www.statistics.gov.uk/Statbase/Source.asp?vlnk=358&More=Y; later versions of the Labour Force Survey are listed as the Annual Population Survey, see http://www.statistics.gov.uk/StatBase/Product.asp?vlnk=10855&More=Y).

Many of the larger sources offer a NESSTAR window for users who want to access the data. A little patience pays off when adapting to using the NESSTAR approach. In this chapter the concept of data extraction is first introduced – mainly referring to making a small subset from a pre-existing large dataset – and then the NESSTAR method of extraction is explained. Future software development may create alternatives which compete with or complement NESSTAR. Once a researcher knows how to explore metadata and derive a list of desired variables (using 'if' statements to select only the desired types of cases), it is easy to adapt to other software.

Extracting data requires a clear focus on a specific research question or task (Dale et al., 2000). The kind of task one might have in mind could include constructing a table with row percentages as background in a qualitative project or setting up a bar chart that compares means across different subsamples (e.g. mean length of marriage for different age groups who get divorced). The complexity of the task will affect the complexity of the data extraction required. According to the task, a list of the variables needed can be generated. These might include demographics, substantive variables and outcome indicators.

To extract data means to take a subset. One might choose all the North East region cases from a dataset about the English Indices of Multiple Deprivation, and then within that choose only the Housing and Unemployment sub-indices as well as the main summary indices. Such an extraction might be visualised as shown in Figure 5.

The data extracted would comprise only the darkest grey areas of Figure 5. This concise mini-database can be brought into the computer via a spreadsheet or a statistical package. Well-known formats include the IBM SPSS .sav and .por formats. Blanks in the dataset will be indicated either by a blank or . or a special symbol such as −99. As it happens, the Indicators of Multiple Deprivation are provided in spreadsheets, so their format is even simpler – it is the Microsoft Excel .xls format.

The resulting matrix is simply a single table of data with the few rows and columns that are needed for this particular project. Localities within the North East might be labelled in a column. That column acts as a row identifier for the small dataset.

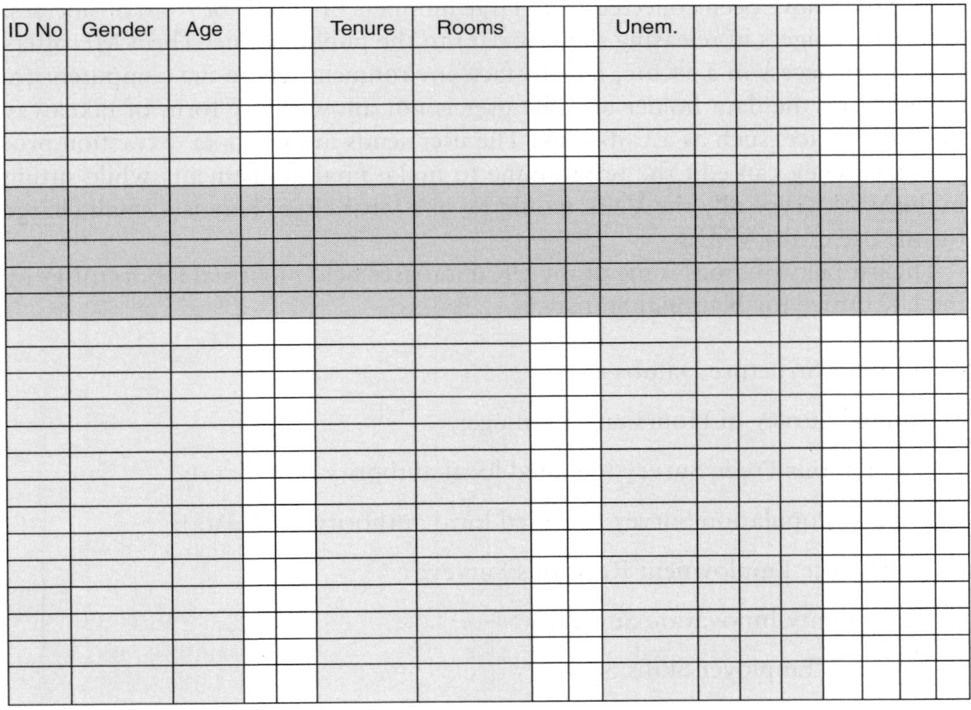

ID No	Gender	Age			Tenure	Rooms			Unem.						

Figure 5   Data extraction using selected rows and columns

Note: Each row here represents a group of cases numbering perhaps tens or hundreds. Light grey shows a selection of variables, and dark grey a selection of cases. When combined, we have a small subset.

Having multiple levels of data collection complicates the extraction of a dataset (Dale et al., 2000). Multiple levels of data exist for many household surveys. Here the data for households are one level and the data for individuals is a second. The number of people will be much higher than the number of households. If your desired dataset is about individual people you may need to replicate the household data for each person. If your desired dataset is about households, and would include household size, household income and type of home tenure, then it is necessary to either omit personal data or else 'collapse' the personal data into household-level summary variables. These are complex data analysis operations. At the data extraction stage a good method is simply to extract two tables, one at each level. Including a household identifier variable and a personal identifier variable in the files will be helpful later on. A little time spent planning the various later tasks of the research will help at the data extraction stage.

A virtual microdata laboratory (VML) is used in some countries to protect the privacy of respondents and the confidentiality of the data in large datasets. A VML is an onsite research access facility for secondary datasets. Where administrative data have been collected from large numbers of people or from businesses, there are dangers in releasing the raw data to the public online. The VML offers temporary access in a secure, face-to-face environment where the computers are provided by the data holder and the user is not allowed any form of takeaway memory device, such as a USB stick. The user sends in their data extraction programme. They can edit the programme to make final adjustments while sitting in the VML. Typically the VML would be in a large city. There is a small charge for the use of the VML.

The list below names some of the UK databases held in virtual laboratories by the UK Office for National Statistics:

- Business Structure Database;

- Annual Survey of Hours and Earnings;

- The Labour Force Survey (detailed local authority level data);

- Annual Population Survey (detailed local authority level data);

- Workplace Employment Relations Survey;

- Community Innovation Survey;

- National Employer Skills Survey.

The VML system presently works as follows. Once the desired data subset has been extracted, the VML will not allow the data themselves to be removed from the site. Instead one must analyse the data and produce the required bar charts, tables, pie charts and numerical results *in situ*. These results pages are handed to the VML managers, who take a few days to check them over. The VML managers look for ways in which the disclosure of these results might perhaps result in a loss of privacy or a breach of confidentiality of an individual respondent or perhaps a sensitive group of businesses. Typically the concerns relate to small groups or unique cases.

The sensitive groups or individuals might appear evident in a tabulated outcome and could perhaps be named by seeking information from a separate public database. The example of a large mansion with 17 rooms can be used to illustrate 'disclosure risk'. If the identity of the owner could be easily discovered, then a table that reveals the whereabouts of this large mansion would be a danger to the owner's privacy. The risk of disclosure from one table depends in part on what information we assume the user has from other data sources such as the publicly available postcode files and the electoral registers. Generally, tables that do not have aggregate counts of less than five units in each row and column tend to be found safer – that is, with less risk of disclosure or identification – than those with low aggregate counts. Once the VML managers are satisfied that there is no risk or a very low risk of disclosure or identification, they will release the tables to the researcher.

So it can be seen that with the VML method raw data cannot be obtained except as an interim product that is used and then left behind at the VML site. As a contrast, with the NESSTAR data extraction method, the raw data can be downloaded directly to the user's computer.

NESSTAR is a software package used by data providers to make data easy for users to investigate.[1] Metadata are produced as labels that describe the data, sampling, variables, cases and case identifiers. Details of survey weighting and missing values are usually provided in well-managed NESSTAR databases. Even if a database is complex, NESSTAR's metadata will describe the full range of background information that a user might need. NESSTAR is a format intended for online access but it can also be used on a desktop computer.

When using NESSTAR software, one first sees a list of databases. After selecting a database, a choice of dates is offered. Clicking through to see the metadata about that dataset brings a range of information: the study description, standard bibliographic citation, study scope, the methodology and data processing used and the data access arrangements. Below the metadata are hotlinked lists of the data. Within a link one finds demographic data, substantive variable lists, survey weighting data and other data. Each link is a list of variables. Summary statistics for each variable can be accessed by clicking on the variable name. Tabs at the top of that sheet allow analysis and cross-tabulation to be done. Icons allow the more experienced user to enter the subsetting and data download areas.

First make the subset. Here the choice of 'rows' involves stating the conditions, which must be true for the rows to be included. These are expressed as values of household or personal variables, Then make the choice of variables. A lot of clicking may be involved for a large data subset. If NESSTAR is not easy to use, it may be wise to check in the metadata to find out whether the dataset might be available as a whole from a data archive. For example the British Crime Survey would typically be held in both NESSTAR and in the UK Data Archive (see www.esds.ac.uk). NESSTAR is most efficient for small subsets extracted from large datasets.

Since NESSTAR is a web-based data-providing service, a bookmark to the NESSTAR web page can be set up. During repeated visits, the user can make graphic images and tables from a familiar survey without having to download any data at all. The graphs can be produced within NESSTAR and then downloaded to the desktop.

The use of weights within NESSTAR is at a high level of sophistication. Care is needed not to produce unweighted graphs or tables with data that require weighting. The tables can be misleading or wrong. Developing expertise in using a dataset may involve checking for other publications that have used the data. It is important to use peer-reviewed publications from reputed publishers, not web-based materials that may have the same typical errors in them that you might be making. Peer-reviewed publications offer a gold standard and can be used to compare percentages and basic outcomes to ensure that the use of NESSTAR is following best practice for a given dataset.

Note

1. NESSTAR is an acronym for Networked Social Science Tools and Resources (see http://www.nesstar.org/). Funded from 1998 as a project within the European Union, involving close collaboration between the UK Data Archive and Norwegian Social Science Data Services, NESSTAR is now the name used for both a company and a product.

5.6 Outliers

The concept of outlying data points is used mainly in the context of continuous variables in survey datasets. These data points, known as outliers, lie either above or below the usual range of a variable. The bell curve or 'normal distribution' has most of its weight in the middle of its range, and as part of its normal shape typically has a few outliers. Other distributions have outliers on one side only (an example of a skewed distribution like the distribution of income comes to mind) or are relatively flat with very few outliers (such as the distribution of age, which hardly ever exceeds 110 years and cannot be below zero). Knowing about outliers is useful for cleaning survey data, because a value like 'age −9' clearly needs to be fixed. Because a range of possible distributions exist – and some do have outliers as a normal part of their range – one has to be careful. In this chapter I review the concept of cleaning by deleting outliers and then turn to more interesting ways of handling them.

To clean a dataset may mean to eliminate whole cases or rows where some key datum is missing or has been refused. When a dataset is cleaned in this way, the rate of non-response is considered to have risen, and the smaller 'clean' dataset may depart from randomness and therefore not be representative. Therefore if the project began with randomness and representativeness as important goals, then cleaning has to be done with partial attention paid, simultaneously, to the effective rate of non-response after cleaning.

A less radical procedure is to clean variables (i.e. columns) by setting up missing-data values such as −99 or −1 which indicate that the outlying value was unexplained. Such missing values are selectively set up by the user and can appear also as little holes or gaps in the raw data table. The use of −1 or −99 is a convenient norm, and software programmes such as SPSS can recognise the values −1 and −99 as special non-existent values for existent cases. SPSS calls them user-missing values. Some packages call them selectively-missing values. On the other hand, if the data cell were simply blank, that might be thought of as a system-missing value: the 'system', i.e. the software, does not know what is supposed to be there. Most software packages will treat the values −1, −99, and empty cells just the same way. A typical trick therefore is to examine each variable, then plot its values on a histogram and recode any value to −1 if its value is simply ridiculously outside the realistic range. One may also check the handwritten surveys or data source to see if the datum can be corrected. Then one can declare the user-missing value −1 for all variables (or at least, being careful, all those where −1 is not the real value) and redraw the histogram plot. It will now have a few less extreme high or low values, and this will be the finalised plot.

Economists and psychologists are sometimes wary of deleting or recoding missing values in these ways. In economics, the concept of stochastic variation explains that an underlying process which is not directly observed can generate a range of values and some may be extreme. If a set of data generally follows a normal plot (i.e. a bell curve), then the economist may not want to see any cases dropped, nor crude recoding or the creation of user-missing data, where there were previously high values.

Take the example of house prices. Suppose the mean price in local currency is 75,000 and the mode is 55,000. The high values may read 655,000, 725,000, 1.5 million or even 10.2 million. Which is the outlier? The value over 10 million, or the values over 1 million? Since the distribution is expected to be skewed any-way, we would tend to accept and not recode or drop very high values.

In a country like the United Kingdom, huge regional variations in house price values means that one's private informal knowledge about them may not cover extreme values like these. Bonus payments too form a highly skewed part of total income distribution across the United Kingdom. A large survey of house prices (or bonuses) can turn up large values like 10.2 million. If – due to prior expectations – the researcher then drops them, they will miss a critical new find-ing from their research! Care is needed when setting up user-missing values for outliers. One certainly needs to consider each variable separately.

There are some alternatives to the deletion and user-missing procedures. These include transforming the skewed variable using ordinal regression; cutting the outliers out of diagrams but leaving them in the data and statistical tables; and testing statistically for bias that might result from omitting the outliers. I will discuss each option in more detail.

Transforming a skewed variable can bring the outlying high values down to reasonable levels. The best-known transformation is the logarithm. The average of log hourly wages is just 2.5 for wages that range from £5.10 an hour upward with an average of about £12.00 an hour. The logarithm is the number to which e should be exponentiated to give the original wage rate such as 12.00 (e is a spe-cial number like π ('pi'); it is 2.71828). The log of 12 is 2.48 and the log of 5.1 is 1.62. For very high wage rates like £75 an hour paid to some consultants, estate agents or bankers (which include bonuses), the log of 75 is just 4.3. The log thus shrinks down the very high values without shrinking the low ones much at all.

There are two problems with using logarithms. One is that the logarithm of zero does not exist, so this transformation can only be used for positive values. That works all right for hourly wage rates, but would not work for weekly earnings or earnings from rents, which might indeed take the value 0 for some individuals. Some alternative transformations are available which might do the same job as the logarithm, but still work for zero-valued cases. For example, one can transform a list of values ranging from 0 upward by using exponentiation: simply take the square root of all values to shrink down the skewness of high values, or square the values to remove skewness from the very low values.

Another solution to a poorly shaped continuous variable is the Box–Cox transformation. Like the logarithm, this transformation requires strictly positive values to begin with. Using transformations is agreeable to an expert audience: they can visualise the transformed variable on its own scaling because they are aware the transformed version is a monotonic function of the original. A monotonically rising result would mean one that increases steadily in tandem with the original. Statistical results from correlation or regression can be comparable with the results from the original, but lack the corruption of distribution shapes that was present in the original variable. This form of cleaning does not remove any data values from the dataset.

A different solution for a statistician is to use ordinal regression. Here the steps in the original skewed variable are considered as steps upward in an ordinal variable rather than in a continuous scale. For example, we might be estimating hours worked per week, which range potentially up to 168 hours. The outliers are from about 100 to 168 hours, and these include wardens, housekeepers and others with live-in jobs. We can keep their weekly working hours values in the dataset, break the data into five-hour groupings and conduct an ordinal regression. Weekly hours on the five-hourly-grouped ordinal scale would decline with the number of dependent children, rise with the education level and perhaps rise with the working hours norms of the occupational group. The regression form called 'ordinal regression' has to assume that each variable's impact is the same across all pairs of values of the outcome variable.

If the following is true then ordinal regression would work as well as ordinary regression:

1. The impact of having dependent children is generally to reduce hours worked per week, after allowing for other factors.

2. The impact of having dependent children is neither smaller nor greater at high hours levels of work than at low-hours levels of work.

The first assumption is a hypothesis and is tested by assessing whether the regression result is statistically significant. The second assumption is rather strong and cannot be tested using the ordinal regression itself.

A third alternative to deleting outliers is simply to cut the outliers out of diagrams by setting the scale to cut off before the outlier level is reached. The downside to this is that diagrams will therefore be a little misleading. However, it would be acceptable if the outliers were left in the data and statistical tables and a note added to each diagram indicating which outliers were removed.

For instance, if working on hourly wage rates one might add a note below a bar chart: 'Wage rates above £75 per hour are omitted here but included in all other statistics in this paper'. If such a note were not present under the diagram, then leaving the outliers out of the scale would be considered seriously misleading.

A final alternative is to test statistically for bias that might result from omitting the outliers. There are two related tests that can be used. Both require careful coding of the outlying values early in the construction of the survey dataset or subsets. Firstly, the outliers can be considered invalid values and recoded to user-missing. During the recoding add a new variable coded 0/1 to indicate that this particular value was missing for this reason (e.g. variable name V5Unreasonable, values 0=no, 1=yes). Now add this new binary variable into regression or ANOVA tests that you are running on V5. The hypothesis is that it is not significant. If it turns up significant, you have a problem of a bias arising from these unreasonably-valued data. If less than 1% of the survey had this problem then it is unlikely to turn up statistically significant. Otherwise the test is needed.

The second test is very closely related to the missing-value test. There are tests for whether data are missing at random, or missing according to some specified, measured causes. The measurement of the causes can only be with variables that are available in the dataset. Therefore one might also consider that the causes are only proxied by variables in the dataset. Take an example: Are all those born abroad showing a missing value for the main variable of interest of the research?

Test for the significance of a gap such as this in the dataset. Take care not to assume this is 'because' of being born abroad, but rather that this measured variable is associated with whatever mysterious factor is causing them to have this unreasonable – and hence user-missing – data value. This method also works for other situations where there are blank values in the dataset. Since it is time-consuming to test whether missing values are missing at random or not, it is wise to have quite narrow bounds on which variables will be examined in such detail.

As a rule of thumb, if less than 1% of values are missing, it is unlikely to be important. If between 1% and 15% are missing, further investigation is needed. If more than 15% are missing, including blanks and user-missing, then you need to reconsider your sample selection and perhaps even question whether using a sophisticated statistical method upon this variable is a good idea. If there is too much missing then maybe the variable should be dropped.

In summary, the concept of outliers leads us into certain methods of cleaning, recoding and transforming a dataset. Outliers and missing values also need close attention if using a method such as regression, which assumes normal distributions for some variables. One golden rule is to check the distribution of variables once the full dataset is available. You may then either clean or transform the distribution. If too many values or outliers are missing, it may be valuable to conduct an analysis of whether the outliers are missing at random. In practice, the use of testing for random missing values is restricted to the absence of values for the dependent variable. However, in some structural equation modelling contexts, more tests may be done. One can even model the 'missingness'. These are advanced statistical methods, but there also is a basic lesson to be learned. Software packages allow for two types of values: blank values, which are system-missing, and user-coded missing values, which reflect outliers that are considered unrealistic for a given column of data. These two types of values can be used flexibly when creating a survey dataset.

5.7 Subsetting of Data

Making a subset of data presumes that a larger dataset already exists. The more resourceful researchers will know how to access large databases. They can glean from them a sensible survey dataset that can be analysed within a reasonable time-frame.

In this chapter, I discuss five types of large databases and where you can find them. I also explain how to access one dataset from a free online source: the American Citizen Participation dataset, available from the Inter-University Consortium for Political and Social Research (1990) at the University of Michigan. The date 1990 given here is the date of creation of the dataset. A dataset is a research product in its own right. It is different from a book or article, but it gets a reference citation just as books do.

1. An enterprise keeps its own employee records or customer evaluation survey data in a growing database. Identifiers for each record include the department, the date, the customer type (or employee grade) and a locality identifier. In large organisations research is usually guided by head-office staff who create a working spreadsheet file from the database. Anonymisation may be required. A textbook which uses business-style datasets to illustrate some aspects of statistical modelling is Hair et al. (2005).

2. Every 10 years many countries carry out a census of their population. The census tables are published online. These tables compare detailed local information on a national scale, so some users – such as local authorities or councils – find them useful to compare different types of local authority in different regions.

    Some countries also offer primary survey data at the individual and household level to users. There may be a fee for commercial users. Anonymisation must be carried out before the census can be provided in raw form. In the UK a small percentage of records are put into a subset dataset for public use. This dataset is known as the Sample of Anonymised Records (SARS; see http://www.ccsr.ac.uk/sars/2001/). Various SARS datasets offer different levels of geographic detail, and there are versions about individuals and versions about households. In addition, for the UK, the CELSIUS project enables linked access to several successive census records for each person using a random sample (see http://celsius.census.ac.uk/). From the CELSIUS subset, the user can either take the whole set (which is very large) or make another subset. The UK tables and primary data access are managed via the URL http://census.ac.uk/. Other countries handle their survey data in varying ways. In India, for example, the National Sample Survey Programme is releasing data more rapidly than the national Census scheme (see http://mospi.gov.in/nsso_4aug2008/web/nsso. htm?status=1&menu_id=28).

3. There are several survey datasets which comprise part of large, multi-country harmonised data collection projects. Examples include:

   • European Social Survey;

   • International Social Survey Programme;

   • World Values Survey;

   • Freedom House Project.

   All of these projects have their own open-access websites. The datasets can be downloaded whole, but it is wiser to select certain countries and dates to make a concerted attempt at a reasonable comparison by theme among selected parts of the world.

4. Data on the sale of houses, court cases, medical outcomes or hospital admissions are held by the relevant controlling authority. Access may be conditional on passing a series of ethical, legal and data protection hurdles. These gateway tests may be applied differently to each category of user. The usual breakdown of users falls into academic, commercial and 'government or other'.

   Once a researcher negotiates access to one of these databases they may discover unexpected complexities or technicalities in the data. At one level these may seem trivial or burdensome. At another level these are the hurdles which one must overcome to open up this gateway to research. In this sense, making a sensible subset is indeed a form of data collection.

5. Finally, there is quite a large number of unharmonised, unique or one-off research survey datasets. Some of these can be accessed from data archives after they have been deposited. For these data, one issue can be that they become out of date before users can get hold of them. Polling data, for example, will only be released after the funding agency has issued its main press releases. Academic data are not usually released until at least a year after a project ends. As time passes, the data are of less use to ongoing social and policy researchers. The agreement to archive the data creates opportunities for comparison over time, though. These datasets can be examined to

identify question wording for one's own survey. There are very many topics and types of survey in the data archives. Some authors also archive the qualitative data for some mixed-methods and qualitative projects.

To improve your grasp of the basic idea of subsetting data, consider Box 8. Consider this a learning task which tests your knowledge of secondary data collection. Your task is to work up a hypothesis that refers to a subset of these particular data. Try to make it a tightly constrained, narrow hypothesis. Remember that a good hypothesis is a statement which is not simply obviously true, nor obviously false, but which, if false, would have an interesting interpretation in terms of some alternative line of argument. Below the box is my attempt at a response to this challenge. Before you read my answer, try to work out a hypothesis and a list of the desired variables for this data subset.

Box 8   Sample Variable List: the American Citizen Participation Study

The study was designed to examine political and non-political civic participation in the United States. Respondents were asked about their interest in politics and their party identification, community involvement, campaign activities and any monetary contributions during any campaign. They were also asked to comment on social, political and economic problems in the United States, and to give their views on why people are not more politically involved. Demographic variables in this study include: education, occupation, religious background, race, ethnicity, age, gender, and union membership.
Variables [also include]:

- Volunteered for 1988 presidential campaign (CW88)
- Monetary contribution to 1988 presidential campaign (CM88)
- Participated in protest in past two years (PT2YRS)
- Year respondent was born (YEARBORN)
- Respondent's gender (GENDER)
- Family income (FAMINC)

This study used a clustered and stratified probability sample.

Source: Taken verbatim from the 1990 American Citizen Participation Study at http://www.icpsr. umich.edu/cocoon/OLC/demcivpart.xml?token-a02.

I immediately thought of age cohorts and wanted to look at the young people. I would take all those born after 1965, giving those perhaps 25 years old and younger. This will be a small sample. The variables I need will have to include a weighting variable if there is one. Otherwise, if none is offered, I need to check that the representativeness of the sample is guaranteed through some complex stratified and clustered sampling methods.

My main hypothesis based on the available data is that young women rather than men will tend to vote for the Democratic Party and identify with its ideas, and the ideas of other parties to the left of the political spectrum. Naturally, your hypothesis might be somewhat different. You might choose to examine ethnic variation in civic participation, for example, or any other topic within the data-set. Confusing hypotheses are worse than clear ones! An even better phrasing of this hypothesis would separate out the role of the Democratic Party from the role of left ideas in general.

The reasoning behind the main hypothesis has to do with values commonly associated with femininity, such as caring, kindness and valuing the underval-ued. These feelings may lead young women to associate with a party that repre-sents liberal values. By contrast, men may be associated with masculine values, which are commonly construed as believing that one should make one's way in the world and be independent of others' help. If that translates into avoiding the help or benefits offered by governments, then young men will tend to support right-leaning political parties which advocate minimal government and low levels of unemployment benefit.

In the background lie two other basic causal processes affecting party affilia-tion. The underlying basic processes are that membership of a trade union makes a person more likely to vote Democrat; and that being a committed Christian makes a person more likely to vote Republican. The effects on political affili-ation of being in a professional occupation or a student are not clear, so by all means one can ignore those aspects for my narrow hypothesis.

The test of the main hypothesis requires a big cross-tabulation that allows for four variables. The first is the support for left- or right-wing parties in the American political system. The second is the gender of the respondent. In addi-tion, two more variables need to be recoded into simple yes/no binaries and used to create four sub-tables:

- control for being in a trade union or not (with students placed in the category 'not in a trade union' in case they do not answer this question);

- control for being a committed Christian (with atheists and agnostics put into the category 'not a committed Christian').

We are now able to look at row and column percentages and use statistical tests for each of the following to examine which young women are more likely to vote Democrat:

- committed Christian women in a trade union;
- women in a trade union who are not committed Christians;
- committed Christian women who are not in a trade union;
- women who are neither in a trade union nor committed Christians.

This approach has the virtue of being clear and simple. It may not satisfy readers, who can turn to the published literature about voting patterns to get much better models and theories. The advantage of the simplified approach I have suggested so far is that, using secondary data analysis and online data, one can generate a rough draft of the results and percentages in a few hours.

A few notes about this subsetting exercise are needed here. It is wonderful that with good advance planning I only need a dataset with eight variables: identification, age, weight, whether Democratic or not, index of left/right identification, membership of a union, being a committed Christian, and gender.

Notice that my main hypothesis does not contrast old against young. If it did, I would need the whole dataset. Instead I have restricted my analysis to the 'young', and have decided to argue that there is a gender difference, and that it matters for political party identification.

It is useful to think a little about hypothesis testing now. For those who want to pursue further in-depth reading on the subject, I would recommend Hunt (1994). Before I run a test, I think over the implications of rejecting the main hypothesis. If it were rejected, I might run the same test on older people because men and women's feminine and masculine (traditional) values might be even stronger in that group. That would involve using another subset. I would certainly want to exclude the mid-age middle group, and take perhaps all the over-fifties for the 'older people' data subset.

If the main hypothesis were rejected, it might also be possible that I have misconstrued femininity and masculinity among the young. That might lead me towards some other research.

Another interesting possibility is that perhaps both young men and young women have a belief in equality which overwhelms any gender tendency they may have. The attitude favouring equality might jar with Republican values and rest easily with Democratic values. Therefore my second hypothesis is that those who believe strongly in social and economic equality will tend to support the Democratic or other left-leaning parties in the USA. To test this I will have to download a variable relating to the belief in (or attitude to) equality and inequality. If I can find one, then I can test this hypothesis. At this stage I am likely to need a multiple regression instead of cross-tabulations. I need to control for gender to allow for – and test for – any small effect it may be having on party affiliation, independent of the belief in equality. Thus when one hypothesis is rejected once, I do not forget to retest it in the next stage. I encapsulate a further test of it just to check, once again, whether it is still being rejected by apparent patterns showing up in the data.

5.8 Survey Weights

Survey weighting matters for data-collection purposes because it allows the researcher to save money on their field data-collection exercise. The use of weights of various kinds can, when used with care, release field researchers from long fruitless trips across difficult terrain and help maximise the efficiency with which the data from a sample of size n can reflect the characteristics of a much larger population of size N.

There are five main types of survey weights: regional weights, stratum weights, non-response weights, frequency weights and combined weights. By describing each one, this chapter helps you grasp the basic concept of weights, while in practice you are likely to use only one or two weighting systems in a single project.

Regional weights allow the calculation of a more accurate national average from a sample chosen in regional clusters or through random sampling at different rates in each region. For an illustration of this main concept, we can compare the four nations of the UK to look at simple averages compared with weighted averages.

The 2007 British Household Panel Survey (BHPS) had 12,053 employed individual adult respondents (background can be found in Taylor, 2001; the online survey is at www.esds.ac.uk; updated information at http://www.esds.ac.uk/longitudinal/access/bhps/L33196.asp). This survey had over-sampled in three regions – Wales, Scotland, and Northern Ireland. The over-sampling was intended to give accurate within-nation estimates for features of the economic and social life within these key parts of the UK.

Looking at employed adults age 16–65, it appears from the unweighted data that 50% live in England, 17% in Wales, 17% in Scotland and 16% in Northern Ireland. The actual percentages are very different: just 4% live in Wales, 9% in Scotland and 3% in Northern Ireland. That leaves 84% of employees living in England.

We can use these data to illustrate the idea of weighted and unweighted averages. First consider a hypothetical example concerning 'hours usually worked per week'. The overall average in 2007 was around 34 hours a week in the UK. If we had four nations with very different levels of hours, we might find this:

Raw averages: 35 in England, 29 in Wales, 30 in Scotland and 30 in Northern Ireland (hypothetical data)

Weights in the population: 0.84, 0.04, 0.09, and 0.03

Unweighted average: $(35+29+30+30) \div 4 = 31$ hours per week

Weighted average: $0.84\times35 + 0.04\times29 + 0.09\times30 + 0.03\times30 = 34.2$ hours per week.

In the hypothetical example the most populous region also has the highest weekly working hours. Therefore the weighted average is higher than the raw average. In this way, if you have received a weighted dataset but then in practice ignore the weights, false averages can be obtained using statistical software or a spreadsheet.

The real data are more complex. There are weights on individual cases within the nations, and then across nations there is also a balancing weight that sorts out the very large over-sampling in three nations. In Table 14, you can see that the weighted and unweighted averages within nations are not very different, and that overall the impact of weighting is ambiguous and could hardly have been predicted. In this realistic but complex example, the average weight was very high in England (1.47 per raw case) and very low in the other areas (0.22 in Wales, for example). These numbers indicate that compared with the UK average, in England cases were under-sampled but in Wales they were over-sampled by a factor of about 5. In simple terms, that means that without over-sampling, Wales would have had just 500 cases instead of 2053 (one-fifth as many).

Table 14 Average working hours per week (usual, 2007, adults), United Kingdom

Nation	Weekly hours, weighted average (accurate)	Weekly hours, unweighted average (inaccurate)	Difference	Number of raw cases
England	32.9	33.4	−0.5	6,037
Wales	32.4	32.6	−0.2	2,053
Scotland	33.0	33.0	0	2,074
Northern Ireland	32.6	32.9	−0.3	1,889
UK	32.9	33.1	−0.2	12,053

Source: British Household Panel Survey, Wave Q.

Reprinted with permission from the Institute for Social and Economic Research

Regional weights have a more formal name – cluster weights – when the researcher has used cluster sampling to choose a series of concrete (focused) geographic sampling points. Here the geographic area might be much smaller – possibly wards or villages of different sizes. Each area will have a different sampling rate which can be optimised to get the best representation and value for money for a given total sample size.

Cluster weights often lead to a wider confidence interval on the estimate of an overall mean because by using clustering the researcher avoids covering every single geographic sub-area of the main area. Instead they may choose 50 or 100 cluster points from among 200 possible points. These clusters can be chosen randomly or purposively, and there are many ways to arrange the sampling. A number of practical issues affect how clusters are chosen. In addition, any known homogeneity among populations can be used to make a cheaper clustered approach to that geographic area.

Stratum weights are used with stratified random sampling. A stratum is a basic unit or group of a certain type such as 'women over age 50 in low-income households'. Whereas clusters are generally delineated by geographic space, strata are delineated within the space by factors known to the researchers. These factors might be the street, postcode or house type (apartments, houses, semi-detached houses and 'other' would be four strata). By carefully selecting cases randomly within the stratum but having a range of strata with different sampling rates, the researcher can adjust the sample to get the most information from their survey cost. In particular, important small strata tend to get higher sampling rates – and therefore lower weights. The weights are inverse to the sampling rate so that the resulting contribution of a particular group to the overall average is just right. If women over age 50 living in apartments were sampled at double the usual rate – say, 3% instead of 1.5% of all such women – then their stratum weight would be 0.5.

Refined calculations of target sample size result in a wide variety of weights for different strata. Stratified sampling tends to narrow the confidence interval for any particular average overall. However, stratifying a sample can be expensive. First, it may turn out to be costly to have to get the information to stratify. In my example, that would mean finding out which people are over 50 and female. Secondly, it can be expensive to visit randomly chosen respondents from the sampling frame or list. With stratified sampling, the geographic spread of the cases will be random within the areas chosen for study and the researcher may have to physically cover a great deal of ground to get their work done. This will have cost and time implications.

Non-response weights are calculated after conducting a survey with non-replacement of those who refuse to take part or who are not available. The BHPS weights we looked at earlier are a combination of non-response weights, cluster weights and stratum weights. The non-response component of weighting requires a specific accurate source of data for each small group within the survey – again, for example, women over 50 in apartments – which is compared with the net out-turn of the random sampling. The non-response adjustment is likely to take account of simple factors such as gender, age and region, and not income, house type or whether their home is rented, owned or subject to some other arrangement.

Thus women over 50 in the South East might get a non-response weight of 0.95 because they are easily accessed by researchers. On the other hand, men over 50 in that region might get a weight of 1.03 since they are, on average, more difficult to access because their rate of full-time employment is higher. Their tendency to refuse the survey leads to low raw numbers and higher weightings. The non-response weight can then be multiplied by other factors, such as 1.2 or 0.85 for clustering or stratification.

The term 'frequency weights' is used within computer software for handling fresh data. You have the data with very exact proportional weighting (p-weights, as STATA calls them). Sometimes the computer software may not accept proportional weights that have decimals when you are trying to create bar charts or other simple statistics. A frequency weight could be used instead.

A frequency weight is an integer (a whole number such as 1, 2, 3, ...) reflecting the number of cases in a group being represented by a single raw case in your data. Frequency weights can be created from proportional weights simply by using a rounding-off or truncation expression.

But beware of rounding off weights below 0.5 to zero. A case with a rounded weight of zero will not be used in most calculations: it will be ignored. Instead adjust your weights, using a rule such as: 'all weights less than 1.5 become 1, and all weights above 1.5 become 2'.

Frequency weights are surprisingly useful. In some surveys they are provided by the producer as very large numbers which allow individual raw cases to be multiplied up to the whole country population. If the population is 50 million and the sample size is 5000, then the average frequency weight will be around 10,000. According to variations in non-response and so on, these are then adjusted so that the whole weighted count of cases is 50 million, with proportions coming appropriately from different subgroups. We use weights like this for the Indian National Sample Surveys to get estimates for the whole of India's population. Pie charts and bar charts using these data can then show the population in both absolute and percentage terms. If you receive frequency weights summing to the population and you want some other kind of weight, then divide the integer weights by the total population. Proportional weights then emerge from the data. Save them in a new variable.

Weights always appear as a variable – that is, a column – in raw survey data. If you are producing a dataset, think carefully about whether you are creating weighting factors before the sampling – *a priori* – and whether you then need to work out a non-response factor afterward – *ex post* – as well. The overall weight would then be the two multiplied together. In most surveys, if the overall weight is over about 4, then it is truncated down to about 4 or 5. Cases with weights higher than this might have unusual values and get too much attention in the survey averages. Examine a histogram of the raw weights to see their spread and then decide whether to truncate any weights. Using truncation, all these values would become the value 4: 4.1, 4.25, 4.5, 7.1, 8.0, 10.3. Care is needed to generate the right truncated value; the old values should never be allowed to get lost.

Here is a useful method to apply in these circumstances. Write a short pro-gramme containing at least three parts as shown below:

- Copy the weight variable to a new variable, called perhaps tweight.

- Recode all values of this over 4.0 to 4.0.

- Plot a histogram of this new weight variable to check its values and see how common the truncation is.

Figure 6 shows a truncated weight variable from the UK British Household Panel Survey.

A few comments on over-sampling (i.e. augmenting a sample) can illustrate several concepts that underpin the decision about how large your samples in different regions should be. In the BHPS sample, if we only had 500 cases for Wales, a small-numbers problem would arise. The small-numbers problem is

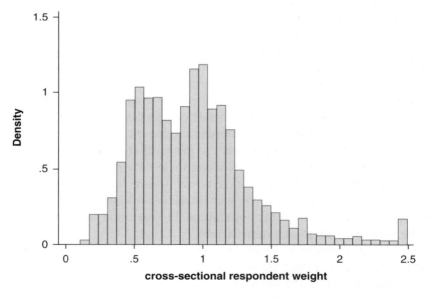

Key: The density is the height of the distribution such that the whole coloured figure has an area of 1. The respondent weight adjusts for non-response, stratification, and clustering. It is called 'cross-sectional' because it allows the weight in a specific year to be correct, but does not adjust for attrition from year to year. The longitudinal weights are not shown here.

Figure 6   Histogram of the weights in BHPS. The variable XRWGHT is graphed for 2007, with the vertical axis representing the frequency of each weight

Source: Author's own calculations, British Household Panel Survey, 2007.

Reprinted with permission from the Institute for Social Economic Research also called the zero-cell problem: in making even simple tables like sex by occupation, we would get zero-cells because 500 cases are being distributed among about 20 cells. Remember that if there are 10 occupations and 2 sexes, we have 20 cells for a single table. Even if the table average is 25 cases per cell, there will in reality be clumping. It is all right for some cells to have 40 or 50 cases, but it causes problems if a few cells have just two or five cases – or none. This is why the zero-cell problem refers to cells that have either no cases or only a handful (less than 5). When taking percentages, ideally we want to have at least 30 cases in each cell before working out a row or column proportion. That allows for oddities and unusual one-off case types to be offset by lots of others.

Further Reading for Part 5

The survey method has been described as dependent first of all on conceptual, theoretical and essentially qualitative prior work (Bryman, 1988). In devoting an entire part of this book to survey methods of data collection, I have not meant to imply that they can reside as a separate set of skills from qualitative and theoretical skills. However, statistical data preparation and analysis are such technical areas that they require a long training and multiple texts. That is why the schism – which is apparent and usually not real – between qualitative and quantitative researchers has developed.

Helpful surveys of introductory data preparation are offered by Bryman and Cramer (2001, 2011), Mukherjee et al. (1998) and Field (2009). Hakim (2000) has presented a summary of research design for social research which is most suitable for quantitative studies. De Vaus (2001) provides a comparable but even more wide-ranging review of how to design a whole research project. Help with hypothesis testing is provided by the short article by Hunt (1994). For international comparisons, a helpful overview was given by Bulmer and Warwick (1993).

Lewis-Beck (1995) is a good starting-point for analysis. Field (2009) offers an overview of methods of data preparation and data description. Breen (1996), Hair et al. (2005) and Tabachnik and Fidell (1996) offer detailed help with statistical modelling. These include explanatory models under the heading of confirmatory statistics and hypothesis testing. To some extent these are also useful for exploratory testing. However, it may be useful to go further, using MacKinnon (2008) or Kaplan (2008) for exploratory statistical research, if mixed-methods research linking up qualitative analysis with statistics is going to be attempted.

On the empirical examples in this part of the book, the related reading includes Beyerlein and Hipp (2006) and Schlozman et al. (1995, 1999).

To put all the skills together, a useful and very advanced text is Danermark et al., (2002). The best idea is always to get experience using the more basic skills of each broad area, including statistics, before trying to do a sophisticated mixed-methods study. The next chapter covers some mixed-methods data-collection techniques.

Part 6

The Case-Study Method of Data Collection

6.1 Case-Study Research

There are three main approaches to case-study research: Yin (1989, 1993) recommends a factual mixed-methods approach; Ragin (1987) and others support a configurational analysis; whereas feminists would argue in favour of a purely qualitative or even dialogical approach – for example, Harding's (1999) strategic realism; see George and Bennett (2005) for a longitudinal approach using qualitative data. This chapter begins by explaining the more traditional, factual approach to case studies. Then it moves towards the complexities of the other approaches.

According to Yin (1989, 2003), a case needs to be studied holistically using a wide range of data sources. The facts should be gathered from multiple sources to ensure that misstatements are offset by others' views. The cases may be diverse, and that diversity creates a challenge for data collection. Therefore a flexible approach is needed. For instance, if government enterprises do not have the same management structure as private sector enterprises, then the sampling of managers for interviewing needs to adapt to this reality of internal structure. Yin's early work tended to argue that mixed methods would help to confirm true results by data triangulation. Yin, like other authors, has more recently moved towards recognising the exploratory and retroductive aspects of research. His argument for purposive sampling, moving from well-known cases to unusual or surprising contrasting cases, is consistent with both broad methodologies. Modern researchers will move away from a focus entirely on 'facts' about cases. We now recognise that how we theorise change and how we formulate our interpretations of texts (e.g. of interviews) are crucial shaping factors for the findings. As explained elsewhere (see 2.5 **interpretation**), not all of social research findings are of a factual nature. To put it differently, the factual content does not exhaust the explanatory or scientific content in the findings. There is also richness in the way things are theorised, the meanings found in data, and the interpretation placed on events. In this sense alone, Yin's early work has become outdated in its approach to facts.

However, Yin (e.g. 1993, 2004) has provided many exemplars of case-study research. These offer useful pointers. In addition, sociologists have widened the scope of case-study research to include the issue of how a case is delineated in the first place (see Gomm et al., 2000; Ragin and Becker, 1992). Byrne (2005) discusses at a theoretical level how cases are embedded in a world full of real complexity. As a result, we would argue, the analysis of causality is not likely to involve simple reductive mathematical formulas but a substantive account of how causality works within different sets of cases (Byrne et al., 2009). The case-study method is illustrated by numerous examples in Rihoux and Grimm (2006).

Ragin (2000) extends the analysis of case-study data by stressing the role of set theory. Set theory is abstract and draws upon selected essential features of cases. The names of sets refer to these real characteristics. Ragin suggests that the use of sets can be helpful both for causal analysis and for simpler comparative research projects that aim to contrast similar (or different) groups of cases. A case lies in a 'set', says Ragin, if it qualitatively matches the features of that set. In crisp-set case methodology, cases can be either 'in' or 'out' of specified sets, and these sets become the dimensional descriptors for the configurational space of all possibilities. In fuzzy-set approaches, the cases are allowed to lie 'partially in' a particular set, and numbers are used to represent the ordinal degree of set membership of each case in each set (Ragin, 2000). The numbers do not reflect a measurement of a probability, but instead are markers of the degree of membership or non-membership in a set. Each set can be depicted as an axis on a diagram, and cases are then measured for their degree of membership in a set of such axes. Qualitative comparative analysis (QCA) is the method used to examine patterns of joint membership in the vector space of all the conditions that define configurations in the qualitative data. QCA textbooks include Rihoux and Ragin (2009) and Ragin (2008). The controversy around QCA needs to be addressed not only by looking at how strongly it is grounded in concrete case knowledge, nor only at its sampling procedures, but also by looking at deeper methodological assumptions about the role of theory (and how theory may be generated) in setting up social research. These issues are treated carefully in various parts of Byrne and Ragin (2009).

The cases may lie in nested sets, such as children in classrooms in schools. Sometimes, however, cases at different levels are non-nested. An example is how secondary school teachers (as cases) handle a series of different children in an N-to-N relationship, because the children move from classroom to classroom. Since the children are not nested within a single teacher's classroom, QCA analysis of multi-level data may be very complex. In exploring this issue in India, I noticed that social classes also penetrate into households through the job that a single individual has, and that therefore a QCA of class would ignore important features of personal experience of class. An individual (as a case) is concurrently in their own social class, by virtue of their job and the employment relations they get involved in, and also at the same time in their household's overall social class which might be different. An employee might be in a self-employed (i.e. petit bourgeois) household, or a self-employed person with employees but might reside in a household that is predominantly earning money through salaried employment. Studies of homogeneous cases at one level need to take into account what is happening among the lower- and higher-level cases, even if the cases are non-nested and quite complex in their interrelationships. Multi-level QCA has not been developed in a detailed software manner, whereas multi-level statistics is rather sophisticated (Hair et al., 2005).

At a higher level of qualitative sophistication, feminists and action researchers would often define a case-study research project in terms of approaching a case and engaging with people and organisations in that scene. Carroll (2004) gives advice for shadowing, participant observation and action research which might qualify as case-study research at the same time. The difference is that the sophistication is in the hermeneutic and ethical aspects, whereas with QCA the sophistication was on the systematising and causal retroduction sides. These methods can be combined, but it is important to recognise what feminists and action researchers are trying to achieve with their case studies. They try to engage in praxis – active interventions in which the processes are in themselves healthy and ethical dialogic meetings. Their outcomes are not restricted to their 'findings' (see 1.2 **findings**, 7.1 **facts**, 3.1 **participation** and 3.2 **praxis**). Strategic realism, as described by Harding (1999), is the activity of naming the objects of a study in order to engage with these objects as they actually interact within a social situation. Harding (1999) suggests that we cannot just be realist for the sake of realism, but always with a social or ethical purpose in mind. Feminists are a good example since most feminists by definition aim to achieve more gender equality. Case-study research is thus a very flexible medium for doing a variety of research activities.

6.2 Comparative Research

In the debates about historical comparative research, a quantitative school and a qualitative historical school can be found. These days, the 'divide' between the two has been worn away because both quantitative data and historical evidence are now widely accepted as useful aids to comparative analysis. In this chapter I describe the middle-way position, then, in which the comparison of different 'units' is done somewhat systematically using a variety of different methods. The first issue is how to work out what the objective of a comparative study is; then to work out what the units are and how to choose the ones you are actually studying; and finally, to gather and analyse evidence.

Choosing a topic for comparative research is like delineating your field of study over both space and time. Being decisive is helpful. Reading around a pre-ferred subject is a useful starting point. Somehow, among all the possibilities, a comparative researcher has to pick a theme and a set of cases to examine. These cases have to be comparable in some way. Being comparable may imply that they are similar in a few respects but not all. Being comparable does not imply that they have a lot of characteristics in common. For example, suppose a study of schools notices that in the public (government) sector there are no school fees. That does not mean one should leave these schools out of the study, but simply that on the question of the level of fees, the public schools are not commensu-rate. Being incommensurate on a few conditions does not stop the set of no-fee schools from lying within the remit of the research. Comparative research is widely know for being arbitrary in the limits it sets on the geography of a study. If you study countries, do you omit the low-income countries? Do you omit China? If you study firms, do you omit the small-scale proprietor-run firms? Do you set a cut-off of 10 employees for a firm to be eligible for the study? The level of cut-off is the part that seems arbitrary to outsiders. Comparative researchers learn to be rather decisive in working out a research design, objectives, and data-gathering approach that suit their aims.

The next issue is to designate as 'units' the various cases in the study. Ragin (2009) has called this 'casing', that is, deciding what will count as cases. I will give three examples to illustrate. First, McCutcheon and Nawojczyk (1995) compared the US General Social Survey with a similar nationally representative survey from Poland to find out how attitudes to abortion differ among Catholics and non-Catholics in these two countries. Their comparative design had as its cases 'the adults of USA and Poland', of which only a random sample were taken into the research design. In the comparative design, a fundamental factor here was that each country had a range of both Catholic and non-Catholic adults. That way, a fair comparison could be made of Catholics in the two countries.

The second example is more ambitious but is not international. The study of homeless people's representation and organisations by Snow and Cress (2000) chose to work in eight US cities, among which 17 organisations were discovered to be working on homelessness. These social movement organisations became the 'cases' in the project. The initial design was narrowed down, however, by choosing eight cities. It was hoped that these would provide a wide range of contrasts as well as commonalities. So far these two examples have shown that some comparative studies are international and some are not. They also show that the concept of a 'case' does not apply at a single level, but at several levels (countries, cities, organisations, and types of people). A book by Rihoux and Ragin (2009) helps with setting up a comparative case-study research project. A helpful chapter by Berg-Schlosser and De Meur (2009) explains how to select cases in such situations.

A third example of a comparative study is Baker et al. (2009). In this study, marriages of two different types of Louisiana couples are examined using both a survey and interview data. The couples are selected from the wedding register and are matched in the following way. First, a couple is chosen who had registered a 'covenant marriage'; then the very next marriage in the register is chosen as a comparable non-covenant marriage, and this one is labelled as standard marriage. Covenant marriages are currently about 2% of all marriages in the state of Louisiana. The state had passed a law in 1997 authorising such marriages. Here is a little background on covenant marriages.

> Some [US] subpopulations adhere to more traditional gender ideologies because of their heightened concern over what they perceive as a societal decline in women's and men's responsible conduct in marriage … Evangelical Christians are one such group. Evangelical discourse routinely focuses on men's authority and the necessity of a marital hierarchy predicated on women's subordination … Rigid forms of this discourse often conflict with mainstream society's increasingly more egalitarian attitudes about gender roles in marriage. In this study, we used a symbolic interactionist perspective to examine whether and how evangelical newlywed couples use the new legal reform of covenant marriage as a symbolic device to signal their beliefs about the benefits of a gendered hierarchy in marriage and their intentions to strengthen marriage as a public institution. (Baker et al., 2009: 148)

In this extract the contrast of evangelical couples with other couples is stated to be the aim of the study. However, among evangelical Christians, due to feasibility issues, it proved possible only to get as a subset those who had married under the covenanted marriage law. In contrast with them are set all other marriages in Louisiana.

As described by Baker et al. (2009: 151), the purpose of a covenant marriage is to stress and be explicit about gendered marital roles.

> Evangelical principles often call on the husband to be the head of the family and the wife to submit to her husband's leadership. As the head of the family, the husband possesses more authority in decisions concerning his family; his ascribed duty is to ensure the physical, spiritual, and emotional health of his family. These studies indicate that evangelicals believe not only in the importance of God in directing their families but also in a necessity for the husband to listen to God.

The researchers contacted the selected married couples, pursuing them through a quantitative and a qualitative stage of research. The issue of developing a comparative case-selection strategy is very vivid in the case of studying marriages. The researcher has to steer a way between the possibilities. Instead of an ambitious wide scope, there has been a strategic decision to have quite a narrow scope (covenant versus all other marriages, in one state in the period up to 2007). This strategic decision helps the rest of the research to run smoothly. In particular, a symbolic interactionist analysis of interviews took place, and a survey was conducted and statistical analysis was done. It was found that strong differences between the two groups existed in their views about Christianity, gender roles and the household.

If comparative research is going to have a quantitative stage, as this third example did, then it needs to have harmonisation of data (see also 1.3 **data**, 3.1 **participation**, and 2.10 **accuracy**).

The conduct of comparative research beyond the initial stages can take a wide variety of research design formats. For example, it can be conducted using mainly quantitative methods, as in Powdthavee (2009), who compared married men with their female spouses in a highly structured statistical analysis. More traditionally 'comparative' studies have a regional comparison within a country, or cover a set of countries. Alternatively, a historical analysis of just two or a few countries or sectors of the economy can be conducted in a comparative mode. Furthermore, it is possible to do comparative qualitative research. Qualitative comparative research sets up a highly structured data table as one part of the research method (see 6.3 **configurations** and 6.4 **contingency**).

6.3 Configurations

A configuration is a set of conditions. The whole set of circumstances is often hard to describe, so configuration specialists – many of whom are doing case-study research – focus on a few key circumstances which are named in theory and sustained by evidence as linked together in important ways. For some configuration specialists, the linkages might be among text units which together make sense in patterns that we can discover and explain using scientific methods (Rantala and Hellström, 2001). For many others, the point of looking at configurations is to see what different effects they have (Ragin, 2008). Hence, one does causal research by looking at causal configurations. According to both views, if one aspect of a configuration is irrelevant, then it can be ignored. In this way we can move from full descriptive detail to a more parsimonious analysis (Rihoux and Ragin, 2009).

The analysis of configurations has been actively promoted by Byrne and Ragin (2009) and Byrne (2005, 2009) because the local context plays a key role for an outcome. Although many social scientists want to generalise across different contexts, Byrne and Ragin say that we need to pay close attention to context in all its detailed differentiation. The configurational approach affects decisions about comparative research method and sampling. I will conclude by using a 'sufficient causal analysis' to illustrate. The topic of this illustration is educational outcomes of schools, and it shows that one can discover key facilitating factors going beyond standard explanations by using innovative primary-data collection methods.

The context for an outcome or indeed any configuration includes the language, local customs, traditions, school system and the history it teaches, which contributes myths and stories to discourses, bodies and their habitual dress and sets of styles which help sustain neo-tribes. In most countries there are both private and public schools, with their organisational cultures, and there are schools supported by religious organisations, as well as government schools with different regulation systems. In the study of schools, outcomes at the personal, classroom, school, regional and school-type levels have been the subject of much statistical study. The configurational approach, however, avoids statistical methods and instead aims to gather qualitative or mixed-methods data.

The contextual factors cannot easily be separated from more proximate causes of outcomes. It is important to understand that causes work in chains, otherwise known as causal processes, and that there are usually a series of distal (i.e. distant) and proximate (i.e. close) causes. Joining a new association and then beginning to follow its rules and guidelines would be an example of a long causal process. Knowing which causes are key factors is crucial. Thus one might ask what made a school join a particular association if 'joining' is thought to be the key moment of change.

An example from demography can be used to illustrate proximate and distal causes. Suppose we wanted to study the age of having one's first or only child – thus whether one has a child and when. The mechanisms include the antenatal care and midwifery, which facilitate a successful birth of a live child; having sex; perhaps stopping the use of contraceptives and thus making the conception possible; having a partner for sex if not for the creation of a child; perhaps marriage; and having an economic basis for planning to have child. Not all of these mechanisms apply in all cases, because there are different patterns of pregnancy. When we are talking about the first pregnancy, in particular, there may be three broad types – accidental, planned outside marriage, and planned within marriage. The broadness arises from the looseness of marriage as an institution. According to Baker et al. (2009) it is becoming 'deinstitutionalised' in Western countries such as the USA. So marriage as a mechanism is not closely linked to having children. Yet it is an important proximate cause for some couples. A configuration is a set of various contextual and proximate circumstances, all leading up to the pregnancy and birth. The reason why it is difficult to separate out specific elements for broad comparison across countries or sub-populations is that the way they operate is not the same, even if the labelling seems to suggest a coherent, consolidated type. Catholic marriage is not construed in the same way as Protestant marriage is. The use of contraceptives among partying students is not the same as the use of the same contraceptives in the context of a two-earner marriage. Not only do the contraceptives have a different meaning in these two different contexts. Their causal power will also be different, in conjunction with closely related factors such as 'will-power', 'conviction about delaying child bearing' and 'consistency'.

The comparative approach to studying causality argues that we can learn which causes really make a difference by comparing both similar and different cases. A case is a 'thing' or object, named as such, with its set of configurational conditions. For example, a school is private, selective, set in a deprived area, not backed by a religious organisation, and co-educational. Describing the conditions, argues Ragin (1994), can be done parsimoniously in a table after detailed qualitative data have been studied. A configuration is then a line in that table. If cases are rather homogeneous, then for one line we can count the number of similar cases within that configuration (N cases). A 'truth table' is a list of all the existing configurations, or permutations of possible combinations of circumstances, covering all the known cases. In addition to the truth table or list, we can also number the remaining 'absent configurations'. These are potential permutations which have not actually been observed, so for them $N = 0$.

In comparative research both historical and systematic data collection methods can be used. The sampling for comparative research will be constrained by time limits if detailed historical or qualitative data are desired. If one is constrained to just 4 or 10 cases, then the choice of cases becomes critical to the overall findings. Having a clear research question and a well-reasoned focus for the research will help these small-N comparative researchers to choose and arrange their configurations carefully and well.

If a lighter-touch data collection is planned, such as filling in tables with a mixture of qualitative phrases and numbers, then the number of cases can be larger and the selection method more systematic. Quota sampling, snowball sampling, or purposive sampling can be used. The advice from the grounded theory tradition is helpful here. In grounded theory, the phrase 'theoretical sampling' refers to choosing first one case, then a strongly contrasting case, then another case which contrasts on a key factor, and so on. This is not snowball sampling because it does not depend on what the agents in the cases think. It is led by the researcher whose focus requires contrasts on a series of key aspects. Theoretical sampling has a lot of flexibility and it requires reasoning throughout the process. The research design can be written up in final form *after* the research has been done. An example of comparative qualitative research with theoretical sampling is Eldar-Avidan et al. (2009). All the cases in that study were in Israel, but within that boundary there was great variety in the experience of a respondent's parents divorcing.

Good sampling enables contrasts and helps the researcher isolate contrasts amid a scene that has some similarities. Usually a limited amount of diversity exists (Ragin, 2000). Therefore one can saturate a category that is rather common and then make sure to cover, at least a little, the rarer categories in so far as they are interesting.

To illustrate this, consider the method used by Byrne (2009) in a study of all the secondary schools in the North East region of England. Byrne chose them all so there was no selective sampling. Because of the regional boundary, no generalisations beyond the North East can be made. A systematic study of the government inspection reports for all these schools led to the creation of a mixed-methods NVivo database. This dataset contained school exam outcomes, indicators of the conditions of the school (religion, deprivation of its locality, selective admissions, whether single-sex or co-educational, and so on). Among the factors recorded were the key dimensions reported as causing good school outcomes as well as key obstacles. Being located in a deprived area, for example, was one part of the configurations that were obstacles to good exam results at the age-16 (GCSE) and age-18 (A-level) stages.[1]

Byrne examined the patterns of causality in the schools' data to find out what the causes of good school performance were. Interestingly, one factor that was important for high outcomes was having a lot of students with special educational needs (SEN). These needs can be 'statemented', after which extra resources are available to the school on a per-statemented-student basis. Apparently the schools with high SEN student numbers also had high exam results. The causal linkages here are subtle and cannot simply be that SEN funds cause higher exam results, because the teaching resources are used on the students at the lower performance levels. It may be that having teaching assistants in the school as a result of SEN makes it possible for a range of students to have higher exam results, or schools organised well to handle SEN students are also organised well to support good exam results. In other words, even when we know that a configuration is sufficient to be associated with an outcome, we still have to investigate the causality qualitatively.

Byrne investigated what caused some schools in the survey (about 12 of them) in a poor-performance configuration to have high exam performance. In other words, the model would have predicted these 12 schools to have low average scores in exams, but they had high scores. In qualitative comparative analysis, this kind of configuration is known as a *contradictory configuration* with mixed outcomes. By looking closely at the text of the government inspection reports, Byrne discovered that one of these schools did well through having an extensive peer monitoring scheme. There may be other reasons why other schools did well. But according to Byrne, even if we find a single case with a new facilitating factor we have made an innovative discovery. The use of retroductive methods was key to this discovery. Mentoring is now being promoted across Britain because it turns out that not only Byrne but also other researchers found peer mentoring to be a useful encouragement to high exam results at secondary level. The retroduction (asking why the data look the way they do) done by Byrne worked like this:

- Gather the data from the government reports – an inductive moment.

- Analyse the systematisable parts of the data – a moment of pattern-seeking analysis.

- Examine the contradictions and non-conforming cases – an exploratory moment.

- Revisit the texts of the reports to explore what may have caused the odd outcome – a retroductive moment.

- Conclude with general statements about education which refer to the concrete cases studied – an inductive moment.

The validity of the results can be checked and rechecked, but is likely to be high because they are firmly grounded. Discussions of the grounding of case-centred research are found in Byrne and Ragin (2009). The retroductive moment was crucial, according to Byrne. We cannot just interpret the data without having any focus to the investigation. The questions we ask provide a focus and help us to steer the inquiry. Blaikie (2000) explains retroduction in detail.

Byrne's argument is that the mentoring of students by students is sufficient to cause higher exam results in a single case. He then suggests that if it was sufficient in a case, in which there was social deprivation in the locality and otherwise the configuration was unconductive to high exam performance, then this may be a key intervention to help schools do better at teaching. The special circumstance of 'mentoring' is a unique way to solve a problem of low performance. Overall, Byrne's study is an example of configurational reasoning. It is about causes, it is retroductive, it benefited from having mixed-methods data, and it is concretely grounded in a specific, named region of one country (UK).

These methods are typical of configurational reasoning studies.

Note

1. An average of the results can be obtained, but only for those students who took sets of exams. Some students take no A-levels, so it is challenging to make a comparison at the higher age groups. The comparisons made are only among those schools which had comparable outcomes, and average scores are typically only calculated among those students who took the exams.

6.4 Contingency

Contingent events are related purely by accident, or in some more complex way through a series of incidents or processes. The word 'contingency' also refers to allowing for multiple possible outcomes. In social research, contingency is an important part of developing causal explanations. If the outcome (which we can designate Y) is always going to follow X, no matter what, then the study of the causality cannot usefully examine X as a possible cause. X would be a 'necessary cause' in the terms introduced long ago and surveyed by Bhaskar (1975). By contrast, Bhaskar urges the researcher to recognise contingent causes as the ones we usually refer to when we explain things. (The basic distinction between necessary causality and contingent causality dates back to Aristotle (1988, 2007), as well as to many other philosophical sources. But it is all too often forgotten when someone starts a fresh research project.) If X is necessarily always with Y and also is sufficient for Y, then, in effect, X is simply part of Y. The example Aristotle gives is that sweating is a sign of fever, and can be cited as a cause of fever, but this mistakes the causality since the two always appear together in cases of fever. To get at the contingent causality, we need to locate cases of sweating without fever (e.g. in heavy exercise). Upon further exploration, we may also find cases of fever without sweating (e.g. in a certain stage of dehydration). Both Aristotle and Bhaskar were keen to apply lessons of contingent causality to the practicalities of doing research and developing convincing, true arguments. For this purpose, a project might not look at sweating but at much more distal causes of fever, such as catching the HIV virus or being exposed to hepatitis C virus, and how these occur.

According to these experts on causality, the study of causes cannot be limited to proximate causes. There are implications for research design. Apart from the study of contrasting cases or survey-data respondents, one may also need to work on explaining how some outcomes at one level of units (or cases) depends on a historically unique conjuncture at the global or macro level. Layder (1993) explains that there are usually psychological, personal, organisational and macro levels to most research studies. Of these, he says, one must focus on just one level but not become ignorant about the other levels. In statistics, a growing branch of technical skills known as multi-level modelling allows individuals, couples, households, social networks, and other 'levels' to be studied in terms of their effects all at one time. Multi-level modelling excels in deriving estimates of cross-level effects, after allowing for effects within each level. This special conclusion in quantitative research can also be mimicked and followed in qualitative research. Thus, the study of contingency leads to strongly innovative claims.

To illustrate a contingent effect of a meso cause in a multi-level qualitative context, suppose a teacher decides to try a new homework routine because the school's organisational cultures values innovation. The teacher knows they have to explain the aim of the homework to both students and line managers. They then await the results. A year later they feel they have got improved marks. But someone has to do a close study of data to find out whether these improvements occurred only contingently because of the teacher's new homework regime, or on a wider scale due to increased discipline or some other encouragement given to all students to learn better. Contingency can work in both proximate causality and in distal causality. The closest X–Y relationships, such as marriage and divorce (marriage being necessary for divorce but not vice versa) tend to have more necessity and less contingency. Nevertheless the key question is 'what kind of marriage is less likely to end in divorce?'. This question is different from 'what kind of marriages did divorced people have?'. The first question is a broad one about the contingencies leading to divorce, and will have a complex answer referring to various configurations (see 6.3 **configurations** and 6.1 **case-study research**). The second question is more narrowly focused and may try to isolate a few key elements in divorced people's marriages. The two questions may seem quite similar, but in their nuances they imply very different sampling strategies. Examine the four sampling strategies in Table 15. Two of them are inferior. These are marked in italics. A discussion of this issue is offered in Ragin (2009).

The sampling issues are an essential step along the way to a successful research project. It does not matter whether it is mainly a quantitative, qualitative, or mixed-methods project, one needs to get the sampling to its optimum range and

Table 15 Sampling and research question relationship under contingent causality

Research question	What kind of marriage is less likely to end in divorce?	What kind of marriages did divorced people have?
Sampling on the outcome	Marriages before divorce and marriages after divorce	Divorcees of all kinds, giving a wide range of marital types
Sampling on the cause	*Marriages of the various types which do and don't lead to divorce (this method of sampling would beg the question of what causes divorce)*	*Marriages of the various types which did lead to divorce (this method of sampling cannot ask the question of what causes divorce)*

coverage. The sample size also has to be adjusted to be a feasible and optimal range of respondents (or cases; see also 6.1 **case-study research** and 1.5 **sampling**). An excellent heuristic approach to stepwise sampling is offered by Levi-Faur (2006).

After the sampling issues have been resolved, it is important to work out what evidence is needed to show that causality exists between some factor(s) and the selected main outcome. Two methods often used are statistical mediation analysis (MacKinnon, 2008) and cross-national comparison with statistical data (Jowell et al., 2007). Contingent effects can best be separated out from necessary and random effects using statistics, according to MacKinnon, if there is either cross-sectional data with clear separation of cause from effect, or panel data for a set of respondents which can isolate the cause and the effect in time. Ideally one would have both, and this implies good operationalisation. It requires clear thinking to develop an argument of this kind:

A and B together are sufficient to cause Y, but neither is necessary for Y to occur.
   In addition, D is a necessary cause of Y.
   Unlike existing literature, E is not always necessary for Y, but E is necessary in most cases where A and B are operating.

Jowell et al. (2007) provide examples such as the causes and effects of certain social attitudes in different country contexts.

In summary, the study of contingency puts stress on distinguishing causes that are not necessarily always present for an outcome Y but which may be causal either alone or in conjunction with other factors (see also 5.3 **causality**, 6.5 **causal mechanisms**, and 6.3 **configurations**).

6.5 Causal Mechanisms

The concept of a causal mechanism is a useful addition to the standard reper-toires of inquiry that have been discussed earlier. In this chapter I hope to clarify what a causal mechanism is so that some mechanisms can be operationalised. By 'causal mechanism' Pawson and Tilley (1997) mean the particular circumstance that makes some outcome more likely to occur, or have a tendency to occur. The model offered by Pawson and Tilley is:

context + mechanism → outcome

This conceptual model assumes that the researchers have clarity about distin-guishing a contextual factor from an outcome, and an outcome from a mecha-nism, rather than mixing them up. Two brief examples help to illustrate this distinction and create a basis for a critical assessment of the 'mechanism' concept:

gender stereotypes + discrimination → lower pay for women in same job

and

domestic division of labour + taking a full-time job → double burden on women

In each case there is much more going on, of course. In both cases there is an assumption that the main focus of attention is on females, but that contrasts with males (and some sharing of work with males) are part of the context. In both cases there is also a slightly narrower phenomenon playing the role of the mechanism – an event or a particular type of act. Discrimination, for example, is hard to pin down, operationalise and measure, because people often try to hide their discriminatory acts and may not even recognise their acts as discriminatory. Therefore in operationalising 'discrimination', it will be necessary to specify even more narrowly (and carefully) what acts, processes or outcomes are meant to be included here. It is not a discriminatory attitude that is being recorded as a mechanism, because that is much broader and might reside in the context. In the second example, taking a full-time job only causes a double burden on women (meaning that their burden then includes responsibility for household chores and responsibilities in the paid work) if women are the main focus of the research. (Otherwise, we can read the second example as applying equally to both men and women.) But as pointed out when discussing the key concept of configurations, it is also important to have men in the frame, either in the sampling frame to offer contrasts or in the qualitative frame to allow a fuller investigation of relationality and interactions. Thus, the second causal claim is focused on women and might be considered to invoke the study of gender before 'double burden on women' can be understood with depth. These background research-design features are extremely important. One can write out the context–mechanism–outcome sets in advance and set up either sampling or a mode of investigation which allows plenty of contrasts and comparisons among relevant groups. There is no need for the context–mechanism–outcome set to follow a lawlike, universal, or overgeneralised pattern of inference.

Pawson and Tilley's point is that the context is part of what enables the mechanism to actually work. They do not urge separating out a single mechanism for very long. Instead they advise that each mechanism can be seen this way, but that there are also many mechanisms located in the context. In a complex world, these various factors offset and obstruct each other. Outcomes are underdetermined in one sense, because there is no certainty that a given mechanism will/did actually lead to an outcome, in the presence of many other mechanisms. In another sense, if we assert that the mechanism is a real tendency for the presence of this thing to cause the outcome, and that there are several mechanisms, then outcomes are also overdetermined – but only if the mechanisms are thought to work deterministically. Pawson and Tilley do not advocate thinking of causes in a deterministic way. They may determine outcomes in a small, encapsulated and restricted time–space combination, but such closed circuits are rare. Most of society, they say, is an open system with organic properties. These ideas broadly lead to some distinct conclusions about causality:

- A mechanism can be sufficient to cause an outcome in some circumstances.

- A group of conditions may be sufficient together to cause an outcome, but each one may not be sufficient on its own.

- The data gathered *ex post* are likely to show a mixture of the outcome of sufficient and not-sufficient causal tendencies. Therefore care must be taken not to exaggerate the definitiveness of conclusions that can be reached using constant conjunctions in data.

The reasoning used in the 'tendencies' approach to causality rests mainly upon two underlying concepts of enabling and inhibiting. An enabling factor tends to cause something to happen. A mechanism – or some feature that is part of the context – can enable future events. This does not definitely make it happen, but it does make it more possible than in the absence of the mechanism. A mechanism – or some feature that is part of the context – can also cause a thing to be liable to do or not do something. The idea of liabilities allows for the obstruction of outcomes, for urges and instincts (private moneylenders are liable to care very much to charge higher interest rates), for tendencies that worry us (the ruling class is liable to impose authoritarian measures to restore order if anarchists or terrorists struggle violently in streets).

The two examples above can be rephrased in terms of enablements and liabilities. In the context of strong gender stereotypes about women's home roles, and what their progression in jobs is likely to be like given their pregnancy leave, managers are liable to discriminate against them at the hiring stage, both by avoiding offering them jobs and by offering them lower pay than a man of similar experience, and this can tend to cause lower pay for women in the same job, through two mechanisms – some women become desperate to get any job, because they have had some rejections, and some women accept a lower pay offer in the job they are moving into because they are afraid of staying on the unreceptive job market.

This rephrasing of the first example definitely leads towards interesting research-design issues. Can a survey or interview be set up to explore the detailed nuances of how the liability of managers to discriminate affects their behaviour? Shall we test whether such a liability is present? How strong is it? Can the same, or a different, project explore women's job search and job acceptance behaviours *ex post*? Pawson and Tilley would suggest that clear thinking about causality helps with setting up a data-collection process.

In the context of a strongly gendered domestic division of labour in which women take responsibility for many more home chores than men, if a woman takes a full-time job she is enabled to pay for child care but she still is liable to feel responsible both for paying for child care and for managing most childcare and domestic chores, and this tends to create a double burden on full-time working women who have dependent children, which is not experienced by children.

This second example is now better specified and includes reference to children. Having dependent children, we might say, is a second mechanism which brings out the double burden phenomenon. This example is now ready for comparative study with contrasts in the degree of the genderedness of the domestic division of labour. Thus not only the mechanism but also the context can be explored in a research project.

Texts that help with research design and analysis of causality in explanatory projects like these include Rihoux and Grimm (2006), Rihoux and Ragin (2009) for the configurational approach, and De Vaus (2001) for the statistical approach. See also Mahoney and Rueschemeyer (2003).

So far I have asserted that causality resides in reality, and that explanatory attempts to draw out a causal explanation can focus in part on mechanisms, and in part on specific features of the context. As argued earlier, the use of retroduction from data to explanation is helpful for this research method. One gathers relevant data around the broad hypothesis or claim, and then examines the data and asks what the world must be like in order for these data patterns and configurations to have emerged. Interpretations of the data are not timeless, but they can take either a definite mode (with reference to a concrete place and time, i.e. descriptive) or an inferential mode (with reference to a wider population, from which a representative sample has been explored). Mixed methods are advised to complement the statistical study of causality. Causes do not exhaust what one might find out, either. But it is possible and feasible to study causality. (It would not be important to argue this point, were it not for some post-structuralist and post-modern authors whose work seems to suggest that causality is purely a matter of stories and representation and does not exist in any real way. See Sayer, 2000.)

Further Reading for Part 6

Ragin's view that case-study approaches can unify and clarify several of the social sciences, overcoming some weaknesses of statistical methods, was also developed in a useful, practical book by Byrne (2002). Byrne and Ragin (2009) have recently collaborated to edit a book on case-centred research. However, these sources on the case-study method do not exhaust the question of causality which is so central to case-study methods. A background paper by Ekstrom (1992) and the full-length book by Sayer (1992) on realist methodology help to fill this gap. In Sayer's book, Chapters 1, 2 and 8 are useful for grasping the problem that statistical methods in themselves, alone, cannot address causality in an adequate way. People grasp causality. Statistical output is an input to an interpretive process. These principles then need to be applied to the case-based methods with suitable modifications. For example, if an inference to a population is not being drawn, then some of Sayer's objections are less salient. But when a general statement is made about several concrete cases in a group (e.g. that there is a 'type' here), one must be careful about what is implied as causal and what is implied as the essential nature of the type. People need to reassess or develop theories which underpin our understanding of each particular social phenomenon. Any simplistic attempt to depersonalise statistical methods through positivist methodological underpinnings creates problems, and the authors cited here help us overcome such problems. For people with qualitative research methodology backgrounds, the issue does not arise so vividly.

For survey data collection, Kent (2007) is a useful guide. Fink (1995) is an excellent guide to creating surveys. Bryman and Cramer (2001) is helpful for the data analysis stage. For those who want to gather data through online surveys, Best and Krueger (2004) offer helpful suggestions.

Whether or not the case-study method or comparative method will be used, each qualitative researcher needs practical help at early stages. Miles and Huberman (1994) offer an excellent overview of how computer software might be useful. Gibbs (2002, 2007) and Bazeley and Richards (2000) go into more detail using the latest types of software. One needs to augment the technical advice with a more interpretive guide: either Miles and Huberman (1994), which encourages creativity and innovation in qualitative interpretation, or general advice about constructing an argument which urges the writer to avoid numerous common pitfalls (Weston, 2002).

Part 7

Concluding Suggestions About Data-Collection Concepts

Part 7

Concluding Suggestions About Data-Collection Concepts

7.1 Facts

In the preceding chapters I have presented concepts arising in the qualitative, quantitative and mixed-methods data-collection processes. I have referred to 'facts' a few times as something that may result from the standard data-collection process. At this point, I want to pause and reflect for a moment on the *factual* status of the findings. It is helpful to know about facts in order to have confidence in building up scientific or ethical arguments. Having clarity about 'facts' has several advantages. For instance, if you have 'facts' then you may be a more convincing author for certain audiences such as journalists or government policy experts. Another advantage of having facts is feeling confident about your own argument, and letting the facts play a role in supporting more complex arguments you may not feel quite so sure about. In this chapter I explore the existence of facts, discuss the kinds of facts that we can be confident about, and conclude with the questioning attitude that makes me think most good science is 'fallible' even if it makes reference to facts.

The challenge today to those who claim to have 'facts' or factual science comes from those who worry about the licence to act that may be derived from this 'factual' basis. This calls for further explanations so that certain kinds of facts can be claimed to be true, whilst arguments – which are not facts – are more healthily set out. A claim is a sentence of longer argument that asserts something is the case; claims can be a mixture of claims about the world and claims that something is the case in general. The former are more testable, while the latter tend to include some normative or ethical assertions, and to be more general or even universal (Weston, 2002). Claims should be based on reasoning, and we reason through a variety of methods rather than just claiming something to be 'factual' when what we really mean is to make a complex argument. Two examples can be used to illustrate simple, factual statements that need to be expressed in a concrete and tightly worded way:

1. A foetus in weeks 1–6 of its development in a uterus has no human consciousness.

2. Statistical estimates show that the wage rise associated with education is not obtained to the same extent by women as by men.

For the sake of this exercise, let us suppose that we have an agreed dictionary of psychology with a widely accepted definition of human consciousness, and that some data do support a regression of the general kind referred to in statement 2. There are three main reasons why statements like 1 and 2 are often *not* considered to be factual.

The first reason is that they are too broad in their apparent coverage to work well as universally or very general factual claims. As a claim, statement 1 seems to apply to any place where we find humans, but a dictionary definition of human consciousness – or any normative definition of human consciousness – is likely to be swayed in one direction or another by local norms embedded partly in the language of that dictionary. Statement 1 might work as a factual statement if it were meant to refer only to a specific linguistic, cultural and regional population. It would need some revision though, perhaps as shown below.

1a. A foetus in weeks 1–6 of its development in a uterus was considered to have no human consciousness as recognised by atheists in the USA in the twentieth century.

Since non-atheists in the USA in the twentieth century would define 'human consciousness' in a different way than their atheist counterparts, the statement would not be true without the specific clause 'by atheists'. I offer this revision only as a rough and temporary illustration of how one might make a statement more concrete, local and particular to enable us to move from a 'false broad' claim to a 'true but narrow' factual claim. Statement 1a is actually about the world. It can be tested. Statement 1, however, is rather abstract. We would move to a search for relevant evidence if we wanted to do further research. We might, for example, start to study evidence for a related claim:

1b. A foetus in weeks 1–6 of its development in a uterus shows no sign of human consciousness as defined by scientists in the USA in the twentieth century.

It should now be clear that the 'factual' nature of a concrete statement such as 1a or 1b could be considered both by atheists and non-atheists to be a matter that could be settled by reference to data. If a statement is not concrete and has a universal or timeless quality, it is more likely to be fundamentally contestable.

A second issue is that the data underlying the statement can be questioned in numerous ways. Statement 2 can be used to illustrate this problem. The data about wages can be questioned in terms of the recording of wages. One might examine whether men's wages are recorded or set differently from women's, perhaps to cover for unpaid overtime which women do not do. If there were more male than female unpaid overtime and wages were adjusted upward to allow for that, then male wages would appear to be higher – but male wages per hour *actually worked* might not be higher. Another issue could be whether some other outside factor explains and causes the difference, and whether, after controlling for this factor (e.g. effort, talent, desire for promotion or ability to plan), the women's wages would be seen as fair. The purview of the statement – which derives a conclusion about a wide population from a sample – could also be exaggerated. The factual reference point is more limited than the general statement seems to imply. Again, a revision of the statement might help a lot to make the statement more factual.

2a. The statistical estimates for the UK in 2004–7 clearly show that the rise in wages (per hour of paid work) associated with education is not obtained to the same extent by women as by men, *ceteris paribus*.

Again this statement has a clear reference to the real world. It is concrete and can be tested. The phrase *ceteris paribus* can be read two ways. It should be translated from Latin to mean 'all else being equal'. That means men's wages exceed women's after controlling for the factors that have been put into the statistical estimate. But *ceteris paribus* can also be read to mean 'all other factors being allowed to vary as they do in the real population', which are not in fact equal at all. Thus many women are unpaid domestic workers and so are left out of the population of waged workers; many men have had several promotions which women have not had, and so on.

The intended reference to the world should really be limited to the exact situation that was the remit of the data collection. With its concrete reference point, giving the country and the dates, the revised statement 2a is much clearer and could be defended more easily as factual – and, indeed, some data do support it.

The third problem with calling something 'factual' is that you might offend someone with the nuances of the statement (Olsen, 2007b). In both statements 1 and 2 there are hints about what is fair and just – statement 1 seems perhaps to relate to operations on pregnant women, and statement 2 seems to relate to an unfairness about the wage inequality. Critics of 'factual discourses' would worry that the use of facts in arguments moves the arguer forward into a territory that they have shaped and mapped out with the statements' discursive tricks. From such a point of view nearly all statements are potentially controversial. Possible responses would be to offer a competing statement, reject the ethics while accepting the 'fact' if it is true, or perhaps create a different venue for a different type of argument. Foucault (1980) and Harding (1999) provide excellent accounts as to why the debates about the framing of facts matter so much. Another useful source is Fairclough (2001) which explains how to do discourse analysis. It is not very useful simply to claim that 'there are no factual statements' without developing any alternative way to gain knowledge and express that knowledge in words. Otherwise nothing could be true and we would never know whether any claim was true or false!

So far I have presented three arguments against the existence of facts. The third is the most compelling. The first two helped give advice about data collection. If you want to gather or develop some facts, then be prepared to quote these facts in a concrete way as narrowly true in a given time and place, supported by evidence, and carefully phrased so as to limit the ambiguity about whom they refer to. It is fine to work through a set of facts, foreseeing criticisms, checking the evidence and working on how they fit together – hopefully without inconsistencies – as a way to make progress on a research project.

But facts are not enough for good scientific arguments. Perhaps surprisingly, facts are not all that arguments consist of. A good argument has a shape or structure and there are many kinds of them (Fisher, 1988, 2001). There are persuasive arguments which urge the reader to take a particular position. These usually move from premises to facts and evidence, concluding with a value judgement and an exhortation. In a persuasive argument, some premises usually invoke a normative position. Another type of argument is the discussion of competing theoretical explanations which concludes that one is better than another. There are several variations on this argument theme: that the best theory is one which encompasses all the others; that the worst theory has false facts underlying it in crucial ways; that the coverage of a poor-quality theory is too limited and that the theory needs to be revised to cover a wider range of cases; and so on.

A third broad type of argument is a scientific test. The structure of this argument might run like this:

We have gathered data consistent with theory A and its sub-element, B.
  We organise the data to test B.
  The test fails and B is falsified.
  Since A implies B, and B is false, A might be false.
  Therefore a new theory will be needed once the alternative to B is examined carefully.

The problem with this argument is rather obvious. Look closely at it and see if you can find its weak point. Read Fisher (1988) or Weston (2002) for more help constructing sound scientific arguments. They advise that you specify the premises very carefully, and perhaps go back and test or re-examine any weak premises. As a result, you develop a chain of explicit reasoning.

The problem with the scientific argument offered is that the whole theory A was not tested. A still stands untested while its spin-off statement B has been falsified. One example would be if a test of statement 1a were conducted by checking whether foetuses in weeks 1–6 of development were able to respond to outside sound stimuli. (That is a better test for statement 1b than for 1a.) Theory A would be the definitional theory of human consciousness that was agreed upon from a dictionary at the start. B could be an implicit statement: babies, like all humans, should respond to external sound stimuli even in weeks 1–6 of their growth in the uterus. If they do not respond, B is refuted. But A is not yet refuted. We can modify A because it does not depend heavily on B and still have the claim that A is true but B is refuted. Quine and Duhem (Quine, 1953) both argued that since scientific falsification arguments typically have a structure like the one given above, they are weak. Whilst keeping scientists busy with experiments, falsification does not solve the greater problem of achieving truth in science. A summary is given by Smith (1998: ch. 3), and there is further discussion by Sayer (1992: chs 1, 2 and especially 8).

In general, good 'arguments' contain a consistent series of statements of which some are premises and some are conclusions. An argument, says Fisher, has both intermediate and final conclusions. The advice Fisher gives arises from a variety of sources, including symbolic logic and some of the philosophical writings of Aristotle, notably *Rhetoric*, written around 300 years before the birth of Christ (Aristotle, 2007). Fisher parses out some longer texts into the skeletal bare bones of their argument. Among his sample arguments, Fisher offers some sweeping statements that usually fall in the list of premises. The reader of a 'fact' within an argument, or a factual argument, will need to be ready to agree to all the premises or else they will need the author of the argument to move backward and prove their premises.

In many scientific arguments certain premises are difficult if not impossible to prove. Examples of sweeping statements include 'the rational choice model of human decisions is correct' as a starting point in economics, and 'the id and ego work together in implicit ways to generate psychological health' in Freudian psychology. In politics a common one is 'country governments act only and always to protect their basic interests'. These basic premises will only be acceptable to a part of the world audience. Many writers compile facts for a limited audience, for example for those in their discipline or sub-discipline or in a particular workplace. An annual report is a set of facts about a firm written by the accountants of that firm. They are factual in that context, but are seen as a social construct by those who do critical accounting and the sociology of finance! The factual nature of a statement or an argument is in large part relative to the standpoint of the group receiving or interpreting the whole argument.

By taking great care in their construction, one can make good arguments that are very hard to challenge. Good scientific arguments have a critical dependence on strongly supportive evidence. Factual evidence plays a role in bolstering arguments but is not enough to make an argument strong. A warranted argument is one which has strong premises, makes reference to the real world and has some evidence in it which has been gathered and can be set out for scrutiny in ways that are consistent with the argument (Olsen and Morgan, 2005).

7.2 Reality

It is important to remember that by doing data collection we are trying to represent reality, not just our own prior concepts and assumptions. It is no good simply having a strong assumption about something, operationalising it, and then proving that the world works just like you thought it did.

Nevertheless, to make sense of the data-collection stage, one has to refine the research question at an earlier stage so that any conceptual framework that is being presumed true is *not* being tested. Such a broad set of assumptions should be reasonable. For most qualitative researchers, that implies trying to start out with almost a blank slate and being prepared to accept almost any new finding. The reason is that each social situation is unique and will show up differences compared with past generalisations. Each qualitative project is unique in its findings.

On the other hand, when we come to more systematically-based projects there is usually a set of claims that need to be accepted from the outset, such as 'suicide arises from a mixture of social, institutional and psychological factors'.

For a qualitative researcher 'suicide' itself is unpicked and explored immediately, and the validity of the initial generalisation cannot be taken for granted. But for the quantitative or statistical stage of a project it may be useful to take this statement for granted and then set up an interesting hypothesis within that frame of reference. One has to stipulate reasonable definitions for basic concepts such as suicide. Making these explicit will tend to improve the research.

An interesting hypothesis would not arise merely 'deductively' as a lawlike prediction from the starting statement. Instead the hypothesis might arise during the literature review from some oddity, exception, difference of experience or ethically worrying oversimplification usually accepted in the literature. For example, if we pursue the project seeking explanations for suicide, we might have this as the controversial hypothesis: 'women's suicides are often misunderstood as psychological, and instead need to be seen pluralistically as affected by institutional and structural factors and not simply as personal tragedies'.

To continue with this, a detailed hypothesis about men might be appropriate, or perhaps we would focus on young women, or some other subgroup. Consider this extension of the hypothesis: 'men's suicides are divided into two groups: young men who are affected by status and dignity issues in a consumerist social milieu, and older men who are distressed by intra-household conflict'. If data were available to explore these hypotheses, then the general research question could be rewritten to encapsulate the whole project.

You can turn this exercise into a research question: 'How do gender and age-group factors influence the causality of suicide, given that suicide's causes are in general multi-level and complex and include both holistic social, local institutional, and personal psychological factors?' Now an interesting project will result. I think of this stage as setting up the project to reflect reality. There are three data-collection techniques which can help both quantitatively-led and qualitatively-led researchers develop their knowledge of the concrete reality during their research project. The techniques are: keeping a field diary, developing expert informants and studying historical and organisational trends.

Keeping a field diary is normal in anthropology, but good operating habits are rarely taught to students in degrees where secondary data analysis is usual.

A field diary is a handwritten collection of thoughts about the scene of the data collection. For a field researcher these will include notes from conversations, addresses of respondents and commentaries on how old theories are being proved wrong by events about which further details will be gleaned.

The field diary usually includes brainstorming and ideas for later tasks. It is a hardbound or spiral-bound book, not a handheld computer. It includes notes about mistakes, problems, translations, misunderstandings, lay talk and slang versus academic concepts, and policy or practitioner responses to the research. The field diary can contain at the front a one-page summary of the project, and at the back a copy of the standard informed-consent form. When meeting new people the field researcher simply shows these documents to defuse any doubts about what they are doing. They can get verbal consent from interviewees prior to starting the interviewing process in earnest. They may give a printed copy of the informed-consent letter to the respondent, or get them to sign a copy. Well-informed verbal consent signifies ethical clearance, and once that has been given the research can in most instances go ahead.

For a secondary researcher, one might say, there is no 'field' of study. There is 'no fieldwork'. Some might say that in that case there is no need for ethical clearance either. These erroneous judgements tend to give us an image that places the researcher on another planet studying the oddity known as Earth. Instead, it is better to consider that we can read the newspapers, magazines, government publications and other sources about the localities that are covered by the data. A field diary then records notes gleaned from these various 'voices' or sources. How their perspective differs from that taken in the research raises serious questions about the usefulness, comprehensibility and validity of the research – or it may suggest that lay writers are actually wrong. The secondary data analyst can also carry out mixed-methods research. They might visit specific field sites under examination, with ethical clearance, of course, so they can discuss the research with people who are typical of those in the secondary data. While in the field they might run focus groups and other supplementary research. For a mixed-methods researcher led by secondary data, a field diary is required. It helps also in recording common misperceptions which may later need to be written about.

The use of expert informants is also typical of field anthropologists and development studies (Thomas et al., 1998).

Anyone can be an expert informant, but there cannot be too many. It is important that these people can and will find the time to sit with the researchers during multiple visits so that various points of interpretation can be cleared up. All researchers need expert informants, and qualitative and mixed-methods researchers need them most.

When using expert informants, note-taking and agreement on the findings are important. No one should collect data covertly, because this would not be ethical. The ethical clearance for a project must include the way that researchers approach other experts. Expert informants often do not want to be quoted. They may have their own reasons for this. They are prepared instead to offer their insights without being formally connected with the project. They may mentor you or offer collaboration.

But be careful about who your expert informants are. Local people are unlikely to have a research background, and people from organisations may have pressing agendas. These require careful and ethically scrupulous treatment. On the other hand, another useful group is academic experts – there might possibly be some in your study area. Academics are widely thought to be public intellectuals who are prepared to have their thoughts put on record (Fuller, 2005). It is polite to check any quotes with them, but they are not like other respondents who may have little public power or voice of their own. In conclusion, getting in-depth knowledge by discussing your research or your findings with local and other experts is an excellent way to broaden the basis of validity of the findings. It may also help you with nuances and subtleties that you might not have thought important beforehand.

Numerous sociologists promote the idea of the researcher as a public intellectual who can then write letters to newspapers, give public talks, engage in participatory or democratic dialogue, give evidence to official committees and sit on public bodies as an expert. The field diary is a way to develop your expertise as a public intellectural – rehearsing arguments with opponents or others; explaining ideas in ways lay people might grasp; reinterpreting what newspapers say in clearer and more concise language to check if they are correct.

Among academics, there may not be a need for the usual written informed consent. If you interview an expert on the record, it may be more like journalism than research. In any case you can get informed consent at the beginning of a meeting by saying politely: 'I am doing a project on ——. Would you mind if I quoted you as making some points in this interview? If so, I assure you I'll send you a copy of the text before it leaves my desk, whether it's a paraphrase or a direct quote. Or would you prefer me to quote your published work?' This polite request offers them a way to give you information secretly if they wish.

It is also important to study history and the organisational culture that sur-rounds your field site. Statistical studies, in particular, sometimes lack a historical background. Most of the 'reasons for things happening' have their origins in the historical events that lie behind today's structures and institutions. Reading up on the political and economic history of a country or region is absolutely crucial for every good research study. Further reading on social, cultural and ethnic factors is very useful too. When doing this background reading, do not just look merely for facts. Notice the viewpoints, standpoints and conceptual frames taken by the various authors. Read widely. Engage with journalists or historians when you can. Discuss the recent past with policy-makers – it may be a really useful chat!

Organisational culture is a subtle but important factor that influences long-term outcomes. The differences of experience – for example, by differing ethnic groups – are often vast but masked by 'official' discourses of equality. Read about the differences between different social groups. Which ones are visibly dif-ferentiated? Which are the minorities? Which are dominant? Which, if any, are isolated – perhaps deliberately so? Why and how is this happening?

These background notes may be useful when you are interpreting your own findings.

So, to summarise: no matter how well planned the research project is, it can usually benefit from some extra investigative techniques. These plug you into an ongoing social reality rather than leaving you in your ivory tower. There is even a danger that too much ivory tower research might leave you stale. That is why in this chapter I have stressed a polarity between the pure ideas explored by an isolated academic in an ivory tower against the grounded, field-tested ideas that are consistent with social reality in a more particular concrete sense.

Keep in mind the three reality-testing techniques presented above:

- Keep a field diary to track your mistakes and surprises.

- Use expert informants as mentors who tell you things you did not know before.

- Read up on the history of your subject to get a sense of how things have developed up to the time of your research.

These pointers are just good sense really, but they also arise from the 'realist' viewpoint. Realists argue that reality – with all its confusing lay discourses – should be valued in itself and that academic ideas should be capable of being tested, because they should reflect and represent that reality.

7.3 Retroduction

The data-collection stage of a research project needs to allow for retroduction to occur. Retroduction means in brief 'asking why', and has already been mentioned several times in this book (see 2.5 **interpretation**, 6.1 **case-study research** and **data**). Retroduction perhaps needs to be set in context, and compared with induction and deduction, so that the data-collection strategy suggested here can be seen as coherently able to mix all three of these approaches to research. In this chapter I explain a coherent approach to induction and deduction that will make the context very clear.

First, no research project can or should be purely inductive. I have argued this point in some depth elsewhere (Olsen and Morgan, 2005; Morgan and Olsen, 2008), as have others before. In theory, a purely inductive project would gather many small details together and then develop a general theory or a series of small generalisations that are grounded on the details. Both grounded theory and content analysis are often portrayed as if they were purely inductive. According to my way of thinking, it is an excellent addition to these methodologies to augment induction by adding retroduction. Thus we would pause half way through a project, review what has been learned so far, and then revisit the data-gathering stage. One wants to keep gathering data to answer questions of the following kinds:

1. What caused the original data to show the patterns it showed? This question includes: why did I start off with the topic that I had set up in the beginning? Were there theoretical reasons? If so, were they good ones, or does that theory have some problems? Or were there ethical reasons, and if so what else do I need to know about in order to develop a strong ethical argument about the topic?

2. What causes unique, unusual, deviant or inexplicable cases to turn out as they do? Here, it may initially seem that speculation is needed. But scientific speculation is also a more formal type of logic which is much more like discernment. We have to ask (a) is it possible that the usual theories can explain the unusual, and if so why was it hidden from us at first? and (b) if the usual

theories do not explain the unusual, then what could? What kind of new theory do I need? What new addition to the lexicon would help me in discerning either meanings, explanations or an overall interpretation that helps make sense of these unusual cases?

3. What are the complex standpoints and viewpoints that are behind the contradictory results in this research? Or in other words, what are the sources of tension, and what have we learned that was not already known about these tensions? How do other people interpret the same data (or events)? Why are their interpretations different from the researchers' findings so far?

The first of these questions is probing the data. The second is avoiding overgeneralisation but searching for reasons and causes. The third of the questions is allowing for contradictory voices. All these three questions are specific forms of retroduction.

Retroduction was traditionally discussed mainly with regard to explanatory modelling (Sayer, 1992, 2000; Bhaskar, 1975). Retroduction implies a number of forms of inquiry that do not fit in easily with a simple inductive method. To see the archetypical inductive method, refer to Blaikie's (2000) treatment of induction which he labels as one of four 'strategies' of research. In his parable of the researchers from outer space, he assumes that the inductive group do not use retroductive methods, the retroductive group do not use deductive methods, and so on. However, if we simply redefine 'retroduction' and 'induction' as modes of analysis in the short term, rather than as whole research 'strategies' or methodologies, we avoid a lot of problems in research. In summary, questions 1–3 are simply short-term modes of analysis, and can lead us towards other modes such as deduction, hypothesis testing, more data gathering, and even back to induction. It seems wiser to mix inductive and retroductive moments rather than to see them as mutually exclusive.

A quick summary of the three questions is a useful way to review retroduction. The researcher asks: why these data, why these things happened this way, and how people interpret things themselves – which implies also asking why people see things as they do. When operating this way, the user of retroduction is not just a scientist, they are also human. They care about what people think but they are not blinded by what people say. They care about the data but are not limited to a single data type or a single dataset. They are inquirers.

In all three ways, retroduction is just one more technique in an arsenal. It is a technique that makes the researchers curious; it does not offer a simplifying protocol but a guide to complexity. Retroduction is also very different from deduction.

According to the usual presentation of deduction as a research 'strategy', one begins with theory and works out some predictions. Then data are collected (consistent with the theory) and the predictions are compared with the data. If they do not match, the deduction is falsified. Even more than with induction, this is evidently a poor research method. It is too limited because it gives no advice on how to generate theory. Most authors advise that induction is a theory-generating method and deduction a theory-testing method. In this book I have presented the case for induction and deduction working alongside retroduction in an overall inquiry approach. The three modes of analysis can be used in any order, repeatedly, with returns to the data (or to new data) at any stage. Like Danermark et al. (2002), I suggest that the steps of research do not need to be a timeline but instead are a guide to activities. Therefore data gathering can happen right up to the last moments of writing up research. In a primary-data study the last few weeks might be spent brushing up on relevant laws, while in a secondary-data study one might decide to visit a field site before finalising the write-up of findings. Deduction in itself can play a part in writing up research because it is useful to know which hypotheses or claims are supported, and which are falsified, by a given set of research findings. It is a helpful mode for presenting results. But it is not sufficient for a whole research methodology.

Blaikie (1993, 2000) adds a serious discussion of 'abduction' ('capturing the phenomenon' from inside, which is like ethnographic approaches) which I will not reproduce here. It is also interesting to note that Potter (1999) sees the four modes as rather mutually exclusive. The reason is that there are whole disciplines and sub-disciplines which are based upon just one of the four modes of analysis. Anthropology usually rests mainly upon abduction, and animal psychology or economics might be seen as resting upon deduction. The reasons why this is an unwise way to set up 'social science disciplines' have been mentioned several times in this book, and can be rather briefly summarised here.

Firstly, the disciplines should be coherent with each other and not contradictory. Secondly, the disciplines should have blendable research themes at all overlapping edges, so training of researchers should not be restricted to just one or two modes of analysis. Thirdly, retroduction is such a good overall technique which aids in planning the research, executing the project, and writing up, that it must not be neglected by any researcher. Fourthly, a whole discipline based on 'induction' would be contradictory since it would obviously be training its students in theories which were passed on by methods other than induction. Fifthly, a whole discipline based purely on deduction would have no way to generate theory, nor could it deal with real anomalies. Finally, a whole discipline based purely upon abduction, if by that we meant immersion in social situations, would lack the expertise that comes from knowing a variety of standpoints while also being able to explain that which people inside a situation cannot see very clearly because they are somewhat blinded by their own viewpoint.

Data gathering is an important part of social research because we have the opportunity to gather empirical evidence to bring to bear on social problems. Thinking about the data and returning to the evidence sources are important stages of research, so data gathering may go on rather longer than you had first realised. It can go on in tandem with thinking, analysing, interpreting, under-standing, learning, acting, voicing and sharing. Data gathering underpins many research projects.

Further Reading for Part 7

In this part of the book I have summarised arguments about science and the development of an explanatory argument. My approach is very ambitious and I hope mainly to make a consistent argument here, not to innovate in this important area of science. Much effort has been spent already in clarifying these issues. Smith (1998) gives a history of the main schools of thought in science. Smith explains the sustained attack on positivism and gives a convincing explanation of why post-structuralism and realism are now so popular in social science. In prac-tice they have replaced positivism. Smith (1998) is the best overview of how some post-modern social science has begun to develop a reputation for being confused or riddled with inconsistencies.

To overcome accusations of a schism, something has to be done about the apparent paradox that induction and deduction (as methodologies) are incom-patible. Worse yet, I have argued, each is incomplete without much more effort being put into a research design and the combining of modes of analysis. Blaikie (2000) offers an excellent parable of Martian researchers who parachute in to Earth to do a research project, then break into four teams. This story is a useful reminder that induction is not enough on its own for research.

For reading the background about choices of research design, it is worth spend-ing time on one of the high-quality methodology books. An easy one to read is Bryman (1988). Like many of the other books mentioned here, this has been reprinted since its original publication because it has been so popular. This book provides a sound underpinning for mixed methods. A broad overview for evalua-tion researchers, also well suited to market research, is offered by Pawson and Tilley (1997). For case-study research Ragin (1994) is indispensable.

Appendix

The appendix has two parts. Firstly, there is a basic health and safety notice for research team members working in a rural setting. Secondly, there is a basic informed-consent form that participants in a project can be asked to sign. These can be used as the basis for more carefully tailored documents to support the ethical clearance stage of data collection in a project that involves fieldwork.

Document A1. Protocol for the handling of health and safety and risk

Regarding the Project on   INSTITUTION LOGO HERE   DATE HERE
ABC (Ref %$£"%)

The personal safety of each researcher on this project is subject to both training and guidance from this protocol.

1. Training

The Research Assistant on this project and any additional research assistants who join him/her are expected to read about 'ethics and informed consent' before they begin any fieldwork. For example, they can read the ethical guidance of the British Sociological Association, and if they desire they can also read the ethical guidelines of the Social Research Association.

Any employed Research Assistant who departs from CITY X in order to do fieldwork on this project is expected to fill out a risk assessment form in accordance with normal UNIVERSITY Y procedures.

Furthermore, the following guidance about safety should be discussed among the research team when going out to the field.

2. Guidance on Safety

When planning to work in villages, arrange the transport before departing for the village, and ensure that you have sufficient water and enough time to return before dark. If you decide to stay overnight in the village, make sure that you have arranged suitable accommodation before it gets dark.

When working in the village setting, be sensitive to any conflicts which have preceded your visit. If you hear about violent conflict, be aware of any implications it may have for your own safety. Furthermore, if you meet any police, security guards, or any person bearing a weapon, please ensure that you are ready to leave the area if necessary to secure your safety. On the other hand, comply with the police if they request you to give any information.

Foreigners are sometimes expected to visit the LOCALITY police offices. You should carry your passport for such a visit. Be prepared by making photocopies of the passport before you go. Be prepared to show evidence of your project and to argue correctly that your activities do match the description that shows in your passport. This may be a tourist or research visa.

During your interviews be aware of any vulnerabilities of the people around you. If someone seems offended or hurt, you need to work out a way to avoid conflict and to resolve the situation so that you are not involved in further conflict. This includes verbal as well as physical conflict. You may not be responsible for the conflict which is occurring. However, you are responsible for not worsening any situation. This may mean ending an interview, leaving the scene, or promising not to continue with some section of the research.

3. Incidents

In case of any incident which threatens the research project itself, please contact Z in CITY X at the earliest convenience. Please ensure that you leave the village until you're able to take advice from local elites or from UNIVERSITY Y staff to protect yourself and others.

Thank you.

NAME HERE   INSTITUTION HERE   DATE HERE

Document A2. Informed Consent Proforma for Signatures

Permission form

A (*the researcher*) is doing more research about LOCALITY agriculture. She has noticed the shortage of water. She is writing about this and she teaches her students about irrigation, renting of land, water pumps, firewood shortage, and how the banks lend to agriculture. She wants to interview tenants, so her student B has agreed to help her with this work. Then B will be starting his own work. She wants you to agree to the following:

- that you would allow us to put the data about you into the computer.

- that we could quote your words when we write.

- that you would be anonymous in these reports (unless you specifically ask to be named).

- that your village will normally be named in the reports.

- that if A or her students come to take photos, these are just for private use, except that

- your permission will be asked before any photo is used in a public place, such as an annual report or a presentation to a public audience. The photos help foreigners to understand how the water problem and the fuel/firewood problem are shared by people in the villages.

- you will probably be interviewed, and your spouse might also be interviewed, and these interviews will be translated into printed English. Students will study these interviews in UNIVERSITY Y.

As you can imagine, it is also possible that A or B will write a book later on. We hope you can agree to have you and your TOWN/VILLAGE/AREA described in this book. By signing here, you agree that your involvement is with full information and with your agreement.

Thank you so much.

You do not have to participate! You can withdraw at any time!

This research is funded by the Council B. The grant is called 'GRANT A'. You can find out more about it by looking on the internet at GRANT A WEBSITE.

Signature: _____ Date: _____

Name spelt out: _____

Hh No. _____

A copy of this agreement is kept by the respondent. The signed copy stays with the questionnaire and returned to UNIVERSITY Y.

LANGUAGE Z1 or Z2 is fine for writing the signature. For those who don't write, it is possible to make a mark above to indicate agreement. Or they can also give verbal agreement and the staff will sign the paper to indicate that the approval was explicit.

References

Alcoff, L. and Potter, E. (eds) (1993) *Feminist Epistemologies*. New York and London: Routledge.

Alfonso, A.I., Kurti, L. and Pink, S. (eds) (2004) *Working Images: Visual Research and Representation in Ethnography*. London: Routledge.

Alvesson, M. and Deetz, S. (2000) *Doing Critical Management Research*. London: Sage.

Antcliff, V. (2000) Television industry contractual terms. Interview text, 15 March. Mimeo, Manchester University.

Antcliff, V. and Saundry, R. (2005) Individualisation, collectivism and the management of risk in a freelance labour market: the case of the UK television industry. Paper presented at the British Sociological Association Conference, York, 21–23 March. http://www.britsoc.co.uk/user_doc/05BSAAntcliffValerie.pdf (accessed July 2010).

Antcliff, V., Saundry, R. and Stuart, M. (2007) Networks and social capital in the UK television industry: the weakness of weak ties. *Human Relations*, 60 (2): 371–93.

Aristotle (1925) *The Nicomachean Ethics*. Oxford: Oxford University Press.

Aristotle (1988) *The Politics*, with an introduction by S. Everson. Cambridge: Cambridge University Press.

Aristotle (2007) *On Rhetoric: A Theory of Civic Discourse*, with an introduction by G.A. Kennedy. Oxford: Oxford University Press.

Babbitt, S. (1993) Feminism and objective interests: the role of transformation experiences in rational deliberation. In L. Alcoff and E. Potter (eds), *Feminist Epistemologies*. New York and London: Routledge.

Baker, E.H., Sanchez, L.A., Nock, S.L. and Wright, J.D. (2009) Covenant marriage and the sanctification of gendered marital roles. *Journal of Family Issues*, 30 (2): 147–78.

Banks, M. (2007) *Using Visual Data in Qualitative Research*. London: Sage.

Barnett, V. (2002) *Sample Survey: Principles and Methods*. London: Arnold.

Bauer, M.W. (2000) Classical content analysis: a review. In M.W. Bauer and G. Gaskell (eds), *Qualitative Researching with Text, Image and Sound* (pp. 131–49). London: Sage.

Bauer, M.W. and Gaskell, G. (eds) (2000) *Qualitative Researching with Text, Image and Sound*. London: Sage.

Bazeley, P. and Richards, L. (2000) *The NVivo Qualitative Project Book*. London: Sage.

Berg-Schlosser, D. and De Meur, G. (2009) Comparative research design: case and variable selection. In B. Rihoux and C. Ragin (eds), *Configurational Comparative Analysis*. Thousand Oaks, CA: Sage.

Best, S. and Krueger, B.S. (2004) *Internet Data Collection*. London: Sage.

Beyerlein, K. and Hipp, J.R. (2006) From pews to participation: the effect of congregation activity and context on bridging civic engagement. *Social Problems*, 53 (1): 97–117.

Bhaskar, R. (1975) *A Realist Theory of Science*. Leeds: Leeds Books.

Bhaskar, R. (1989) *The Possibility of Naturalism: A Philosophical Critique of Contemporary Human Sciences*. Hemel Hempstead: Harvester Wheatsheaf.

Blaikie, N. (1993) *Approaches to Social Enquiry*. Cambridge: Polity.

Blaikie, N.W.H. (2000) *Designing Social Research: The Logic of Anticipation*. Cambridge: Polity Press.

Blaikie, N.W.H. (2003) *Analyzing Quantitative Data*. London: Sage.

Breen, R. (1996) *Regression Models: Censored, Sample-Selected, or Truncated Data*. Thousand Oaks, CA: Sage.

British Sociological Association (2002) Statement of Ethical Practice for the British Sociological Association. http://www.britsoc.co.uk/equality/Statement+Ethical+Practice.htm (accessed July 2010).

Brockington, D. and Sullivan, S. (2003) Qualitative research. In R. Scheyvens and D. Storey (eds), *Development Fieldwork: A Practical Guide* (pp. 57–76). London: Sage.

Bryman, A. (1988) *Quantity and Quality in Social Research*. London: Routledge.

Bryman, A. and Bell, E. (2007) *Business Research Methods*. Oxford: Oxford University Press.

Bryman, A. and Cramer. D. (2001) *Quantitative Data Analysis with SPSS Release 10 for Windows*. London: Routledge.

Bryman, A. and Cramer, D. (2011) *Quantitative Data Analysis with IBM SPSS 17, 18 and 19: A Guide for Social Scientists*. London: Sage.

Bulmer, M. and Warwick, D.P. (1993) *Social Research in Developing Countries: Surveys and Censuses in the Third World*. London: UCL Press.

Burnham, P., Lutz, K.G., Grant, W. and Layton-Henry, Z. (2008) *Research Methods in Politics*. Basingstoke: Palgrave Macmillan.

Byrne, D. (2002) *Interpreting Quantitative Data*. London: Sage.

Byrne, D. (2005) Complexity, configuration and cases. *Theory, Culture and Society*, 22 (10): 95–111.

Byrne, D. (2009) Using cluster analysis, qualitative comparative analysis and NVivo in relation to the establishment of causal configurations with pre-existing large-N data sets – machining hermeneutics. In D. Byrne and C. Ragin (eds), *The Sage Handbook of Case-Based Methods*. London: Sage.

Byrne, D. and Ragin, C. (eds) (2009) *The Sage Handbook of Case-Based Methods*. London: Sage.

Byrne, D., Olsen, W.K. and Duggan, S. (2009) Causality and interpretation in qualitative policy-related research. In D. Byrne and C. Ragin (eds), *The Sage Handbook of Case-Based Methods*. London: Sage.

Carroll, W.K. (ed.) (2004) *Critical Strategies for Social Research*. Toronto: Canadian Scholars' Press.

Charmaz, K. (2006) *Constructing Grounded Theory: A Practical Guide*. London: Sage.

Chiapello, E. and Fairclough, N. (2002) Understanding the new management ideology: a transdisciplinary contribution from critical discourse analysis and the new sociology of capitalism. *Discourse & Society* 13 (2).

Cooke, B. and Kothari, U. (eds) (2001) *Participation: The New Tyranny?* London: Zed Books.

Creswell, J.W. (2003) *Research Design: Qualitative, Quantitative, and Mixed-Methods Approaches*. London: Sage.

Creswell, J.W. (2009) *Research Design: Qualitative, Quantitative, and Mixed Methods Approaches*, 3rd edition. London: Sage.

Creswell, J.W. and Plano Clark, V.L. (2007) *Designing and Conducting Mixed Methods Research*. Thousand Oaks, CA: Sage.

Crompton, R. and Harris, F. (1998) Explaining women's employment patterns: 'orientations to work' revisited. *British Journal of Sociology*, 49 (1): 118–49.

Crompton, R., Brockmann, M. and Lyonette, C. (2005) Attitudes, women's employment and the domestic division of labour: a cross-national analysis in two waves. *Work, Employment and Society*, 19: 213–33.

Dale, A., Fieldhouse, E. and Holdsworth, C. (2000) *Analyzing Census Microdata*. London: Arnold.

Danermark, B., Ekström, M., Jakobsen, L. and Karlsson, J.Ch. (eds) (2002) *Explaining Society: Critical Realism in the Social Sciences*. London: Routledge.

De Vaus, D.A. (2001) *Research Design in Social Research*. London: Sage.

Economic and Social Research Council. (2005) *Postgraduate Training Guidelines: A Guide to Provision for Postgraduate Advanced Course and Research Students in the Social Sciences*. London: Economic and Social Research Council. http://www.esrc.ac.uk/ESRCInfoCentre/Images/Postgraduate_Training_Guidelines_2005_tcm6-9062.pdf (accessed January 2010).

Ekström, M. (1992) Causal explanation of social-action – the contribution of Weber, Marx and of critical realism to a generative view of causal explanation in social-science. *Acta Sociologica*, 35 (2): 107–22.

Eldar-Avidan, D., Haj-Yahia, M.M. and Greenbaum, C.W. (2009) Divorce is a part of my life ... resilience, survival, and vulnerability: young adults' perceptions of the implications of parental divorce. *Journal of Marital & Family Therapy*, 35 (1).

Engels, F. and Kelley, F. (1892) *The Condition of the Working-Class in England in 1844*. London: S. Sonnenschein & Co.

Fairclough, N. (2001) *Language and Power*, 2nd edition. Harlow: Longman.

Fals-Borda, O. (1988) *Knowledge and People's Power: Lessons with Peasants in Nicaragua, Mexico and Colombia*. Delhi: Indian Social Institute (in association with ILO).

Fals-Borda, O. and Rahman, M.A. (1991) *Action and Knowledge: Breaking the Monopoly with Participatory Action-Research*. New York: Apex Press.

Field, A. (2009) *Discovering Statistics Using SPSS*, 3rd edition. London: Sage.

Fink, A. (1995) *The Survey Handbook*. Thousand Oaks, CA and London: Sage Publications.

Fisher, A. (1988) *The Logic of Real Arguments*. Cambridge: Cambridge University Press.

Fisher, A. (2001) *Critical Thinking: An Introduction*. Cambridge: Cambridge University Press.

Flyvbjerg, B. (2001) *Making Social Science Matter: Why Social Inquiry Fails and How It Can Succeed Again*. Cambridge: Cambridge University Press.

Foucault, M. (1977) *Discipline and Punish: The Birth of the Prison* (trans. A. Sheridan). London: Allen Lane.

Foucault, M. (1980) *Power/Knowledge: Selected Interviews and Other Writings, 1972–1977* (ed. and trans. C. Gordon). New York: Pantheon Books.

Frankfort-Nachmias, C. and Nachmias, D. (2000) *Research Methods in the Social Sciences*. New York: Worth.

Freire, P. (1993) *Pedagogy of the Oppressed*. New York: Continuum.

Friere, P. (1996) *Pedagogy of Hope: Reliving Pedagogy of the Oppressed*. New York: Continuum.

Fuller, B., Caspary, G., Kagan, S.L., Gauthier, C., Huang, D.S.C., Carroll, J. and McCarthy, J. (2002) Does maternal employment influence poor children's social development? *Early Childhood Research Quarterly*, 17: 470–97.

Fuller, S. (2003) *Kuhn vs. Popper: The Struggle for the Soul of Science*. New York: Columbia University Press.

Fuller, S. (2005) *The Intellectual*. Thriplow: Icon Books.

George, A.L. and Bennett, A. (2005) *Case Studies and Theory Development in the Social Sciences*. London and Cambridge, MA: MIT Press.

Gershuny, J.I. (2000) *Changing Times: Work and Leisure in Postindustrial Society*. New York: Oxford University Press.

Gibbs, G. (2002) *Qualitative Data Analysis: Explorations with NVivo*. Buckingham: Open University Press.

Gibbs, G. (2007) *Analyzing Qualitative Data*. London: Sage.

Glaser, B.G. (1978) *Theoretical Sensitivity: Advances in the Methodology of Grounded Theory*. Mill Valley, CA: Sociology Press

Glaser, B.G. and Strauss, A.L. (1967) *The Discovery of Grounded Theory: Strategies for Qualitative Research*. Hawthorne, NY: Aldine de Gruyter.

Gomm, R., Hammersley, M. and Foster, P. (eds) (2000) *Case Study Method: Key Issues, Key Texts*. London: Sage.

Greene, W.H. (2003) *Econometric Analysis*, 5th edition. Upper Saddle River, NJ: Prentice Hall.

Greenwood, D.J. and Levin, M. (2004) Local knowledge, cogenerative research, and narrativity. In W.K. Carroll (ed.), *Critical Strategies for Social Research* (pp. 281–91). Toronto: Canadian Scholars' Press.

Hair, J.F., Black, B., Babin, B., Anderson, R.E. and Tatham, R.L. (2005) *Multivariate Data Analysis*. Upper Saddle River, NJ: Pearson Prentice Hall.

Hakim, C. (2000) *Research Design: Successful Designs for Social and Economic Research*. London: Routledge.

Hamilton, L.C. (2004) *Statistics with STATA*. London: Thomson Learning.

Hammersley, M. and Gomm, R. (1997) Bias in social research. *Sociological Research Online*, 2 (1). http://www.socresonline.org.uk/socresonline/2/1/2.html (accessed January 2010).

Haraway, D. (1988) Situated knowledges: the science question in feminism and the privilege of partial perspective. *Feminist Studies*, 14 (3).

Harding, S. (1993a) Rethinking standpoint epistemology: what is 'strong objectivity'? In L. Alcoff and E. Potter (eds), *Feminist Epistemologies*. New York and London: Routledge.

Harding, S. (1993b) *The 'Racial' Economy of Science: Toward a Democratic Future*. Bloomington, IN: Indiana University Press.

Harding, S. (1999) The case for strategic realism: a response to Lawson. *Feminist Economics*, 5 (3): 127–33.

Harrison, J.S. and Freeman, R.E. (1999) Stakeholders, social responsibility, and performance: empirical evidence and theoretical perspectives. *The Academy of Management Journal*, 42 (5): 479–85.

Heron, J. (1999) *The Complete Facilitator's Handbook*. London: Kogan Page.

Heron, J. (2000) *Co-operative Inquiry: Research into the Human Condition*. London: Sage.

Heron, J. (2001) *Helping the Client: A Creative Practical Guide*. London: Sage.

Hickey, S. and Mohan, G. (eds) (2004) *Participation: From Tyranny to Transformation? Exploring New Approaches to Participation in Development*. London: Zed Press.

Holland, J. and Campbell, J. (eds) (2005) *Methods in Development Research: Combining Qualitative and Quantitative Approaches*. London: ITDG.

Hunt, S. (1994) A realist theory of empirical testing: resolving the theory-ladenness/objectivity debate. *Philosophy of Social Sciences*, 24 (2).

International Social Survey Programme (2006) Role of Government module IV. http://zacat.gesis.org/webview/index.jsp (accessed September 2009).

Inter-University Consortium for Political and Social Research (1990) *Demographics and Non-Traditional Civic Participation: A Data-Driven Learning Guide*. Ann Arbor, MI: Inter-university Consortium for Political and Social Research [distributor], 2009-04-16. doi:10.3886/demcivpart.

Jowell, R., Roberts, C., Fitzgerald, R. and Eva, G. (eds) (2007) *Measuring Attitudes Cross-Nationally: Lessons from the European Social Survey*. London: Sage.

Kaplan, D.W. (2008) *Structural Equation Modelling: Foundations and Extensions*, 2nd edition. London: Sage.

Kendall, G. and Wickham, G. (1999) *Using Foucault's Methods*. London: Sage.

Kent, R. (2007) *Marketing Research: Approaches, Methods and Applications in Europe*. London: Thomson Learning.

King, I. (2008) RBS chief Fred is not dead. *The Sun*, 23 April.

Kirkpatrick, G. (2009) Technology: Taylor's play between worlds. In F. Devine and S. Heath (eds), *Doing Social Science: Evidence and Methods in Empirical Research*. Basingstoke: Palgrave Macmillan.

Kozinets, R.V. (2010) *Netnography: Doing Ethnographic Research Online*. London: Sage.

Krieger, N. (1994) Epidemiology and the web of causation: has anyone seen the spider? *Social Science and Medicine*, 39 (7): 887–903.

Kuhn, T.S. (1970) *The Structure of Scientific Revolutions*. Chicago: University of Chicago Press.

Kvale, S. (1996) *InterViews: An Introduction to Qualitative Research Interviewing*. Thousand Oaks, CA: Sage.

Lamont, M. (2000) *The Dignity of Working Men: Morality and the Boundaries of Race, Class, and Immigration*. Cambridge, MA: Harvard University Press.

Lamont, M. (2005) Peer evaluation in the social sciences and the humanities compared: the United States, the United Kingdom, and France. Report prepared for the Social Sciences and Humanities Research Council of Canada. Online mimeo, http://www.wjh.harvard.edu/~mlamont/SSHRC-peer.pdf (accessed 2006).

Laws, S., with Harper, C. and Marcus, R. (2003) *Research for Development*. London: Sage (in association with Save the Children).

Lawson, T. (1989) Abstraction, tendencies and stylised facts – a realist approach to economic analysis. *Cambridge Journal of Economics*, 13 (1): 56–78.

Lawson, T. (1997) *Economics and Reality*. London and New York: Routledge.

Layder, D. (1993) *New Strategies in Social Research*. Cambridge: Polity Press.

Lenin, V.I. (1964) *The Development of Capitalism in Russia*. Moscow: Progress Publishers.

Levi-Faur, D. (2006) A question of size? A heuristics for stepwise comparative research design. In B. Rihoux and H. Grimm, H. (eds), *Innovative Comparative Methods for Policy Analysis: Beyond the Quantitative-Qualitative Divide*. New York: Springer.

Lewins, A. and Silver, C. (2007) *Using Software in Qualitative Research: A Step-by-Step Guide*. Los Angeles: Sage.

Lewis-Beck, M.S. (1995) *Data Analysis: An Introduction*. London: Sage.

Lobe, B. (2008) *Integration of Online Research Methods*. Ljubljana: Faculty of Social Sciences Press.

MacIntyre, A. (1985) *After Virtue: A Study in Moral Theory*. London: Duckworth.

MacKinnon, D.P. (2008) *Introduction to Statistical Mediation Analysis*. New York: Lawrence Erlbaum Associates.

Mahoney, J. and Rueschemeyer, D. (eds) (2003) *Comparative Historical Analysis in the Social Sciences*. Cambridge: Cambridge University Press.

Marx, K. (1969) Theses on Feuerbach. In *Marx/Engels Selected Works*, Volume 1 (pp. 13–15). Moscow: Progress Publishers.

Marx, K. and Engels, F. (1998) *The German Ideology: Including Theses on Feuerbach and Introduction to The Critique of Political Economy*. Amherst, NY: Prometheus Books.

Mason, J. (2002) *Qualitative Researching*, 2nd edition. London: Sage.

May, V. (2009) Family: Bengtson et al.'s How Families Still Matter. In F. Devine and S. Heath (eds), *Doing Social Science: Evidence and Methods in Empirical Research*. Basingstoke: Palgrave Macmillan.

McCutcheon, A.L. and Nawojczyk, M. (1995) Making the break: popular sentiment toward legalised abortion among American and Polish Catholic laities. *International Journal of Public Opinion Research*, 7 (3): 232–52.

McNiff, J. and Whitehead, J. (2009) *Doing and Writing Action Research*. London: Sage.

Mikkelsen, B. (1995) *Methods for Development Work and Research*. London: Sage.

Mikkelsen, B. (2005) *Methods for Development Work and Research: A New Guide for Practitioners*, 2nd edition. New Delh: Sage.

Miles, M.B. and Huberman, A.M. (1994) *Qualitative Data Analysis: An Expanded Sourcebook*. Thousand Oaks, CA: Sage.

Morgan, J. and Olsen, W.K. (2008) Objectivity as a second-order 'bridging' concept, Part 2: Bridging into action. *Journal of Critical Realism*, 7: 107–32.

Mukherjee, C., White, H. and Wuyts, M.E. (1998) *Econometrics and Data Analysis for Developing Countries*. London and New York: Routledge.

Office for National Statistics (2005) 2001 Census for England. http://www.statistics.gov.uk/census2001/census_form.asp (accessed September 2009).

Olsen, W.K. (2005) Poverty and Problems in Salford (mimeo), Salford, The Community Network. 56 pages.

Olsen, W.K. (2006) Globalisation, liberalisation and a paradox of social exclusion in Sri Lanka. In A.H. Carling (ed.), *Globalisation and Identity: Development and Integration in a Changing World* (pp. 109–30). London: I.B. Tauris.

Olsen, W.K. (2007a) Structure, agency, and strategy among tenants in India. Global Poverty Research Group Working Paper GPRG-WPS-080. http://www.gprg.org/pubs/workingpapers/pdfs/gprg-wps-080.pdf (accessed February 2011).

Olsen, W.K. (2007b) Pluralist methodology for development economics: the example of moral economy of Indian labour markets. *Journal of Economic Methodology*, 14 (1), 57–82.

Olsen, W.K. (2010a) Realist methodology: a review. In W.K. Olsen (ed.), *Realist Methodology*, Vol. 1 (pp. xix–xlvi). Los Angeles: Sage.

Olsen, W.K. (2010b) 'Poverty' as a malaise of development: a discourse analysis in its global context. In A. Boran (ed.), *Poverty: Malaise of Development?* Chester: Chester University Press.

Olsen, W.K. and Morgan, J. (2005) A critical epistemology of analytical statistics: addressing the sceptical realist. *Journal for the Theory of Social Behaviour*, 35 (3): 255–84.

Olsen, W.K. and Neff, D. (2007) Informal agricultural work, habitus and practices in an Indian context. Global Poverty Research Group Working Paper GPRG-WPS-079. http://www.gprg.org/pubs/workingpapers/pdfs/gprg-wps-079.pdf (accessed February 2011).

Olweus, D. and Alsaker, F.D. (1994) Assessing change in a cohort-longitudinal study with hierarchical data. In D. Magnusson, L.R. Bergaman, G. Rudinger, and B. Törestad (eds), *Problems and Methods in Longitudinal Research: Stability and Change*. Cambridge: Cambridge University Press.

Outhwaite, W. (1987) *New Philosophies of Social Science: Realism, Hermeneutics and Critical Theory*. Basingstoke: Macmillan Education.

Pawson, R. (1998) *A Measure for Measures: A Manifesto for an Empirical Sociology*. London: Routledge.

Pawson, R. and Tilley, N. (1997) *Realistic Evaluation*. London: Sage.

Payne, G. and Payne, J. (2004) *Key Concepts in Social Research*. London: Sage.

Pink, S. (2006) *The Future of Visual Anthropology: Engaging the Senses*. London: Routledge.

Pink, S. (2007) *Doing Visual Ethnography*. London: Sage.

Pink, S. (2009) *Doing Sensory Ethnography*. Los Angeles: Sage.

Popper, K.R. (1963) *Conjectures and Refutations: The Growth of Scientific Knowledge*. London: Routledge.

Potter, G. (1999) *The Philosophy of Social Science: New Perspectives*. Harlow: Longman.

Potter, J. and Wetherell, M. (1987) *Discourse and Social Psychology: Beyond Attitudes and Behaviour*. London: Sage.

Powdthavee, N. (2009) 'I can't smile without you': Spousal correlation in life satisfaction. *Journal of Economic Psychology*, 30: 675–89.

Prosser, J. (1998) *Image-Based Research: A Sourcebook for Qualitative Researchers*. London: Falmer.

Quine, W.V.O. (1953) *Two Dogmas of Empiricism from a Logical Point of View*. Cambridge, MA: Harvard University Press.

Ragin, C.C. (1987) *The Comparative Method: Moving beyond Qualitative and Quantitative Strategies*. Berkeley: University of California Press.

Ragin, C.C. (1994) *Constructing Social Research: The Unity and Diversity of Method*. Thousand Oaks, CA: Pine Forge Press.

Ragin, C.C. (2000) *Fuzzy-Set Social Science*. Chicago: University of Chicago Press.

Ragin, C.C. (2008) *Redesigning Social Inquiry: Fuzzy Sets and Beyond*. Chicago: University of Chicago Press.

Ragin, C.C. (2009) Reflections on casing and case-oriented research. In D. Byrne and C. Ragin (eds), *The Sage Handbook of Case-Based Methods* (pp. 522–34). London: Sage.

Ragin, C.C. and Becker, H.S. (eds) (1992) *What is a Case? Exploring the Foundations of Social Inquiry*. Cambridge: Cambridge University Press.

Ramachandran, V.K. (1990) *Wage Labour and Unfreedom in Agriculture: An Indian Case Study*. Oxford: Clarendon Press.

Rantala, K. and Hellström, E. (2001) Qualitative comparative analysis – a hermeneutic approach to interview data. *International Journal of Social Research Methodology*, 4 (2): 87–100.

Reason, P. and H. Bradbury (2009) *The Sage Handbook of Action Research: Participative Inquiry and Practice*, 2nd edition. London: Sage.

Reason, P. and Rowan, J. (1981) *Human Inquiry: A Sourcebook of New Paradigm Research*. Chichester: Wiley.

Richards, L. and Morse, J.M. (2007) *Readme First for a User's Guide to Qualitative Methods*. London: Sage.

Ricouer, P. (2003) *The Rule of Metaphor*. London: Routledge.

Rihoux, B. and Grimm, H. (eds) (2006) *Innovative Comparative Methods for Policy Analysis: Beyond the Quantitative – Qualitative Divide*. New York: Springer.

Rihoux, B. and Ragin, C. (eds) (2009) *Configurational Comparative Analysis*. Thousand Oaks, CA: Sage.

Risseeuw, C. (1991) *The Fish Don't Talk about the Water: Gender Transformation, Power and Resistance among Women in Sri Lanka*. Delhi: Manohar.

Sayer, A. (1992) *Method in Social Science: A Realist Approach*. London: Routledge.

Sayer, A. (2000) *Realism and Social Science*. London: Sage.

Scheyvens, R. and Storey, D. (eds) (2003) *Development Fieldwork: A Practical Guide*. London: Sage.

Scheyvens, R., Scheyvens, H. and Murray, W.E. (2003) Working with marginalised, vulnerable or privileged groups. In R. Scheyvens and D. Storey (eds), *Development Fieldwork: A Practical Guide* (pp. 167–96). London: Sage.

Schlozman, K.L., Burns, N., Verba, S. and Donahue, J. (1995) Gender and citizen participation: is there a different voice? *American Journal of Political Science*, 39 (2): 267–93.

Schlozman, K.L., Burns, N. and Verba, S. (1999) 'What happened at work today?': A multistage model of gender, employment, and political participation. *Journal of Politics*, 61 (1): 29–53.

Scott, J. (1990) *A Matter of Record: Documentary Sources in Social Research*. Cambridge: Polity Press.

Silverman, D. (2000) *Doing Qualitative Research: A Practical Handbook*. London: Sage.

Silverman, D. (2001) *Interpreting Qualitative Data: Methods for Analyzing Talk, Text and Interaction*. London: Sage.

Smith, M.J. (1998) *Social Science in Question*. London: Sage.

Snow, D. and Cress, D. (2000) The outcome of homeless mobilization: the influence of organization, disruption, political mediation, and framing. *American Journal of Sociology*, 105 (4): 1063–1104.

Stanley, L. and Wise, S. (1993) *Breaking Out Again: Feminist Ontology and Epistemology*. London: Routledge.

STATA (2003) *STATA 8 Reference Manual*. College Station, TX: STATA Corporation.

Tabachnik, B.G. and Fidell, L.S. (1996) *Using Multivariate Statistics*. New York: HarperCollins College Publishers.

Taylor M.F., with Brice, J., Buck, N. and Prentice-Lane, E. (2001) *British Household Panel Survey User Manual: Volume A: Introduction, Technical Report and Appendices*. Colchester: ESRC Research Centre on Micro-Social Change. http://www.esds.ac.uk/longitudinal/access/bhps/L33196.asp (accessed July 2010)

Teddlie, C. and Tashakkori, A. (2009) *Foundations of Mixed Methods Research: Integrating Quantitative and Qualitative Approaches in the Social and Behavioral Sciences*. London: Sage.

Thomas, A., Chataway, J. and Wuyts, M. (1998) *Finding Out Fast: Investigative Skills for Policy and Development*. London: Sage.

Treanor, J. (2008) RBS chief's £1.2m salary deal revealed. *The Guardian*, 5 November.

Wetherell, M., Taylor, S. and Yates, S.J. (eds) (2001) *Discourse as Data: A Guide for analysis*. London: Sage.

Weston, A. (2002) *A Rulebook for Arguments*, 4th edition. Indianapolis, IN: Hackett Publishing.

Williams, M. (2000) *Science and Social Science: An Introduction*. London and New York: Routledge.

Wisker, G. (2008) *The Postgraduate Research Handbook*. Basingstoke: Palgrave Macmillan.

Wodak, R. and Meyer, M. (2009) *Methods of Critical Discourse Analysis*, 2nd edition. London: Sage.

Wolfe, A. (1989) *Whose Keeper? Social Science and Moral Obligation*. Berkeley: University of California Press.

Wooldridge, J.M. (2002) *Econometric Analysis of Cross Section and Panel Data*. Cambridge, MA: MIT Press.

Yin, R.K. (1989) *Case-Study Research: Design and methods*. London: Sage.

Yin, R.K. (1993) *Applications of Case Study Research*. Newbury Park, CA: Sage.

Yin, R.K. (2003) *Applications of Case Study Research*. London: Sage.

Yin, R.K. (2004) *The Case Study Anthology*. Thousand Oaks, CA: Sage.

Index

978-1-84787-907-3

978-1-4129-2226-5

978-1-84920-417-0

978-1-84860-034-8

978-1-4129-7517-9

978-1-4129-7457-8

978-1-4129-7044-0

978-1-84920-595-5

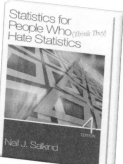

978-1-4129-7959-7

Find out more about these titles and our wide range of books for students and researchers at **www.sagepub.co.uk**

EXCITING RESEARCH METHODS TEXTS FROM SAGE